JANE COCHRANE

Odysseus' Island

Isometric reconstruction of the Megaron (main hall) of the Palace of Odysseus at Agios Athanassios - School of Homer in Ithaca

ISOMETRIC DRAWING MADE FOR ASSOCIATE PROFESSOR OF PREHISTORIC ARCHAEOLOGY LITSA KONTORLI-PAPADOPOULOU BY THE ARCHITECT DIMITRIS SKIRGIANNIS.

KEY

1. Entrance
2. Court
3. Altar
4. Hall
5. Hall of throne
5a. Fireplace
6. Chimney
7. Storage rooms
   (below ground floor)
8. Carved staircase to upper level
9. Carved external staircase to upper level
10. Wall upper level
11. Sanctuary?

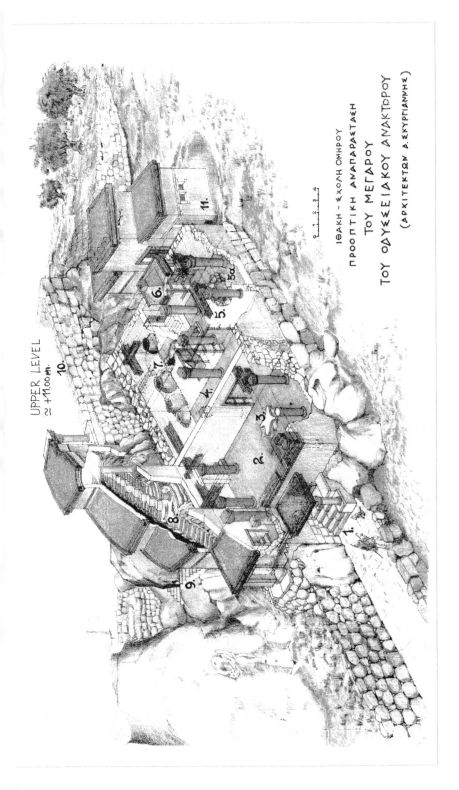

UPPER LEVEL
≃ +11.00 m.

ΙΘΑΚΗ - ΣΧΟΛΗ ΟΜΗΡΟΥ
ΠΡΟΟΠΤΙΚΗ ΑΝΑΠΑΡΑΣΤΑΣΗ
ΤΟΥ ΜΕΓΑΡΟΥ
ΤΟΥ ΟΔΥΣΣΕΙΔΑΚΟΥ ΑΝΑΚΤΟΡΟΥ
(ΑΡΧΙΤΕΚΤΩΝ Δ.ΣΚΥΡΓΙΑΝΝΗΣ)

A CIP catalogue record for this book is available from the British Library.

ISBN 978-1-9162923-1-4

Cover painting and illustrations by Jane Cochrane

Typeset by Loco Design

Jane Cochrane trained as an architect at the Architectural Association in London. As an architect she worked principally on existing buildings, at a housing association and as a Conservation Architect. For several years she taught at the Bower Ashton School of Art in Bristol. She writes, paints, draws, and sometimes makes pots as well. Together with her Greek-speaking husband, Alec Kazantzis, she repaired an old house in Ithaca. She has been visiting the island since 1982.

This book is written in loving memory of Alec Kazantzis

As you set out for Ithaca
hope the voyage is a long one,
full of adventure, full of discovery.

From 'Ithaca' by Constantine Cavafy 1897

Contents

Map 1 10

Map 2 11

Map 3 12

Map 4 13

Introduction 14

1. Nostos 16

2. Ithacan Landscapes 37

3. King Agamemnon comes home to Mycenae................................61

4. Back in Ithaca..82

5. Denis comes home 101

6. Immigrants...118

7. Conflict 138

8. Others plan to come home..154

9. A threat from outside...179

10. Three deaths and a miraculous escape 197

11. Keeping memories 218

12. Some light on the subject 233

13. Odysseus and Telemachus come home 252

14. The story of Eumaeus the swineherd...266

15. The Palace of Odysseus and Penelope 287

Epilogue 312

Acknowledgements...314

A note about transliteration 316

A note about the characters 317

Selected bibliography 318

Notes 322

Map 1

MODERN ITHACA

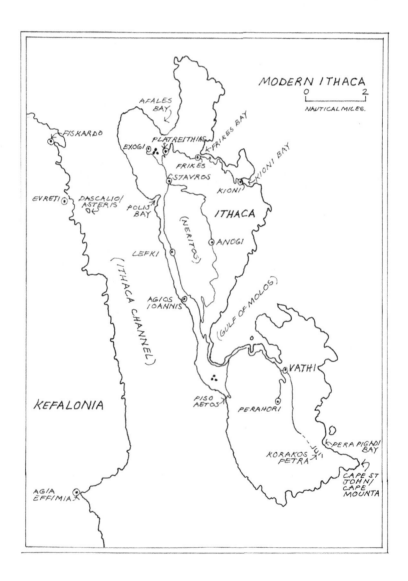

Map 2

SKETCH MAP OF THE IONIAN AND AEGEAN SEAS AT THE TIME
OF ODYSSEUS

Map 3

TELEMACHUS' ROUTE FROM PYLOS BACK TO ITHACA

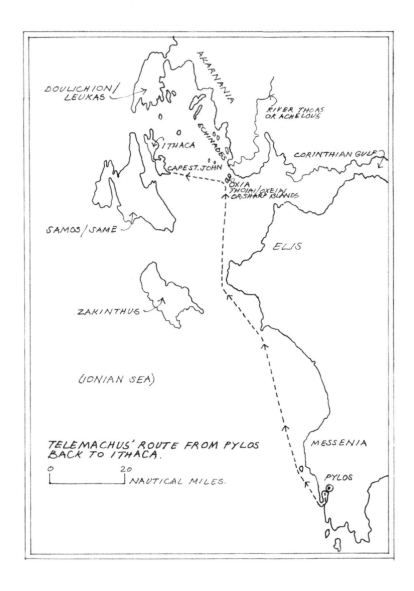

Map 4

HOMERIC ITHACA

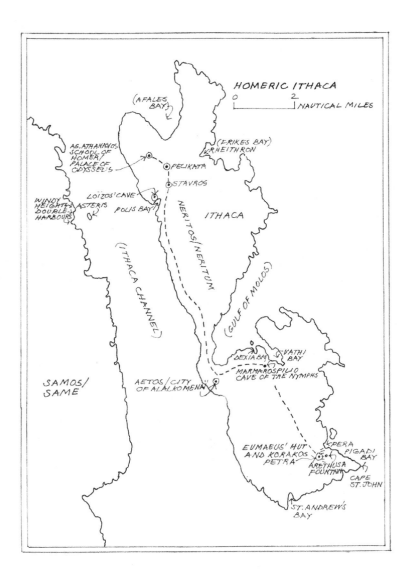

Introduction

My husband Alec Kazantzis first came to the Greek island of Ithaca in 1975. He immediately began to search for the Palace of Odysseus. The palace was thought to have stood on one, or other, of two known ancient sites in the north of the island.

He and I first came together to Ithaca in 1982. We bought and repaired a ruin in the remote village of Kioni. We were the first foreigners to do this. Alec spoke in Greek to the villagers in this isolated traditional community and I recorded some of these conversations in the little blue exercise books that Greek schoolchildren use. Together we shared their old stories, their grape picking and their winemaking, and I too began to speak a bit of Greek.

In 1994, Greek archaeologists from the University of Ioannina began to excavate one of the two sites on Ithaca previously pinpointed before World War Two by archaeologists from the British School at Athens. But simultaneously, several high-profile theories claimed that the centre of Odysseus' kingdom lay in the neighbouring larger, and richer, island of Kefalonia. Alec was watching this situation. When, in 2010, the archaeologists on Ithaca announced their discovery of the Palace of Odysseus, their conclusions were energetically challenged. Around this same time, Alec's health began to deteriorate, and I became his scout. Back in London I researched the archaeology on the island, and soon I was hooked.

Alec's death, on April 11 2014, was sudden and shocking. After his funeral, and a memorial service, I closed down his maritime arbitration business, and dealt with his will and probate both in England and in Greece. These things were both time-consuming and tricky, which was lucky in a way. The intense mental activity required prevented me thinking of very much else.

INTRODUCTION

As I completed this work, I looked again at the row of blue exercise books sitting on a bookshelf at our home in London. They recorded the changes in the village of Kioni and the island of Ithaca over the period of thirty years that Alec and I had been visiting. As I wrote up these stories I listened to a BBC series *The History of the World in a Hundred Objects*. Following this format, I decided to describe a few objects, all dating from well before Christ, which can be seen in the two museums on Ithaca. I felt these provided a direct link between the modern island of the same name and the ancient hero Odysseus. They prove, I believe, that Modern and Homeric Ithaca are one and the same, and that Ithaca was the true home of Odysseus.

As this subject area is tricky, I searched for someone more expert to check the detail of my conclusions. A recommendation from Professor Robin Lane Fox led me to the home of another professor, George L. Huxley, an eminent classicist, philologist and archaeologist, and an expert in precisely this field. With his help I was able to grasp the arguments underlying the Kefalonian claims. He also pinpointed the particular areas in Ithaca that scholars have associated with the texts of The Odyssey. They fitted so perfectly that I began to agree with the many scholars who have suggested that, to make such accurate observations, Homer himself must have visited Ithaca.

Meanwhile, archaeological work on Ithaca came to a halt and the main archaeologist died. It was practically impossible to obtain information about the excavation. Finally, I managed to complete Alec's search and to locate, with some certainty, the Palace of Odysseus described by Homer.

1
Nostos

As we set out for Ithaca, in the summer of 1982, the omens were good. The boat was small, but our skipper was competent and the sea was calm. Clouds of tiny fish shimmered below its glistening turquoise surface. As we headed for deeper water, the wind blew up. Alec hid behind the heaps of yellow fishing nets and the small boxed motor, chatting in Greek to our skipper, but I stood with my two teenagers in the bows. The waves smacked onto the small craft, drenching them with cooling spray so their straight blond hair hung in strings. Their sodden clothes clung to their slim shapes, silhouetted against the sea. We passed several desolate inlets to the north of the island before turning into a deep quiet bay. In the distance a scatter of pitched-roofed houses clustered round a harbour. They were wrapped around by an amphitheatre of steeply sloping hillsides, thickly covered in bushes of many different greens. When we reached the village, our skipper tied up amongst the other fishing boats at a small stone jetty.

NOSTOS

The harbour was the centre of the village. There was a taverna, a church, a shop, and a mint-green hut where the legal documents were stored. By day, when the sun blasted down from a clear blue sky, old men sat in the shade of a large eucalyptus tree. They chatted as they played backgammon, or clicked the beads of a komboloi through their fingers. Little old widows darted to and fro in the shadows between the houses. Their worn black dresses were mended and their cardigans darned. In the morning, after the bread was baked but the old wood-fired oven was still warm, they carried wide round dishes of herb-scented hand-stuffed tomatoes, peppers, or aubergines to the communal bakery behind the church. This was a place unaffected by modern life. A place where time moved slowly.

It was August, the height of the tourist season but, back then, we were the only tourists in Kioni. When we came back from the beach we showered and ventured out for supper in the taverna. The room was dominated by a black barrel-shaped cast-iron stove from which a stove-pipe rose, turned at right angles and looped its way across the room suspended from the ceiling by knotted wires. It left through a broken pane of glass above the entrance door. Behind the stove Aphrodite, the proprietress, hunched over a cauldron. It was balanced precariously on a two-ring tabletop hob linked by a tube to a large Calor gas canister below. From there she screeched orders at her husband, who leaned languidly against the outside wall. He seemed oblivious to her commands. We peeped inside her cooking pot, according to Greek custom, and came face to face with fish, that only that morning had been swimming in the sea. Their heads, bones and tails were all on show amongst a collection of roughly chopped onions, garlic, carrots and potatoes. At home the teenagers and I were vegetarian. I always insisted they eat fish or meat if it was offered, but Aphrodite's fish soup proved rather a sticking point. The teenagers joked about it late into the night. Luckily she also served sumptuous chips fried in hand-made local olive oil and tomatoes and peppers stuffed with rice, onions and herbs, all cooked in the village bakery. On feast days her husband turned the carcass of a whole goat on an iron spit above a half barrel of smouldering charcoal and Alec, who was a keen meat-eater, tucked in with enthusiasm.

The taverna was the centre of village gossip. Immediately the villagers gathered round and questioned Alec.

"How do you speak Greek?" asked one old man.

"I was born in England, in London, but my parents were Greek and we spoke Greek at home," he replied.

My teenagers and I stood by and watched. Alec and the old man were both of medium height and skinny, but Alec was particularly thin. When he took off his shirt his chest had a hole in it.

"Like a polo mint," I told him.

They both had large ears, and Alec's were particularly prominent. They both had thick fingers, another Greek characteristic. Alec was fifty-two when we first got together, nine months earlier, and I was a few days short of my fortieth birthday. The age difference worried him, but I assured him that it didn't matter to me.

"I prefer someone with a bit of maturity," I said.

Now, I think, Alec had brought us to this quiet and beautiful place to cement his relationship with my children. We didn't understand his conversation, which went on in Greek, but when we sat down he explained that the questioning had followed a predictable pattern.

"Where do you live?" the old man had asked.

"I live in London."

"What work do you do?"

"I am a lawyer but I specialise in arbitrating in shipping disputes."

"Which boat brought you to Ithaca?"

The fisherman's boat was called the 'Moby Dick'. I had puzzled over the name, which was spelled Mompi Ntik.

"Is this your first visit to Ithaca?"

Alec had been to Ithaca once before in the 1970s, when he stayed in the main town Vathi in the south of the island. The island, which is some fourteen miles long and four miles wide at its widest point, is squeezed in the middle as if someone had twisted the two ends in opposite directions. A narrow isthmus joins the north and the south parts of the island. On that first visit Alec had searched without success for the remains of the Palace of Odysseus, but nobody seemed precisely certain where it once stood. Yet the feel of the place fascinated him and, seven years later, he brought us to Kioni, in the north of the island. The village was as remote as could be. You could say it was at the end of the road but, at that time, only a dirt track existed to the village. We came by sea, as others had arrived there from time immemorial.

The people of Ithaca were still recovering from a succession of tragedies. During World War Two, the island had been occupied first by the Italians and then the Germans. The horribly divisive Greek Civil War followed. Finally, in 1953, a terrible earthquake had left only thirty houses standing in Kioni. Newly built or badly repaired houses were still interspersed with ruins. Dotted amongst them were pre-fabs the English had put up as a temporary measure. The villagers told us that after the earthquake, with nothing left of the village, the able-bodied had left for Australia, South Africa or the USA. They left the elderly to live precariously on small pensions from their time as seamen. Those who were left kept boats and did a bit of fishing and some grew vegetables for themselves. They tended their vines and made wine and later, through the winter, they picked their olives and crushed them into oil. The daily lives of those left on the island ran on as they had for centuries. Maybe millennia. This was a village cut off from the modern age. It was lost in a previous time.

By day, we marvelled at the purity of the light and swam in the jewelled sea. At night, the silence was broken only by the regular poop-poop sound of Scops owls and by the occasional barking dog. At dawn, the cockerels woke us with their crowing. After the hurly-burly of our crowded lives in London we felt we had arrived in paradise. The villagers went on with their questions.

"Where did your parents come from?"

"From Kastoria in Northern Greece."

"Oh, a lovely place! Do you still have relations there?"

Many Greeks have strong feelings of rootedness to the island of their origins but Alec's parents didn't come from Ithaca. He was only a visitor. Yet Ithaca has a particular tradition of homecoming stemming back to the return of Odysseus. A hero of the Trojan War, Odysseus, who the Romans later called Ulysses, is the main character of Homer's epic tale, *The Odyssey*. He is said to have come from this island. Alec had brought with him a copy of E.V. Rieu's Penguin Classics edition of *The Odyssey*. One evening he read aloud the passage where Odysseus' son Telemachus questions the goddess Athena when she appears disguised as a man on his home island.

> 'But tell me honestly who you are and where you come from. What is your native town? Who are your parents? And since you certainly cannot have come on foot, what kind of vessel brought you here? How did the crew come to land you in Ithaca, and who did they claim to be? And tell me the truth – I'd like to know – is this your first visit to Ithaca?'
>
> (1: 168-178 Rieu)

Telemachus' questions were hauntingly similar to those the islanders were still asking now, as if little had changed here in three thousand years.

By day we settled into a conventional seaside holiday. At that time the pebbly beaches of Ithaca were covered in flotsam and Alec made a large collection of washed-up shoes he discovered amongst the debris. I wonder now, over thirty years later, if the sea-shoes chimed with his feelings about his own life at that time. I was a lone parent of some standing but only two years had passed since Alec's first marriage had shattered, and his feelings were still raw.

"Each single shoe," he said, "is an emblem of past dreams, now lost and wrecked." Their huge platform soles fanned out in layers and thin straps unwound and stiffened into contorted snakes. "Once long ago," he said, "each shoe carried a young girl high above her natural height tottering out to find her man."

My children and I helped Alec with his sea-shoe search. We found dozens of singletons amongst the piles of seaweed, driftwood, and old plastic tubs along the seashore. We picked suitable stones and built a specially designed 'museum' on that steeply sloping beach. Each shoe had its own display stand to show it off to its best advantage. As the children of two architects my teenagers knew exactly how to do it.

At this time, when he was feeling a bit at sea with his life, Ithaca, with its long tradition of nostos, may have exerted a particular pull on Alec. The Greek word 'nostos' means 'heart-ache for homecoming'. It is the root of our word nostalgia. Homer's *Odyssey* tells the story of Odysseus' homecoming to Ithaca. It is known as a 'nostos poem' and perhaps there was something about this particular island that tied Alec back to his own Greek roots. He was always carrying a big fat book and *The Odyssey* epic was particularly important to him. He could even have he felt it tied him back to the origins of civilisation itself. Perhaps his sea-shoe collection was a symptom of his need, at that time, to reconnect with the past, but this is surmise and now it's too late to ask him.

Towards the end of our holiday, an old man we hadn't met before approached us. Panayiotis Païzis had recently returned from South Africa, where he had lived since his late teens, to organise and repair his property on Ithaca. The few foreign tourists who visited Kioni at that time mostly dropped by in a yacht. So the old man's eye fell on us landlubbers and he decided we should buy a house from him. We were curious, and had time to spare, so we went along to have a look. We followed him up the hill at the back of the village. Panayiotis was asthmatic. He wheezed and coughed as he struggled along in front of us. We climbed up and up, around hairpin bends, higher and higher above the harbour. A tatty old dog, snoozing in a pool of sunlight in the middle of the road, twitched an ear as we passed. Chickens and turkeys jostled and scratched amongst the hostile stems of prickly pears in the dried-out gardens on either side. In the upper part of the village the headland topped out. This part of the village was called Rachi.

"Rachi is the Greek name for that part of the upper human back which slopes around the shoulder," Alec explained. "In this case it describes the shape of the land."

Old people were sitting in a row on a bench. They leaned their backs against a battered stone wall. Men and women sat close, side-by-side, chatting amongst themselves. A few just gazed out to sea. Their clothes were clean, but darned, and their rugged faces had seen life. As we approached, they halted their chatter and greeted us with the utmost cordiality then, almost immediately, they turned to interrogate Alec in much the same way as the villagers down by the harbour. They asked him his name, how he spoke Greek, whether this was our first trip to Ithaca, which boat had brought us, and the rest. Alec answered their questions and we shook a hand of each in turn.

Then the old man led us along a narrow earth path, cut into the side of the steep slope of the mountain, which led towards the house he wanted to show us. We walked in single file, sometimes clambering over stones tumbled from the broken walls to our right. Above them, ancient olive trees grew on neglected terraces, their exposed roots huge and twisted. To our left, the land sloped steeply down to the harbour. The sun still shone down there, although up here we were in shadow. Rubbish had been tipped down the hillside. A dog leaped out barking and set off the mournful song of a donkey. The old man was gasping for air. Three hundred yards along the track he stopped in front of a gaping, bulging, semi-detached stone ruin. It towered, deep grey and ominous, at the top of a slope of scree.

"This is the house where I was born," he said.

Panayiotis Païzis peered out at us through round steel-framed, thick-lensed spectacles. Their arms rested on large low-slung ears. His thin white hair was greased and combed back smoothly. Although he had lived most of his life in South Africa his English still wasn't good. He told us he had worked there as a carpenter but, in spite of this physical job, he wasn't muscly and I could see that this dusty work hadn't been good for his asthma. He was wearing a formal suit and tie while Alec was wearing a sporty shirt and very short shorts. For Panayiotis this was work, but for Alec it was a game, or so I thought.

We scrambled up the fallen stones to the broken door of the ruin. It creaked open into a windowless ground floor workroom built into the hillside. Inside it was cool. As our eyes grew accustomed to the dusky light, we saw around us the remnants of a life lived on these islands for hundreds of years. Across the back of the room stretched a grape-treading area behind a low wall. From the base of the enclosure a carved stone spout once took the grape juice into a circular stone-lined pit about a metre deep in the earth floor, a kind of wine well. We dipped a tin can into the liquid at its base and smelt the sharp vinegar smell of the old wine. Against a side wall stood a battered wooden washstand with a hole in the top for the long-vanished bowl. Above it a nest of rusted iron bands, once used for wine barrels, hung from a large nail hammered into the wall. Nearby stood a rocking cradle, handmade from the same strips of steel.

"My mother rocked me in that cradle when I was a baby," said Panayiotis Païzis.

To the right of the door was a massive container hewn from a single piece of stone. What strength must have had been needed to move such a stone down the mountain and what skill was needed to carve it out.

"My family used it as a container for olive oil," the old man said.

At one corner of the room an area was partitioned off with a flimsy wall, its daub plaster had crumbled to reveal rough horizontal laths. In the enclosed area, the floor was roughly paved with flat stones, though the rest of the floor was just earth, and there was a makeshift stone hearth. It was some kind of a kitchen, perhaps. I set out through a broken doorway into a roofless, bramble-filled side ruin, but the old man called me back.

"There could be snakes out there," he said.

I had already found another square stone container and, across the corner, a massive stone bread oven.

An open-tread wooden staircase, steep as a ladder and rotting, led up from the main room to a trap door in the boarded ceiling. The old man went ahead. As he opened the trap, a shower of droppings fell down and a flurry of bats flew away. We crept gingerly after him into the room above where light shafted down through a hole in the roof. A heap of tiles lay below, around a corresponding rotten hole in the floor where the rain had come in. The whitewash on the walls was flaking to reveal a strong blue colour. In some countries, that blue paint is said to discourage mosquitoes.

Panayiotis Païzis stood with his back to the wall, but Alec and I wanted to see what lay in the second room to the front. We skirted around the edge of the broken floor to a room with a boarded ceiling painted pale grey. A crack in one wall was big enough to put my fist through, but we gasped as we looked out through the shattered upper window. The view was breathtaking. In the centre of our vision, above the cobalt blue sea, was a mysterious island with a band of white at its shoreline. It was floating like a ship.

"Would it be possible to mend this ruin?" Alec asked me.

Nearly all my working experience as an architect had been with existing buildings and I particularly liked a fine old ruin. But this one would be a challenge.

"Well, in England we might be able to strap the walls together and reinforce the stonework," I replied, "but here I am not sure. We are in an earthquake zone. I would have to ask the advice of an engineer, and not just any engineer. He would need to be a specialist."

We scrambled down the stairs and emerged into the light. Panayiotis Païzis' ruin was set into the steep hillside and a long flight of irregular stone steps followed the land up beside it. We climbed the steps, leaving the ruined house to our right. To our left he pointed out another patch of overgrown land, where a neglected almond tree and an ancient olive stood in a field of thistles and brambles. He wanted to include this in the sale. Higher up, to the right of the steps and behind the house, we found the 'water sterna'. This huge underground water cistern had been used to collect the winter rainwater from the roof of the house. From the top it looked like a well surrounded by a paved area. The top of the sterna was ringed with a carved stone like a huge dough-nut, its inner hole grooved over hundreds of years by the ropes of buckets drawing water from the chamber below. I wondered if it still held water, so I dropped a stone into it. It landed way below with a dull echoing thud. No water.

"You would need to mend the water sterna," the old man commented.

In the early evening light, we walked back down the rickety stone steps and stood with our backs to Panayiotis Païzis' ruin. We looked down at Kioni harbour with its jolly tiled roofs, its church, its taverna, and the town clerk's mint green hut. The stone ruins and little pre-fabs that interspaced them were not so obvious from up here. On the slope below us, small seed-eating birds twittered in huge untended olive trees, their sound mingling with the high-pitched bleat of cicadas. The air was scented with wild thyme, sage and catmint. We gazed over the peninsula behind the harbour to the magical island floating on its white shoreline. The faded mountains of mainland Greece stood silently beyond it. We had turned our backs on the ruined house but the old man broke into our reveries bringing us quickly back to earth.

"You can have it for a million drachma," he said.

It was about £6,000.

"Are you interested?" insisted the old man.

Alec stood there quietly. He was thinking.

"It is possible," he said.

When we got back to England we were busy. We both had full time jobs and teenage children to care for but we often talked about Ithaca. Something about it had caught our imagination. The following year, in the summer of 1983, we went back. This time we came in a larger group with Alec's sister Helen, her writer husband Gerry, and a group of six teenagers: theirs, Alec's, and mine. We wanted to cement these wider family relationships. We didn't stay in Kioni, but in the neighbouring village of Frikes.

This time we hired small boats so we could reach more distant beaches. Alec brought watermelons to eat, so wasps besieged our picnics. The teenagers raced to the sea to escape them and, at our favourite beach, swam to a rocky outcrop far out in the bay. After a scramble up the barnacled rocks they reached a tiny chapel and inside, although it seemed miles from anywhere, they found a bottle of olive oil and a small oil lamp burning. The local people were guarding their memories and someone had come out by boat to keep the flame alight.

One day three stout women stripped off their clothes and wallowed in a lake of rotting seaweed behind our favourite pebbly beach. We tried to hide our interest as they ran for the sea covered in mud like shiny black hippos. Later they emerged clean, dried off, and pulled themselves into old-fashioned flowered silk dresses fitting their ample bosoms as tightly as sausage skins. Then they approached, greeted us warmly, and asked Alec in detail about himself and his family according, it seemed, to Ithacan tradition.

"My mother came from Frikes," the lead woman said. "When I was a child, she told me this seaweed purifies and tightens the skin like nothing else on earth. Now I live in Athens but I come back every year and bring my friends to bathe in this pool."

A few days after our arrival that second year, as Alec was steering our little boat ashore, we saw from a distance the same old man standing by the harbour wall. Panayiotis Païzis was waiting for us. Alec leapt out to shake his hand, leaving the practicalities of securing the boat to me. Panayiotis was puffing and wheezing from his seven-kilometre walk to Frikes along the dirt road from the village of Kioni, where we had stayed the previous year. Alec led him across the road and sat him down at a table in front of the only taverna in Frikes. He offered him a Greek coffee, a glass of local wine, or a bowl of olives, but the old man turned them down. He had more important business to discuss. As I joined them he was saying.

"I have been waiting all year for you to come back to buy my house in Kioni. Until you buy it, I can't repair my other house down by the harbour, or return to my wife and children in South Africa."

He got up from the table as soon as he finished his speech. We watched his back as he tramped off into the distance, a sad but determined figure.

For over three thousand years, since Odysseus finally returned to Ithaca there has been a tradition that people come back. The old man had expected that we would too, and he was right. He had discovered we were back on his island and come to make his case. Alec's minimal show of interest had been enough, it seemed, for him to wait all year for our return. We were filled with guilt.

We began to turn Panayiotis Païzis' suggestion over in our minds and to discuss it with Alec's sister Helen and her husband Gerry. Alec began to think about the legal side of things. It was not encouraging. There was no system of land registration on the island. Ownership of land was just known, not centrally recorded, and we could see this created problems. All over the island, even in the most remote parts, we found rocks where people had painted their initials in red paint to indicate their ownership of the surrounding land. Sometimes the ownership of land was just based on the area of ground below the branches of an olive tree; the land itself was deemed of no value whereas the olive was the basis of the village economy. Then there was the principle of joint inheritance by every one of a man's descendants. Alec, Helen, Gerry and I had all heard of English people who finished the repair of their houses on other islands only to receive a visit from a Greek neighbour who said, "Thank you very much for all your hard work, and now go home as this house is mine."

Panayiotis had told us he could give us absolute ownership.

"I once had two brothers," he said. We knew that either of them, or their children, might have a claim to his ruin. "But," he continued, "they were both killed in Australia in their twenties before either of them married or had children. Nobody but me myself, and my children, have any claim to this house and I can guarantee these rights will be handed over to you."

We wondered how we could be sure of this. Alec and I walked from Frikes along the dirt road by the seashore and up the hill into Kioni to have another look at Panayiotis' ruined house. At the end of the footpath, the old people were still sitting on their bench, observing and commenting. They were still looking out to sea just as they had the previous year. They sat where their mothers and fathers sat before them and their grandparents sat before that. Once they had been to school together in the little school building down by the harbour. Now it was closed. There were no children left in Kioni. The old people gossiped about everything that went on in the neighbourhood, the village, the island, and the world. They turned over every small item of news received by letter from their families overseas. They were waiting for them to return. They commented like the Greek Chorus in the ancient plays by Euripides, Sophocles and Aeschylus, and we soon began to call them 'the Greek Chorus'.

When we reached Panayiotis' house it looked as formidable as ever, but there was no denying the view was spectacular. Alec left me there to measure the ruined walls, the garden, the dry water sterna, and the steps. I dropped plumb lines down the walls and measured their height and the angle by which they leaned from the vertical. I took a film of thirty-six slide photographs. Meanwhile, Alec knocked on the doors of each of the neighbouring houses in turn. Everybody was at home and they welcomed him with traditional hospitality.

First Alec visited Maria. She lived alone. Neat featured and intelligent she welcomed him into her sparse kitchen. She went outside and lowered a tin bucket into her water sterna so she could offer him fresh water with a saucer of homemade fig jam. Next, he visited the little house opposite. There large Cassandra smiled broadly, revealing her three remaining teeth. Her skinny husband, Dimitris, joined her in insisting that Alec sit down and make himself at home. They offered him a sweet Greek coffee (which the English might call Turkish) and, when he refused it, a glass of wine. All three neighbours agreed immediately that Panayiotis alone owned his ruined house, as well as the 'garden' on the far side of the steps. They all knew the sad story of his two brothers, childhood friends of theirs, who both died young in Australia. These two had never returned.

Back in Frikes, we discussed Panayiotis Païzis' ruin with Helen, Gerry, and with whichever children felt like joining in. This became a conversation not just about the old house but about the villagers too. They were very self-sufficient, and this was necessary. There was no mains water supply to either Kioni or Frikes, so the winter rain, collected from the roofs of their houses, had to last them through the summer. There was no rubbish collection, so rubbish was rotted down or buried or, as we had discovered, sometimes just thrown down the hill on the edge of the village. In the dry summer weather, it wasn't safe to light a fire. The only telephone in Kioni was communal. It was placed in a small mint-green wooden shed with a heavy pan-tiled roof down by the harbour. The shed doubled as the Town Clerk's office and housed dusty heaps of ancient documents and manuscripts.

Alec and I were attracted by the simplicity of the villagers' lives, but Gerry was less sure. In England, he and Helen lived in a remote part of Devon that was already quiet. We loved the August weather but Gerry found it too hot. In Ithaca ragged mongrels begged at our taverna table and this disturbed Gerry. At home he had a pedigree dog, which he took for walks on nearby Dartmoor. He was too polite to come right out with it but we sensed Gerry thought we were mad to spare a second for Panayiotis Païzis' suggestion, so Alec and I tried to pin down what attracted us to Kioni.

It was more than its peace and exquisite beauty, we thought. It was something about the way the society worked in the village. It seemed stable, permanent, unchanging. The shared hardship and isolation of the people had brought them a degree of cohesion, co-operation and self-reliance which, if it had ever existed in England, would certainly now be a thing of the past. We felt that Kioni, so cut off from city life by road, rail or air, nevertheless contained all the elements of a perfect existence. Here, beside the ever-changing sea, was the church, the shop, the bakery, and the legal office. Everybody knew about births, deaths and marriages, of the even-handedness of the mayor, of the severity of the priest, of loves and betrayals. The village had its history, its festivals, and its rivalries. Everything needed was here.

Yet I couldn't entirely agree with Alec.

"It is stunning here. Just perfect," I said. "I can't think of anywhere I would prefer to be. But all the same, there are lots of beautiful places in the world. If we buy this ruin on Ithaca we'll always have to come back here for our holidays and, who knows, we might feel like going somewhere else some day? Besides we've just spent all the money we have, and a lot we don't have too, on our place in London. We shouldn't allow ourselves to indulge in these fantasies."

Alec didn't argue, but he didn't take much notice of what I said either. He just went on quietly talking about Ithaca as if it had somehow got under his skin. I'm not sure what Helen was thinking. She kept her thoughts to herself.

We compared the larger village of Kioni with smaller Frikes, where we were staying that second year. Frikes was cold in winter, we had heard, and torrents of water filled a dry channel, which came down through the valley behind. Sometimes the land behind the harbour flooded. Kioni had over a hundred people living there through the winter whereas Frikes had less than a dozen permanent inhabitants. It seemed to us that Kioni had a more solid social structure whereas Frikes wasn't much more than a harbour where a small ferry from Lefkas came in daily. The local simpleton pretended to guide it in. He wore a hat, blew a whistle, and cried out "Mitsotakis, Mitsotakis!" (Mitsotakis was a right-wing politician in Greece at the time.) The sailors humoured this self-appointed port official as they manoeuvred the ferry up against the harbour wall.

The island was a paradoxical place. The local people were poor, yet many had seen the world travelling with the Greek merchant navy, or working for Aristotle Onassis who used the island as his main recruiting ground. They were almost completely cut off, yet they were well travelled and seemed very much in touch. They were rough yet sophisticated. They had a confidence coming from knowing who they were and where they belonged. They were friendly and welcoming and, of course, it helped that Alec and Helen could speak their difficult language.

Alec and Gerry were competing in bird spotting. By day, we watched red kites flying above us and in the evenings we listened to the strange calls of Scops owls. Alec saw a bright blue kingfisher skimming over the rocks. Gerry saw a hoopoe.

One evening Alec scrambled up a rocky headland and watched an eagle soaring over the hilltops. At supper he read us a passage from *The Odyssey*.

'Zeus the Thunderer urged two eagles into flight from the mountain-top. For a while they sailed down the wind with outstretched pinions, wing to wing. But as soon as they were directly over the meeting-place, where the sound of voices filled the air, they began to flap their wings and wheel about, glancing down at the faces of the crowd with looks of foreboding death, Then with their talons they clawed at each other's cheeks and neck, and so swooped eastward over the house-tops and busy town. The people stared at the birds in amazement, and asked themselves what was to come of it.'

(2: 145-56 Rieu)

It was a sign that Odysseus would return.

On September 1, 1983 a lorry came to pick up the rented tables and chairs from the one taverna in Frikes. The short tourist season in Northern Ithaca was officially over. We wondered whether or not we would come back again. That night Helen made us an offer.

"I will lend you the money if you want to buy Panayiotis Païzis' ruin," she said. "You can pay me back when you can afford it."

On the last day of our stay Alec walked from Frikes to Kioni one more time. He found Panayiotis Païzis and told him we would buy his ruined house.

When we returned to Ithaca in the summer of 1984, we brought with us the money Helen had lent us. Kioni looked just the same. The Greek Chorus were still sitting at the end of the track chattering about the slightest bit of news. Panayiotis Païzis was still waiting for us. He hadn't managed to find anyone else to buy his ruin.

During the winter Alec had written to the Australian authorities who, in due course, sent him copies of the death certificates for both of Panayiotis Païzis' brothers and confirmed they had no descendants. Meanwhile, I drew up my survey of his ruin. I took my drawings and photographs to the seismic design department of the engineering firm Ove Arup in London. I managed to catch the earthquake specialist on his return from Mexico where he had been assessing the effects of a recent huge earthquake. He considered my photographs, drawings and measurements in detail, and came to the conclusion that, with careful reinforcement of the existing stonework, it would be possible to save the old house and to make it safe. I was reassured by his assessment and incorporated his proposals into my drawings.

That year, we made friends with another Païzis, apparently not closely related to Panayiotis. Captain John Païzis lived down by the harbour in Kioni. He had returned to live in his home village after a lifetime abroad. Newly retired as captain of Onassis' fleet, Captain John was an immensely capable, practical, energetic, and kind man. Everyone treated him and his wife Loula with love and respect, which they richly deserved. They had huge authority in the village and became our chief source of advice and information. Now they recommended a lawyer in the capital Vathi, twenty-four kilometres away on the southern part of the island. Taxis were cheap in Ithaca in those days and, like taxis in many Eastern countries, they filled up with as many other people as they could squeeze in on the way. The road had been newly repaired and now, although it was still narrow and precipitous, it was tarmacked all the way to Vathi. (See Map 1)

Vathi is a small town with a long deep harbour. In fact, the name

Vathi means 'deep'. The lawyer Kandiolotis was an elderly man who, like our prospective neighbour Cassandra, had very few teeth. Maybe he had none at all. We had noticed this was another feature of the island. Obviously there was a shortage of dentists, but we wondered if it might also be the result of a lifetime of drinking soft rainwater collected from the roofs. Alec handed over my drawings of the site and went through the legal details with Kandiolotis. They spoke in Greek and I couldn't understand their conversation, but the lawyer's office was pleasant with a spectacular display of shells and other sea ephemera. Sea-shoes were not included.

After the lawyer Kandiolotis had prepared the papers, we came again to Vathi, this time with Panayiotis Païzis, to register the purchase. Together we walked a short way round the harbour to the notary's office. It was in a wooden shed with a heavy (much too heavy) pan-tiled roof similar, but a bit larger, than the legal shed in Kioni.

At first, as we came in out of the bright light outside, I could see very little. The atmosphere was strange. The shed had a musty tomb-like smell. As my eyes adapted, I realised we were looking down its length to a large, dilapidated and dimly illuminated desk at the far end. On either side, shelves dipped under the weight of mouldering ancient books, and papers tied with faded ribbons. Spiders had built elaborate nests amongst them. Stacked around the edges of the floor below the shelves were so many books, and bulging old files, that only a narrow passageway remained. Many of these ancient papers, we later discovered, were archives from the three hundred years of Venetian rule of the island from the end of the fifteenth century. At the far end of the hut a tiny, pallid, bespectacled head peered out from behind the papers piled high on the desk. It belonged to the notary.

The notary looked carefully through our two copies of hand-typed documents and discussed them at length with the lawyer Kandiolotis. Some handwritten notes were made. Panayiotis added his signature. The notary fumbled in the drawers of his desk and produced postage stamps of many different colours and sizes. He stuck them to each page of both documents and rubber-stamped carefully over each one. Alec took bundles of drachma notes from a carrier bag and handed them over. We all shook hands. The deed was done.

That evening Alec and I went for a meal in Aphrodite's taverna down by Kioni harbour to celebrate the occasion.

"I bet some of our papers go missing from that notary's office," I joked. And many years later we discovered that had indeed happened. Luckily the lawyer, Kandiolotis, had given us a second copy.

Our friend the sea captain John Païzis came and sat down beside us. We didn't need to tell him our news as he had already heard it on the village grapevine. He congratulated us saying:

"You have not bought a house, you have bought an extra ten years to your life."

We hoped he was right.

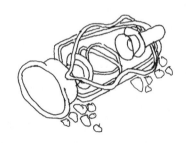

2

Ithacan Landscapes

ANDREAS
COMINOS

After the purchase, we set about clearing the brambles and thistles from our two sites, one on each side of the steep stone communal steps. It was on one such bramble-clearing mission that we found a chubby middle-aged man in jeans and a striped tee shirt under our almond tree collecting nuts. Alec approached him in a very friendly way but the man, who we later knew as Mimis, seemed embarrassed and upset. We felt his mistake was perfectly understandable. Our 'garden' was a long-abandoned, unenclosed patch of hillside. It would have been a shame to let our almonds go to waste and possibly he, unlike us, didn't have the money to buy almonds at the shop. He apologised profusely and told us he was the son of the priest. He didn't stay long and spoke in Greek without admitting to his fluent English.

The old priest was a tall, cultured and distinguished man, but rather severe. Mimis, short for Dimitris, was his eldest son. We had often noticed the priest striding about the village amongst his small flock. He looked all the taller for his black cassock down to the ground and the high black hat on his head. An embossed silver crucifix around his neck was partly concealed by his long white beard. We had wondered if he was happy in this remote spot or if he was sometimes lonely. Mimis told us later that he had a sister and two brothers, although their mother had unfortunately died. We were glad to find the priest had a family.

Mimis hadn't known about our purchase but, now that I know how quickly news spreads about the village, I find this surprising. In a community where houses are divided equally between the children on the death of the parents, and passed on through the generations, ours was the first property to be sold to a foreigner. Perhaps Mimis hadn't heard the news as he himself had only just returned from America. It was ironic that after thirty years abroad he had finally fled that mobile rootless society only to be caught scrumping on land recently bought by foreigners in his home village.

We discovered things hadn't worked out for Mimis in America. He had married and divorced. He had lost touch with his only daughter, which is unusual for a family-minded Greek. Now he had returned to live with his father. There was no work available in the village, but soon after he arrived the old town clerk died of a heart attack and Mimis took over his job in the mint-green wooden hut with the tiled roof down by the harbour. Along with the local legal files, he took charge of the temperamental communal telephone. It was the only phone in the village, so there was always a queue of locals waiting to use it. As the number of foreign tourists slowly increased there were also usually some visitors waiting too. Calls to neighbouring villages were possible but calls to Athens were difficult, and overseas calls practically impossible. Mimis struggled to make a connection with the outside world and Alec liked to watch his delight when the occasional young American or Australian girl with long sun-tanned legs and short shorts came into his little hut and presented him with a really big problem.

"Monkeys on the line," he would comment, as the phone squeaked and grunted and failed to make a connection with the outside world.

Mimis acquired a dog, which he aptly named Bully. Bully was often involved in dogfights outside Mimis' little green hut.

We soon discovered Mimis had a gift for storytelling. He took it upon himself to explain to us, and to any other foreigners who now occasionally made their way to his village, how things worked in this tight-knit society. One evening, as dusk fell, he told us a story about the German occupation during World War Two. Everyone in the village knew how, he said, if the Germans caught a Greek resistance fighter, they would torture both him and his family. Sometimes they would burn down his whole home village. Several local men were resistance fighters, or andartes, and everyone knew where they were hiding in caves in the hills. The German forces were based in the capital Vathi that was linked to Kioni only by a donkey track over the mountains. This was, at that time, the main route from the north to the south of the island. The path winds up the hill from Kioni to Anoghi, continues along the high spine of the northern part of island past the monastery at Kathera, across the narrow isthmus where the two halves join, and on to the southern part of the island and Vathi.

Everyone was short of food during the war. Nothing was brought in from outside and sometimes the Italians and Germans raided the local people and took what little they had.

"We were better off than our relations in Athens," said Mimis, "where huge numbers died of starvation. In Kioni we ate sea urchins, snails, and edible weeds. Many of the older people live like this still. There was no food in the shops, but here, by the sea, we could catch fish. We grew our own maize and ground it in the windmills, which were all still working in those days. We baked bread but we often ran short, so then we used to trade our fish with the people of Anoghi, who had larger fields and could make more bread."

This is how, one day, Mimis and his mother came to be climbing up the long steep footpath from Kioni up to Anoghi. The name Anoghi means the 'land above'. On their backs they carried panniers full of fish. They set off up the hill, past the top end of Kioni, past the vineyards, and on through olive groves and wild woodland. They walked for over two hours until at last they reached Anoghi. Mimis was eight at the time. His mother swopped their fish for bread and they set out again on the downward path towards Kioni. They were passing through woods when they heard a thumping sound in the distance. Mimis wondered if heavy animals were stamping over the hills. His mother pulled him into the scrub beside the path where they crouched behind a large bush.

Mimis began to look nervous as he told us the story.

"The noise came closer and closer. A troop of men were marching in unison with heavy boots. My mother was shivering with fear. A column of German soldiers carrying weapons came marching towards us. Their faces were a blur under their helmets. They walked right by the place where we were hiding. I could see their strong brown boots through the base of the bush. My heart was thumping so loudly I wondered if they might hear it. I held my breath. I was terrified I might sneeze and we would be discovered. What would they do if they found us? Tramp, tramp, tramp. More and more. They came on and on. About two hundred of them. Finally, the terrible sound faded into the distance and the quiet of the mountain returned. Where had they gone? We didn't know. When we were sure it was all clear, we crept out from behind the bush and hurried back down the path into the village."

When Mimis and his mother arrived back in Kioni there was no sign of the soldiers. His mother alerted his father the priest, who immediately went to tell Captain John Paizïs' father, who was the mayor. The priest and the mayor were the two most important men in the village. They discovered the German soldiers were still up in the hills that surrounded the village on all sides.

Mimis told us how the Greek resistance fighters immediately crept out of the village and made their way to secret caves in the hills. He pointed to the house by the harbour where they kept their arms and ammunition in the two storerooms on the ground floor. Then another group of men moved the weapons into one of the storerooms, leaving the other empty but locked. As soon as the job was complete those men too slipped away quietly and hid in the hills. They left only the priest, the mayor, the women, and the children in Kioni.

Early the following morning, the German soldiers came down from the hills into the village. The priest and the mayor came out to meet them and shook hands with the officers who approached.

"Where are your people?" asked a German officer who spoke Greek.

"They are all away just now," replied the priest.

"You're lying, priest."

"Aren't you ashamed to say that a Christian priest would lie?"

"Do you have any arms or ammunition?"

"We did have some here but the resistance fighters came and took them," answered Captain John's father the mayor.

"Where were they stored?"

"I will show you the room."

The mayor led the soldiers to the recently emptied storeroom. On the other side of the central dividing wall the arms and ammunition were piled high.

"This is where they were," he explained, "but now they have been taken away."

Mimis explained to us in detail exactly how his father managed not to lie while, at the same time, not giving away the position of the guerrilla fighters or their store of weapons. The Germans continued their search but found nothing. Finally, they turned round and marched back up the path towards Anoghi.

"Your stories are fascinating," I told Mimis. "You should write them down."

"Oh no, I'm not a writer," replied Mimis. "I just pass on stories by word of mouth."

"Like the bards of ancient times," said Alec.

Alec and I came back to Kioni each summer. It had a choice of lovely places to swim and sometimes we hired a small boat and made trips to nearby beaches. We were happy to explore the places the villagers described. We didn't hire a car. Even after the road from Kioni to Vathi was tarmacked it was narrow and very precipitous and Alec was a remarkably bad driver. He'd gaze around at the landscape as he zigzagged to and fro across the road. He seemed totally unaware of the danger into which he was putting himself and his passengers. I didn't want to shame him by insisting I took over the task, and agreed readily to making any necessary journeys by taxi or on foot.

We spent a lot of time walking. We explored the footpaths around and beyond our ruined house. They were often overgrown. They forked. They were not well marked and we often lost our way. Some tracks were marked with blobs of red paint on a rock to show the route. Some were blocked with bundles of brushwood where a shepherd wanted to keep his goats or sheep to one side or the other. Once we found a tree full of goats, all gazing down at us from its branches. Often, goats spotted us before we saw them, scattering behind the rocks as we approached. We discovered makeshift goat shelters; their roofs made from re-used, rusted corrugated metal, their doors and gates from oddments of sticks, or discarded cast iron bedsteads tied together with tangled wire. Inside these improvised shelters donkey saddles hung on pegs. Outside the ground was soaked with goat pee and sprinkled with droppings. Sometimes we found local people in the most remote places and if we lost our way they were always happy to help.

One time a flimsy gate blocked our path. Posts on either side of it supported a ragged fence. The gate was tied to each of the posts with crazy tangles of knotted wire. We puzzled over the knots, both sides looked equally difficult to untie. Finally we made a decision and had almost completed the task when we heard galloping hooves approaching. A boy riding a small grey pony stopped behind us. He was riding bareback without any bridle. We recognised each other immediately as he was the nephew of Aphrodite, who ran the taverna down by the harbour, the son of her brother the goatherd. He sat on his pony watching carefully while we finished untying the knots.

"In Greece," he said, "we normally open a gate by the latch, not the hinge."

It was unusual, on Ithaca, to find someone riding a pony. There are not many ponies on the island. The pathways are treacherous and the hills are too steep for a pony and cart, but a sure-footed donkey can scramble up these rocky paths with panniers slung across their backs to carry bunches of grapes or branches of olives. The owner walks by its side. In Homer's *Odyssey*, Odysseus' son Telemachus turns down the gift of three horses and a splendid chariot offered by the rich King Menelaus of Sparta who lived on the fertile plains of the Peloponnese. Telemachus replies:

> 'Horses I will not take to Ithaca. I'd rather leave them here to grace
> your own stables. For your kingdom is a broad plain, where clover
> and galingale grow in plenty, with wheat and rye and broad-eared
> white barley; whereas in Ithaca there is no room for horses to run,
> nor any meadows at all. It is a pasture-land for goats and more
> attractive to my eyes than any sort of land where horses thrive. None
> of the islands that slope down to the sea is rich in meadows or suitable
> for chariots, Ithaca least of all.'
>
> (4: 601-8 Rieu)

Alec and I checked the path Mimis had taken with his mother to barter their fish for bread. It was a difficult uphill walk and at that time it was rather overgrown. After leaving Kioni, a stepped and cobbled track passed through an area of well-kept vineyards and terraces of olive trees. As it left the village, the track turned into a narrow dirt footpath and entered a dense forest where spiders made huge webs. Insects had left their skins when they moved on to something larger, leaving perfect transparent replicas of themselves on the branches. Crusty wide-headed crickets integrated themselves with the bark of the trees. Only their high-pitched cries revealed them in spite of their camouflage. We discovered hundreds collected on one tree trunk.

Sometimes a brightly lit opening in the trees revealed a long view down to the sea where, far below, we saw little fishing boats moored in sheltered bays. Beyond them, over the sea, lay scatterings of islands, as Ithaca is surrounded by other islands. Heading inland the dark forest enveloped us again. The trees closed over our heads and dried-out brambles reached towards us from either side. Suddenly, far from anywhere, the path led us into a fertile, sunlit valley surrounded by hills with another group of vineyards, goat enclosures, well-tended olives and an ancient water sterna. This valley was silent, strange, ancient and mysterious. The landscape was just as the goddess Athena had described it in *The Odyssey*.

'The long hill-paths, the welcoming bays, the beetling rocks and the leafy trees'.

Overhanging rocks beside our path, the ones the goddess called 'beetling', made good hiding places for goats. Sometimes they concealed the entrance to a cave. As we finally approached Anoghi the stones had been cleared into walls around small fields and a few cows were grazing. As the goddess said:

'Corn grows well and there is wine too. Rain and fresh dew are never lacking; and it has excellent pasture for goats and cattle, timber of all kinds, and watering places that never fail'.

(13: 243-5 Rieu)

A 'menhir' stands to the left of the path as it approaches Anoghi. We could see the ancient rock rearing over the landscape beyond a vineyard where a man was working, and when Alec approached to ask him the way and he gave us a bunch of ripe grapes. Beyond his vineyard the ancient standing stone towered above us with one huge rock fitting snugly on top of another. The massive upper stone is carved with vertical ridges. It stands in a moonscape of similar stones. Some have fallen on their sides. Behind it lies another fallen stone with similar ridges. The standing stone, which the locals call Irakles (or Hercules) is believed to date from before the time of Odysseus, from around the time of Stonehenge, but nobody exactly knows.

The menhir outside Anoghi

When Alec and I reached the village of Anoghi, most of the houses were deserted. Traditional stone water sternas crumbled beside them. The shop-cum-drinking-place was a relic from past times. Travel posters, nailed up in the 1950s, drooped from the walls. A talkative parrot called greetings from his cage. A few packets of biscuits with old-fashioned Greek lettering were neatly displayed on the shelves at the back of the shop. A larger bird with outstretched wings, long dead and stuffed, glowered down from the top of the shelving. It may once have been an eagle but, with the feathers dropping from its neck, it looked more like a vulture. Maybe it was always a vulture. There, Nikos and his wife sold us a Greek coffee or a bottle of water and, when Captain John asked especially in advance, they would cook us a chicken stew with roast potatoes. Alec and I would borrow the key from Nikos and go to look at the stunning frescos in the church next door. They were painted when, under the three hundred year rule of the Venetians, Anoghi was once the capital of the island, but now only thirty people remained in the village.

In Ithaca you can feel, all around you, the ghosts of people who lived thousands of years before. Our teenagers were particularly interested in the pirates who were an ever-present danger in ancient times. The settlement of Anoghi, like all the more ancient habitations in Ithaca, was built on high ground so the people could escape from them. Yet who were these pirates? After reading *The Odyssey* I began to wonder if Odysseus himself was a bit of a pirate.

> *The same wind that wafted me from Ilium brought me to Ismarus, the city of the Cicones. I sacked this place and destroyed its menfolk. The women and the vast plunder that we took from the town we divided so that no-one, as far as I could help it, should go short of his proper share. And then I said we must escape with all possible speed. But my fools of men refused. There was plenty of wine, plenty of livestock; and they kept on butchering sheep and shambling*

crooked-horned cattle by the shore'.

(9: 39-47 Rieu.)

As Odysseus' men cooked meat and drank wine on the beach the Cicones called for help from their inland neighbours, who were good fighters. Six of Odysseus' men from each ship were killed. He lost about seventy-two men, and when he managed to escape with the others, to punish him further, a terrible storm blew up.

Another day, we took a different inland walk. We set out on the track past our newly purchased ruin and found several other substantial ruins in an even worse state than our own. It was clear that, like the village of Anoghi, Rachi was once a much larger community.

Further up our track we found just one inhabited house, with an old couple living there, then we walked on through wooded land and neglected olive groves, and reached an opening with fresh green vineyards on either side and blue sky above. The grape vines were carefully tended and we recognised members of the Chorus working there. A path from there led steeply uphill through overgrown olive groves, past improvised goat houses, old water sternas, and walls once carefully built with cut stone archways and niches. After about an hour and a half on foot, we reached the Vigla. This open place had ancient fields, olive groves and a tiny chapel. It was a lookout place for spotting the pirates, who once terrorised the inhabitants of these islands.

To amuse our teenagers we tried to discover a bit about the pirates. The authors of Classical Greece often mentioned pirates cruising the Ionian Sea and Plutarch told how pirates sacked nearby Lefkas. In the fifth century BC the historian Thucydides explained how, in order to avoid danger from the sea, the oldest inhabited sites were built high up on land hidden from view. Watchtowers and lookout forts were positioned so sentinels could keep a constant watch. The smoke from their beacons, or their flames at night, gave early warning of an attack. This was the place we had discovered.

During the Roman occupation of Ithaca, which continued for nearly 600 years from 180BC onwards, there was such a rise in piracy that the seas were virtually closed and trade was brought to a standstill. Only when Rome itself was threatened with famine the Romans appointed a proconsul specifically charged with the task of dealing with the pirates. He did so by manning 270 warships and mobilising 100,000 troops. As a result of this radical policy, piracy in the Mediterranean was kept in check for around five centuries.

Piracy flourished again after the Byzantines disbanded their imperial fleet in 1182. Pirates joined Venetian ships in the sea-lanes and attacked both ships and coastal towns. By this time, the Ithacans referred to pirates as 'Saracens', implying they were not Greeks but Arabs or Turks. We were told that Saracen pirates lay in wait in hidden coves and made surprise attacks on ships sailing in the strait between Ithaca and Kefalonia. Yet there is still a bay in Kioni called Sarakinari, indicating that pirates operated from there, as well as a bay called Sarakiniko near Vathi.

It seemed that when Homer called Odysseus the 'Sacker of Cities' it had no derogatory overtones. He was admired as a hero. I wondered if some of these later pirates might also have been Greek. I didn't quite like to mention this to Alec, although later I discovered this was certainly so.

Alec left the practical side of repairing the ruin to me. The engineer I consulted at Ove Arup in London was a world expert. He was critical of the rigid concrete frames used for so many modern buildings in Greece as he had often witnessed them failing when subjected to the actual horizontal shaking forces of an earthquake. He was particularly critical of the cheap perforated red bricks the Greeks so often use in their new buildings. He advised that the walls could be strengthened with stainless steel mesh within their mortar joints to make them safe.

"Particularly," he advised, "you must be careful to preserve the corners of the building which are beautifully built with large, specially cut corner stones. Also, you must be careful to keep the good wide bearings on the lintel stones you have over the windows and doors on the front elevation. Then you must insert a reinforced concrete ring beam around the top of the building. You can do it on the inside of these thick walls without it showing."

His advice made a lot of sense and on this basis I drew up plans for the repair of our ruin. In 1985, I took my set of drawings out to Ithaca to apply for planning permission and we discussed with Captain John Païzis how we should proceed. He advised we should go to Vathi and speak to Massos, the best architect/engineer on the island, and ask him how to submit our plans. Massos was friendly but quite definite in his total rejection of my ideas.

"You, as a British architect, are not allowed to present plans to the planning authorities in Kefalonia," he said. "Even an architect from Athens cannot put in a planning application here. It has to be done by an architect from Ithaca or Kefalonia."

The second problem arose as soon as Massos looked at my drawings. His response was swift and decisive.

"You can't do this. The first thing you will need to do is to knock out the corners of your building. You must have concrete columns in each corner of the house."

In vain, I begged him to believe that the seismic specialist at Ove Arup knew what he was talking about. Did he really mean we must knock out the strongly built stone corners and leave the wobbly walls unsupported? This made no sense.

"There has to be some alternative," I suggested.

"The only alternative is to line out the whole interior of the ruin with 15 cm. of reinforced concrete."

"Like a bomb shelter," I said. The walls were already over two foot thick.

The regulations in Ithaca may now have been updated to include some less brutish way to repair and strengthen an existing house, but at that time there was, it seemed, no other way we were allowed to do it.

In the following weeks, Massos made some drawings of a new and totally different two-storey house with a concrete frame, perforated red brick infill panels and a rendered finish in the standard modern Greek style. But we weren't interested in building a new house, and our inaccessible site was clearly unsuitable for such a project. Even if we managed to barrow our builders' rubble 200 yards along the narrow, overgrown dirt path to the road, there was no rubbish tip on the island.

"We have plenty of stones, and they are already there, for free," I pointed out. "It would be absurd to cart all those good stones down to the road by barrow to replace them later with holey red bricks, which we would then have to bring by barrow all the way back up the track. It would be cheaper, as well as nicer, to re-use the stones we have already to mend the building."

Massos was getting fed up with me.

"You are not allowed to repair this building at all," he said. "First, I have to apply for permission to demolish it entirely."

Things were getting worse. Finally, some compromise drawings for a two-storey house were sent off to the planners in the neighbouring island of Kefalonia, but neither he nor I were happy with the proposals. I was an outsider making unconventional suggestions on Massos' home ground. Moreover I was a woman, and I didn't even speak Greek. It was a bad start. We went back to England.

Ten months later in London Alec met a maritime lawyer who happened to come from Kefalonia. He asked for news about our ruin in Ithaca.

"Nothing is happening at all," replied Alec. "We eventually agreed that the local architect should put forward some compromise scheme, we paid his fees in advance for the whole job and he said he'd put it in for planning permission. Now month after month passes by and we haven't heard a thing."

"How many months have passed?"

"About ten."

"I think," the lawyer said, "there is a local law that says if the planners don't respond to an application within six months permission is automatically granted."

Alec passed the details of this law to Massos, who wrote to the planners. Permission, he told Alec when he rang him from England, was granted. So the following year when we came out to Ithaca we hoped it would be plain sailing. We couldn't have been more wrong.

Captain John explained to us how we should pick our builder.

"You have to employ people from Kioni to build up your house, or the local people will take offence. Then, if you ever need them to repair it in the future they won't come."

He recommended George and Spiros Papalexis, stonemasons from the village, to do the structural work. He introduced us to the brothers and explained how the partnership worked; thin George did the brainy work while large Spiros provided the physical strength. After the walls were built, the client had to employ his own roofer, buy his own windows and doors, and act as building foreman. I wondered how I was going to do that without telephone contact, when I didn't speak Greek, and as well as my full-time job in England.

At Aphrodite's taverna down by Kioni harbour Alec and I met up with Massos the architect and George Papalexis the brainy brother to discuss the repairs needed to our house. George agreed to take on the work. I hoped he would turn out to be as brainy as John had described but, in any case, there appeared to be no alternative. Alec passed on to him in Greek that the first thing he needed to do was to mend the water sterna. In this way, we could collect water over the winter so work could start the following spring. George ignored this. He had something else on his mind.

"Where are the papers?" he asked Massos. "How can I be sure that these people really have planning permission?"

"You can take my word for it," Massos replied. "They have planning permission."

George looked dubious.

"Look," Massos said, "there is the chief planner sitting over there. We will go and ask him."

The taverna had grown a bit since we first knew it. Now it had several tables outside by the sea as well as inside with Aphrodite's cauldron of fish soup. Our little group of four walked over and confronted the planner who just happened to be sitting at a neighbouring table.

"So have they got planning permission?" asked George.

The planner scowled. "Unfortunately, yes. These people dug up some ancient law that hasn't been used for decades and we were obliged to give them planning permission. They shouldn't have got permission to do anything on that site. That building is an ancient monument. Now I have had to give permission for it to be first demolished and then re-built. I must see to it that law gets repealed."

The sun had long left our side of the mountain and the air was cool when George, the brainy builder, came up to our site to discuss the work. Alec and I stood with him on the rough paving stones surrounding the top of our water sterna. We shook hands politely, assured him our children were well, and made all the formal greetings usual in Greece, then we got down to business. I was concerned that some things might get lost in translation, so I was trying to keep things simple.

"First we need to mend the water sterna this autumn," I repeated to Alec, "so we can collect the rain over the winter. We'll need the water for the building work when we mend the house next year." Alec translated this into Greek. There was a long silence then an extended conversation in Greek. I could see from their body language things weren't going well.

"Surely it is obvious we have to mend the water sterna first?" I said to Alec. "Doesn't he accept the logic of that?"

"Yes, I think he accepts that," replied Alec, "but he has a lot of problems. He is wondering why we don't want to build the house in perforated bricks. He knows a place where we can buy them very cheaply."

"You must explain that we have decided to use the local stone," I said, "not only because it is beautiful but because it is here. Even if we wanted to use those bricks, which we don't, how would we ever get them up the track? Then we'd have to get rid of all the stone we've got here already. That would be silly, I think. Could you explain that to him?"

I wished I could understand what they were saying. I was baffled to see how such a simple point could generate so much discussion. Finally, Alec asked me another question,

"Where can he put the rubbish from the old tiles and mortar and any little stones too small to re-use?"

"He should first build up a retaining wall in front of the house beside the track," I replied, "then he can fill the space behind it with his building rubble, up to the ground floor level, to make a terrace in front of the house."

Another long conversation in Greek followed. Alec seemed to be pleading with George, who put his hand to his head and began to look quite distressed. Finally, George dropped a stone down into the water sterna and it fell, as before, with a dull thud into the base. He looked gloomily down the hole after his stone.

"We must be sure to preserve this lovely stone ring around the top," I said. "If it has to be taken off to get access to the chamber, he must carry it carefully and put it somewhere it won't get damaged. Then, when the sterna is mended, it must be replaced in the same position. Can you explain that Alec?"

Alec explained. George still looked glum.

"Then we must take up these paving stones and put them carefully in a pile," I added, "because we want to use them on the terrace out the front of the house."

Another conversation in Greek followed.

"He is asking where we want the pile," said Alec.

We decided on a position for the pile of stones and for the ring from the top of the sterna.

"Before we can do any other building work," I repeated yet again, "we'll have to mend the water sterna so we can catch some water over the winter."

George was still scratching his head.

"He says he will need water before he can mend the sterna," said Alec.

"Surely this can't be beyond the wit of man," I said.

I was beginning to wonder whether, if George was the brainy brother, what the other one must be like. Or was he taking the mick?

"What does he usually do in these situations?" I asked.

I watched while another long conversation took place.

"He says he doesn't usually build up houses which are this far off the road."

"Well perhaps he could bring an old tank along the path with a barrow and then bring the water in jerry cans to fill it?"

The conversation in Greek went on and on and George was still scratching his head. Alec, who was normally very calm, began to gesticulate. George said something I could see was a final pronouncement. He smiled as he stretched out his hand to shake each of ours in turn. Then he turned and walked away quickly down the track.

"What did he say?" I asked Alec.

"He said we will talk about it again next year when we come out," replied Alec.

"TALK about it. AGAIN?" I expostulated, "NEXT YEAR WHEN WE COME OUT? At this rate we might decide to go somewhere else!"

Yet each summer we came back to Kioni and rented somewhere down in the village to stay. Years passed by. Our teenagers were growing up, one was already at university, but we never lost faith. We often walked up and looked at our dilapidated ruin. We cleared the garden but no work was ever done on the house.

We got to know the Greek Chorus on the bench at the end of our track. Alec particularly enjoyed talking to them about the heroes of Ancient Greece. They had preserved so many of the old traditions, as well as the philosophy and superstitions from those ancient times, and Alec amused himself, and them, by talking to them about it. I was intrigued by his conversations and I wondered if I could record some of them by writing them down. In this quiet place, so far from our hectic life in London, these conversations seemed important.

Late one afternoon, as we walked up the track beyond our ruin in the last of the sunshine, I was deep in thought. I had had a brilliant insight and I wanted to record it in the blue school exercise book I had bought. Could I capture it or would it vanish like a dream before I could write it down? Would it still seem important the following day? Or when we got back to England? Then I stopped dead. My heart was banging inside my chest. I was looking straight into two bright yellow eyes with strange horizontal pupils and they were looking straight back at me. We both leaped back. The billy-goat was the same height as me. His horns spiralled out on either side of his head. My precious idea, whatever it was, had totally vanished.

Andreas Cominos, member of the Chorus and the owner of the billy, followed close behind his animal. He was elderly and his hair, both on his head and his beard, was balding in patches, but he still looked handsome. As Alec talked to him I had time to look at his face. Creases from a lifetime of smiles fanned from the outer edges of his eyes. Deep indentations ran from each side of his nose down either side of his mouth, but under his leathery skin, which pulled in ridges up his neck, were high cheekbones, even features, and a classical Greek nose.

Andreas often wore neatly cut Viyella checked shirts. He looked like a model in a fashion photograph for Vogue magazine as he sat amongst the rest of the Greek Chorus on the benches at end of our track. At first, we put this down to his innate good taste, but later we heard he had a son in Germany and we wondered if it was he who brought back those wonderful shirts for his father.

That evening, Andreas had four goats with him: two massive billy-goats with shaggy heads and spiralling splayed horns, one delicate white nanny-goat and a much smaller grey kid. He told us the two large billies were both sons of the elegant white nanny-goat. The grey kid at her heels was the child of the nanny-goat and one of her own sons. Andreas was shocked by their incestuous behaviour but he excused them.

"They are only goats so they know no better."

"Humans were no better in ancient times" replied Alec.

He knew Andreas was interested in the old Greek stories, and Captain John had told us he wrote poetry, so Alec justified his response by telling him the story of Oedipus.

Oedipus, he said, was the son of the king of Thebes who, soon after the birth, was told by a fortune-teller that his new baby would grow up to kill him and therefore he must be slaughtered immediately. So the king gave his tiny son to one of his servants to carry out the terrible deed. But the man took pity on the baby and gave him away to a peasant family in the Peloponnese. They brought him up as their own, and he grew into a fine young man.

Travelling across the northern side of the Gulf of Corinth Oedipus had an 'incident' with a fellow traveller. An arrogant man coming from the other direction wanted the entire road to himself, and in the fracas that followed Oedipus ended up killing him. He continued on his journey to Thebes, where he found the whole country in mourning for their king who, inexplicably, had been murdered on a lonely road. Thebes at that time was troubled by a sphinx, which would only cease to threaten the city if her riddle was solved. The riddle was:

"Which creature has one voice and becomes four-footed, two-footed, and three-footed?"

Oedipus correctly guessed that the answer was man. A baby crawls on four legs, a grown man has two, and an old man like Andreas uses a stick and so he has three. After Oedipus solved the riddle and rescued Thebes from the sphinx he was the hero of the day. He fell in love with the widow of the king and, since the whole world was now open to him, he married her. We all know, Alec said to Andreas, the Oedipus Complex is when the son has an unhealthy sexual love for his mother.

"Well," said Andreas, "the young are no better these days."

"Oh?"

"They sometimes marry on a Saturday."

"Does that matter?"

"When a couple marry on a Saturday they celebrate and drink wine and then they go to bed. Later the man makes union with his new wife and a baby is conceived. A Sabbath child will always be defective in some way."

"Oh," said Alec, politely disguising his scepticism, "I didn't know that."

That evening Alec explained to me that 'man' was often the answer to an ancient Greek riddle. The Greeks believed, as the philosopher Protagoras had maintained, that 'man is the measure of all things'.

This focus suited Alec. Unlike most men, he was particularly clever with people but no good at all with anything mechanical.

Nothing was happening to our ruined house so we had plenty of time to get to know the Greek Chorus. They always greeted us with friendliness and interest when we passed them at the end of our track, and Alec always stopped to have a chat with them. They asked us simple and direct questions about ourselves and about England. When Margaret Thatcher was prime minister one member regularly asked us:

"What do you think of the Iron Lady?"

They watched as we explored their footpaths. Alec explained where we had been and they seemed pleased, adding snippets of information. But I was still completely tongue-tied. I'm no good at languages and a bit shy. At first I found it hard to differentiate one word from another and it seemed like a continuous stream of sound with a regular hammering tone. I am ashamed to say this went on for several years until, listening to Alec speaking, I found that I could understand quite a bit, but I still couldn't say a thing. Then one day, when Alec was having a conversation at one end of the Chorus, and I was standing silently a bit behind him, I overheard a conversation between two old ladies sitting at my end of the bench:

"And what about his wife?" asked the first. "She has been coming out here for years, doesn't she speak any Greek at all?"

"No, nothing. Nothing. Not a word!" replied the second.

"Is she a very stupid woman?" asked the first.

"No, I think he must be a very bad teacher," said the second.

Neither Alec nor I came well out of that exchange, so later I signed on to an evening class in Modern Greek at Holland Park Comprehensive in London. An interpreter, whose main emphasis was on rote-learning the hideously complicated Greek grammar, taught the course. In spite of my best efforts I made slow progress and when I tried to speak in Greek to Alec he immediately dropped off to sleep.

"You're so boring when you try to speak in Greek," he explained.

His response was honest but not very polite. Alec had a great many wonderful qualities and skills but the Chorus were probably right that teaching languages wasn't one of them.

3

King Agamemnon comes home to Mycenae

At Easter Mimis' father the priest presided over the three Kioni churches; the main church, rebuilt after the earthquake, down by Kioni harbour, the older church up at Rachi, and the small church, once attached to a monastery, down by the beach at Mavronas. Church celebrations were important in this traditional community.

During Lent no animal products, not even milk or butter, were eaten in Ithaca. Only vegetables, bread and other wheat products, dried beans, fruit and shellfish were allowed. Although Alec had been brought up as Greek Orthodox he only occasionally went to church in England. On the other hand he was a keen meat eater. In the Iliad, the Greek heroes eat meat to make themselves strong and perhaps Alec, who was never physically strong, felt it would do the same for him. Whatever the reason he was never in any way flexible on this matter.

During Lent one year in Ithaca we went out to lunch at a restaurant in the neighbouring village of Stavros and, to my embarrassment, Alec insisted they cook him meat. The restaurateur eventually agreed and, after a long delay, served him up something that looked like a large piece of pale beige fur coat. I think it must have been tripe, but it was cooked in a particularly unappetising way. Even Alec found it inedible. I thought it served him right.

The Easter services went on hour-after-hour and night-after-night. The people walked in and out but they tried to be there at the holiest moments. As they came in they lit small candles. Then women sat on one side with the men on the other. Alec and I stayed in the middle so we could be together. I felt a bit of an intruder in this traditional Greek scene. The old priest sang on and on. His son Mimis had inherited his father's beautiful strong voice. He stood across the aisle from Aphrodite's husband and their energetic son Costa singing the strange notes and repeats of the ancient Byzantine chant, now dissonant, now harmonious, tossing the sound from side-to-side across the church.

At the end of the Good Friday service we swarmed out onto a terrace where a stuffed effigy of Judas (in the manner of Guy Fawkes) was set alight, and up he went with a great flame while firecrackers jumped and banged amongst our feet. They sang as they carried the epitaphios, a bier thickly decorated with white flowers and topped with lit candles sticking out in all directions. The church bells rang as it was carried out of the church. Then we joined in the procession around the harbour, led by a man carrying a crucifix topped with a crown of thorns followed by the blazing epitaphios. Red smoke wafted into the night air as we approached the little stone jetty where we had first arrived.

On Easter Saturday we took the last boat off the island with our hired car as, although several people had invited us, we didn't want to intrude on their Easter celebrations. As we reached the mainland town of Arta the people were gathered together in groups, roasting whole sheep on spits, just as they were back in Kioni. The people were celebrating in the same way that, in *The Odyssey*, Odysseus' men feasted to celebrate their brief victory over the Cicones.

Ancient traditions were firmly observed in Kioni although some Greeks, especially those who had spent much of their lives abroad, found the concept of God, or gods, hard to believe. Captain John, a firm communist, was one of these. The roots of the words agnostic and atheist are Greek, the prefix 'a' indicating the negative. The word atheism comes from atheos, godless, and agnosticism from agnostos, or unknown. Socrates, a philosopher (or lover of wisdom), was one who thought long and hard about the concept of gods, and got into trouble for his conclusions. In 399BC, he was sentenced to death for refusing to believe in the gods recognised by the state, for introducing other divinities, and for corrupting the young. Back then most Greeks believed in not one but many gods, who had supernatural powers to do both good and evil. The Greek gods and goddesses play a large part in the story of Homer's *Odyssey*, which begins with a command to the goddess muse to help the bard Phineus:

'*Tell me, Muse, the story of that resourceful man who was driven to wander far and wide after he had sacked the holy citadel of Troy.*'

(1: 1-3 Rieu)

That resourceful man was, of course, the Ithacan hero Odysseus.

Alec was always interested in other people's beliefs. He was happy to engage with stories about mythological creatures such as fairies, laestrygonians or the sphinx, and he often spoke to the Chorus about the old Greek heroes. He was interested to find they all knew the story of Odysseus and they were particularly proud of the idea that their island had been his homeland. But, I used to wonder, how many of Homer's ancient stories were based on real historical events and how many were myth and legend?

My children and Alec's were inclined to dismiss the whole story of Odysseus and his travels as mythological, and we discussed this with them. Luckily for us, around this time, the historian and broadcaster Michael Wood put his mind to this question. In 1985 he made a six-part television series for BBC TV *In Search of the Trojan War*. Wood began his series in Berlin. There he searched in vain for the gold treasure found by the German pioneer archaeologist Heinrich Schliemann at the site of Troy in the 1870s. He showed photographs of the Royal Museum in Berlin reduced by allied bombing to a pile of rubble at the end of World War Two. The huge hoard of gold cups and jewellery found by Schliemann at the site of the Trojan War had been on display there at the outbreak of World War Two, but now it had vanished.

"Probably it was smashed by the bombing," Wood said, "and looted a second time."

He looked at a few replica cups but the original hoard of gold was nowhere to be seen.

Wood turned to explain about Schliemann. Heinrich Schliemann had a nose for gold. His childhood was troubled. His mother died when he was young and his education was cut short when his father, a Lutheran Minister in Germany, was accused of embezzlement of church funds. But the young man was energetic and hardworking. He soon became rich wheeling and dealing as an international businessman. He had an amazing talent for languages. By the time of his death he could converse in fourteen languages including Greek, Russian, Turkish, Arabic and Polish. In California, where he started a bank at the time of the gold rush, he made a fortune, but (and in this he may have taken after his father) he was accused by the local agent of sending short-weight consignments of gold. Schliemann made a swift get-away. By the age of thirty-six, he was wealthy enough to retire. He dedicated the rest of his life to following his dream. He aimed to prove the words of Homer were based on real history, not on mythology, and he set out to find the sites described by Homer in

The Iliad and *The Odyssey*.

The ancient city of Troy held a critical position guarding the straits of the Dardanelles, which run between the Black Sea and the Mediterranean in modern Turkey. (See Map 2) By Schliemann's time the old city had vanished. The historian Michael Wood, driving a boxy little car and sporting the long hair and tight jeans fashionable in the 1980s, followed Schliemann's trail. He walked all over the mound of Hisarlik and looked at the massive trench dug by Schliemann in the 1870s. The reckless Schliemann had hired 120 men, and supplied them with picks and shovels to dig the trench. He believed the Trojan War was the beginning of history, so its remains would be found deep at the base of the hill. There, at the level now known as Troy II, he struck gold, literally, and lots of it. He named it 'King Priam's Treasure' after the king who, according to Homer, was ruling Troy at the time of the Trojan War. He believed the pure gold necklaces, tasselled earrings, and broad golden headdresses he found had been worn by the beautiful Helen who, in Homer's story, was the cause of the war.

"But," asked Wood, "was this the actual jewellery worn by Helen of Troy?"

No, it wasn't. Human history went back much further than Schliemann had imagined. He had trenched right through the level of the city besieged at the time of the Trojan War, largely destroying what remained of it in the process, to a level from a thousand years earlier. Then he tried to smuggle his huge hoard of gold out of the country, but his appetite for publicity got the better of him. He dressed his new young Greek wife Sophia, thirty years younger than him, in the jewels, and had a photograph taken. It was this photograph that, unfortunately for Schliemann, alerted the authorities. He made a deal with them to pay a fine and to keep a large share of it. This treasure eventually made its way to the Royal Museum in Berlin from where, sometime during World War

Two, it vanished.

Schliemann went on to find another hoard of gold at Mycenae in the Peloponnese, the home of the great King Agamemnon who, according to Homer, led the Greek troops into the Trojan War in thirteenth century BC. Homer described Agamemnon's city as 'Mycenae rich in gold' and, sure enough, Schliemann found it. He walked into the citadel, through the lion gate that still stands there, and dug down in the grave circle immediately to his right. There, in the ancient burial site, he found the remains of royalty and nobles buried thousands of years earlier along with another heap of treasure. He pulled the golden mask from the head of one corpse and, he said, the face beneath it was still intact. Schliemann was thrilled. He immediately wrote a message to the King of Greece.

"I have gazed," he said, "upon the face of Agamemnon."

"But," asked Michael Wood again, "had he really found the grave of the great king Agamemnon?"

No, he had not.

These graves were (as it turned out after research by subsequent, more careful, archaeologists) also from an earlier time, from a time some 300 years before King Agamemnon. But, like Troy, Mycenae was clearly an important royal site. Ancient kings lived in both these places even before the Trojan Wars and the time of the heroes whose names we still know: Achilles, Agamemnon, Nestor, and Odysseus.

Schliemann's hoard of gold treasure from Mycenae can still be seen in the large main hall of the Archaeological Museum in Athens, where it is an extraordinary sight. Many people label Schliemann a thief and a liar, as he undoubtedly was, but his discoveries went a long way to prove his basic premise that Homer's epic poems were based on historical truth.

Homer's poems were the first real literature to be written down after the new flexible Greek alphabet made this possible. The new alphabet was developed from that of the seafaring Phoenicians, but this was already some five hundred years after the War of Troy. At the time of Odysseus, a hero of the Trojan War, the writing used by the Mycenaean Greeks was Linear B. When, in 1952, the architect Michael Ventris deciphered this, he found that the syllabic writing of Linear B was used principally for recording lists of items stored, or to be sold, rather than for literature.

Not long after the Trojan War there was a collapse of civilisations right across the known world from Greece through to Babylonia, and this is worth bearing in mind. The kingdoms of the Mycenaean Greeks fell, many of their palaces were burned to the ground, and several hundred years of 'dark ages' ensued. Only after these dark ages came the remarkable flowering of Classical Greece that we think of today, with its fabulous architecture, philosophy, geography and democratic ideals.

"So how," asked Michael Wood, "were the stories recorded in *The Iliad* and *The Odyssey* passed on through the five hundred years between the time of Odysseus and that of Homer?"

In the 1930s, it was fairly conclusively proved, by an American scholar Milman Parry, that the stories were passed on by word of mouth by illiterate poet bards. Wood went off and filmed some poet bards still in existence, one on the west coast of Ireland and a couple working together in Anatolia. In ancient times, long before books, and longer still before films and television, the bards were the chief entertainers of their day. Wood went on to look at several sites on mainland Greece recorded in ancient writings. The local people directed him to one site after another and they seemed to fit remarkably well. He started his search as a sceptic but, by the end of his television series, he was convinced that Homer's account of the Trojan War was based on a genuine historical event. He even speculated that some recently deciphered tablets, thought to be contemporary with the Trojan War and written in the cuneiform language of the neighbouring Hittites, might also refer to the fall of Troy. By 2005, when a paperback edition of his book was published, his hunch had been confirmed.

"But where then," our teenagers asked, "is the Palace of Odysseus and Penelope on Ithaca?"

We couldn't answer this question with any certainty. Alec had searched for the site, without success, way back in 1975. He had heard that Heinrich Schliemann made a brief visit to Ithaca even before he went to Troy. We didn't know what he found or what he took away with him from Ithaca.

"Perhaps it was better that he didn't find Odysseus' Palace as his methods were seriously destructive. Modern archaeologists," we explained to our teenagers, "sift the soil layer by layer brushing the earth carefully from each of their finds and recording its location so the site is not destroyed and the historical evidence is preserved. Mercifully they no longer move in with a hundred and twenty men with picks and shovels to dig a huge trench."

There is a postscript to the story of Schliemann's golden treasure from the site of the Trojan War, which vanished from Berlin at the end of World War Two. In 1994 it was put on display in the Pushkin Museum in Moscow. It turned out that when the Russian army entered Berlin at the end of that war, they discovered the hoard of gold hidden in a bunker under the Berlin Zoo. They took it back to Russia, where it was hidden for fifty years before they admitted what had happened. Alec and I never went to Moscow to see Schliemann's cache of gold from Troy, still wrongly called 'Priam's Treasure', but I believe it can be seen in the Pushkin Museum to this day.

My spoken Greek was progressing slowly. Work on our ruin was moving forward even more slowly still. Each autumn we arranged again with

George Papalexis for our water sterna to be mended over the winter, but year-after-year we found nothing had changed. We first discussed our project with George in 1985. In 1986 and 1987 we spoke with him again. Each year he agreed that over the next winter he would mend our water sterna but each spring, when we came out, we found nothing had happened. The only thing that changed was that we agreed with Massos, our architect from Vathi, that we should carry on without his help:

"Now you have planning permission you can build what you like," he said.

With those instructions we might have built the Empire State Building, but instead we were getting increasingly pessimistic about our plans to repair our ruin in Greece. To be on the safe side we decided we would reduce our proposed house to one storey. Also, after experiencing some of the loos on the island at that time (many of them were squatters and some were quite smelly), we decided we would not have our loo opening from inside the house. We would approach it from the garden and plant a sweet-smelling jasmine directly outside the door, just in case. I re-drew the plans yet again and, when we next went out to Greece, we discussed the revised plans with George Papalexis the builder, and with the Chorus.

"In Kioni," they told us, "the men used to help each other with their building work. Before a man could get married he had to collect up enough stones for his house and bring them down the mountain to his site. When he had collected his stones, and done all that he could on his own, his relations and neighbours got together to help him build a house before the wedding."

They pointed out that we foreigners had a perfectly good house back in England where we could go and live so why should the local people do any work for us?

"Why do you need another house?" They asked.

It was a fair point, I thought. But Alec wondered if first we had to establish a reputation for paying on the nail before any work would be done for us. Yet how could we pay if nothing was ever done? For years we had been trying to ignore the lack of progress on our house. We had enjoyed our conversations with the Chorus, but finally frustration caught up with us. When we came out in 1988 to find George Papalexis hadn't even begun work on our water sterna we had had enough.

"It seemed like a good idea at the time," we said to each other, "but it didn't work out."

Three days after our arrival we took a taxi to Vathi and made our way by ferry to continue our holiday on the nearby island of Zakynthos. At last we accepted the situation. These people in Kioni had neither the time nor the inclination to do any work for a foreigner, and neither would they hear of any builder from outside their village undertaking the work. It was all just talk. We decided that now we had Planning Permission we would sell our ruin and see if the new owner fared any better. We were still, as far as we knew, the only foreigners who had ever tried to build in Kioni, and maybe the locals had their own way of making this impossible.

Zakynthos was welcoming, mild and rather civilised. Its fields were more fertile, its rocks less rugged, its olive trees more pastel-coloured, its little stone churches more elegant than those of Ithaca. Small seedless grapes were drying to currants on mats in the sun. Their museum, rebuilt since the earthquake, was filled with superb old icons. We had decided to sell our ruin in Kioni yet, after a week, something we couldn't explain pulled us back to the craggy hills of Ithaca.

Perhaps the finality of our feelings, or something we had said, had at last impressed George Papalexis and his strong brother Spiros. When we returned a week later we found that work on our ruin had begun. Not only had it begun, but our old ruin had been practically razed to the ground. The beautifully built stone corners, the strongest part of the house, and the whole front wall with its stone lintels with their adequate bearings were just a pile of stones. We looked on in dismay.

"What a terrible mess," I said. "Now we can't even sell it."

A large group of people had gathered on the communal steps by the shattered remains. We tried to hide our feelings as we sat down amongst them. Some were the neighbours we hadn't yet met from the small house further up the communal steps opposite our water sterna, and others were involved in the demolition. Three young men from Kioni were there, and two from neighbouring Frikes. Our new neighbours were watching the ruthless destruction of the house we had hoped to repair. They introduced themselves as Ilias and Vasso. The voluble Vasso came from the village. Her quieter husband was a banker in Athens where they lived for most of the year. A skeletal cat completed the party. She had belonged to the old couple further along the track who, we discovered, had both died over the previous winter. The cat had a neat triangular face, long ears, and impeccably good manners as she stood quietly by us with one front paw lifted in a request for food.

"She is called Grizoula," Vasso told us. "Little grey."

The Papalexis brothers were both there too and soon they all got to work again levering the walls apart with picks and creating huge piles of stones and rubble. In the centre of the track below the house was a large steel water tank half filled with water, just as I had suggested for the mending of the water sterna so often over the years. The water sterna itself remained dry.

I had annotated my new drawings for the one-storey house with an outside loo with simple overall dimensions and clear notes in Greek, but I had no idea how things would go once we went back to London. Would the brothers stop? Or would they carry on? I wasn't sure which would be worse. And it seemed that nothing Alec said, or that I drew would affect what they did one way or the other.

That evening in Aphrodite's taverna we ordered ourselves a large carafe of local wine made by our once intended neighbour Maria. We had discovered she picked the grapes from her vineyard further up our track and trod them with her own feet in the 'katoï', or workshop, on the ground floor of her house. All the old houses in Kioni were built in this way, as ours had been too, with the living and sleeping rooms on the first floor and the grape-treading area and the storage of wine and olive oil in the 'katoï' below. The wooden barrels Maria used were not airtight and the resulting oxidised wine was not to everybody's taste, yet we found it gave quite a rapid hit. It had no additives and left no hangover and I had become quite fond of it over the years. Alec was never much of a drinker but even he tucked into Maria's wine that evening.

As we sat in Aphrodite's taverna wondering what we should do next Captain John Païzis approached us. He had a direct line of vision up the hill from his front balcony on the far side of the harbour and he had noticed that work on our ruin had begun. We couldn't believe our luck when he offered to keep an eye on the work over the winter, as he did for his relations, and to handle regular payments to the builders. I hugged him. When John took pity on us we knew our luck had changed.

Back in London, we received regular updates from Captain John on the progress of our building work. He negotiated incredibly reasonable prices for the walls, the windows, the plumbing, the electrics, the roof, and finally for the wonderful marble slabs for the floor (cheaper than ceramic tiles, we had discovered). He kept meticulous accounts and insisted that he himself should be paid nothing.

Captain John took responsibility but, on the other hand, he also did things his way. I had hoped to keep the large old bread oven in our 'bedroom', but it came out. I had arranged for the tank to collect the water from the roof to be on the north side of the house away from the communal steps, but he decided to move it to the south side. It wasn't that he didn't know what I wanted; it was just that he liked to decide these things for himself.

"Much as I respect Jane's skills," he wrote to tell us, "I decided together with Thanasi to put the tank in a more convenient position over the communal steps."

Captain John had appointed a local man, Thanasi Kotsis, to do the plumbing work on the house. A later letter told us how our neighbours Ilias and Vasso from the house above had objected to the position he had chosen for the water tank and, to pacify them, he reminded Vasso that her old school-friend Thanasi had done the work. When we came back the following Easter the walls were built and a concrete ring beam cast around the top. The wall by the track in front of the house was built up, there was a terrace in front of the house, and the sterna was full of water.

In the end the house was small, and looked on the outside roughly as shown in my latest set of drawings for a single-storey house with a stone exterior. I was a bit dubious about it in some ways, but Alec was happy and I reckoned it was the best we could do under the circumstances. Some dimensions above ground were a foot or two out, and at the time this upset me, but I bit my tongue and re-designed the windows, kitchen, and shower room to suit the spaces as built. Our long wait had taught us to be grateful that anything was built at all.

Alec had a sentimental attachment to the old style, and I agreed the vernacular style fitted well with its surroundings. This was also the way to get the best work out of the local builders. I took photographs of traditional stone walls, windows, or doors to show what we wanted. Other photos, which I marked with a large cross, showed what we didn't want. Our builders never followed the photographs precisely, but interpreted them in their own way. Nothing was ever done exactly as I had worked out and drawn. I just had to accept it and be pleased.

Some years later, when the Papalexis brothers built a house down the road for our South African friends Piers and Lynda, I realised just how lucky we had been. When Piers arrived from Johannesburg to see how their new house was going he thought someone had built a hotel on their site. The Papalexis brothers had asked Mimis to ring him several times to ask for extra money. As he knew Mimis was an honest man Piers had paid up without discovering the reason, but now he realised the brothers had built his house twice the size of that shown on their drawings. Piers and Lynda were patient. They accepted their double-sized establishment, re-planned the interior, and brought a couple of builders over from South Africa to finish it off.

The Greek Chorus watched every twist and turn of the work on our house and kept up a running commentary on everything we did. On the whole they approved, but when we topped the house off with a simple tiled roof, like others in the village, they were unanimous in their condemnation.

"You have built an English roof," they pronounced in unison.

Whatever did they mean? We thought we had built our house in perfect old-fashioned Greek style. Eventually we discovered what was bothering them. During the years we had waited for work to start we had stayed in many different houses in the village. One thing they had in common was a shallow pitched tiled roof and we noticed these leaked if it rained and the wind got up simultaneously. To the dismay of the Papalexis Brothers I insisted that our roof should be built to a slope of 30°, the minimum for a tiled roof in England.

"We won't be here in the winter to mop up the water from our floor when it rains," Alec explained, "so we want a steeper slope to be sure our roof doesn't leak."

We had quite a job to get the brothers to build the gables to a higher pitch but finally, while we stood by exerting constant pressure and reassurance, they did it. They must have grumbled to the Chorus, who questioned us endlessly about it. Some years later Martha, a regular Chorus member, fell and broke her arm whilst mopping up the rainwater from her tiled floor after a storm. Then one of the Chorus said to us, "It must be nice to have a roof which doesn't leak in the winter.

"It is," we replied.

As the years went by, we noticed some other roofs were built to a slightly higher pitch. It was a small triumph but we were touched.

Our little house took a very long time to repair so we had plenty of time to get to know the local neighbourhood and its history. From 1504 to 1797, the Venetians ruled Ithaca from the high town of Anoghi. During the eighteenth century they began to make progress in freeing the seas from pirates. As the seas grew safer, people moved down from their strongholds up in the hills, but they didn't immediately move right down to the harbour. At first they just moved to the upper part of Kioni, to Rachi where we had bought our ruin.

The Païzis clan moved down to Rachi around 1735. By this time we had met several Païzis. The first was Panayiotis Païzis who sold us the ruin and later we met Captain John Païzis who helped us with the building work. Now, in Rachi, we discovered a shop run by Costa Païzis and his wife Panayiota. Costa's shop doubled as a local meeting place and bar for the people of Rachi, just as Aphrodite's taverna was a meeting place for the people who lived down by the harbour, and Alec soon discovered it was another centre for local news and gossip.

Costa had inherited the shop, and thus a living, from his father, while his three brothers went to sea in the merchant navy. The Rachi shop was run in the old style. When it rained the Chorus sat in there on mis-matched chairs at tables covered in flowered plastic to continue their con-versations. Around them, the walls were lined with green painted shelves. They displayed rat traps, boxes of nails, translucent boat paint in beautiful bright colours and pure turpentine to dilute it. Donkey harnesses hung from nails hammered into the walls. Below them picks and shovels stood around the edges of the room along with sacks of rough white sand or lime putty.

When Alec asked if he could buy some wine and olive oil Costa took two empty screw-top Coca-Cola bottles down to his basement katoï. He filled one with his own homemade wine from the barrel and the other with oil crushed from his own olives. Then, as a meze to go with the wine, he spooned some olives from a large colourful tin into a plastic bag and tied it up neatly with a ribbon.

Two windows punctured the thick stone wall at the back of the shop. They framed exquisite views down through an olive grove to the harbour of Mavronas way below. Alec and I often walked down there to swim. Mavronas is smaller than the main Kioni harbour. It is on the other side of a headland and safer from the winter storms. All year round it is a working harbour where fishing boats are repaired and painted. The beach is a communal open-air workshop. In those days lanterns, used to attract fish by night, lay broken on the shoreline. Brushes, dustpans, rags, and scrapers were stacked in an open shed along with lengths of rope, bright yellow fishing nets and floats. A pot of caulking material hung from a convenient sawn-off branch of a scraggy eucalyptus. Men broke off from their work to swim round the rocks and pull out octopi, then they brought them back to the small stone pier and beat them against the rocks to tenderise them for their supper. They singled out the female sea urchins and ate their delicious eggs. They sat down to rest and chat in the shade of a small group of tamarisk trees.

Behind the beach stands the small monastery church of St Nicholas. The monastery of Mavronas was established in the 1650s to celebrate a local victory over pirates, but the church is all that remains of it. In Ithaca, this monastery was an early, maybe the first, habitation at sea level. At the end of the nineteenth century, it was abandoned and, after its handsome buildings were damaged by the earthquake of 1953, only the church was repaired.

The door of the church was unlocked so Alec and I went in. The atmosphere was cool and peaceful. The ornate wooden iconostasis, or rood screen, was hand-carved in spiralling plant forms. Its arched openings contained stiff-limbed saints, and Christ figures with large bows of wedding-veil incongruously pinned to their heads. An upper layer of saints, supported on carved Corinthian columns, was topped off with winged sea-dragons painted a vivid green. Incense thuribles hung in clusters from the ceiling and several pots of plastic flowers stood on the steps below the alter. A column, after which some say Kioni was named, was hidden behind curtained openings in the screen in a place where women are not supposed to go. We could see the church was well used. New candles were planted in many-branching candlesticks ready for the next service. Naïve modern prints nestled amongst ornate older carvings. Rush-seated chairs and small plastic-clothed tables stood clean and stacked by the back door. A small icon of the panaghia, the Virgin Mary, was hung with pressed tin images of a leg, a heart, a head, and even ships, to accompany prayers for those things. We put a few coins into the wooden box to buy a couple of candles. We lit them from others already burning there and stuck them into a sand-filled tray while we remembered friends and relations no longer with us.

Now that our new house had a roof and windows a generous and handy

English friend knocked up a rudimentary kitchen for us. There were no screws available on the island so he fixed its wooden frame with nails from Costa's shop. We followed him out, stopping off in the Athens flea market to buy a bed with a cast metal frame and a bed head topped with dented copper balls. The bed was delivered by caique to the tiny stone pier (now long since replaced) down by the harbour in Kioni. There we assembled it to see if all the parts had arrived. Then we lay down on it side-by-side. We were showing off. We expected the villagers would come and crack jokes and tease us, but they looked the other way and walked past. They took no notice at all as we lay by the sea wall on our bed until finally we got embarrassed. Sheepishly we dismantled the bed and carried it up the hill. There the Greek Chorus inspected it scornfully.

"Why," they asked us in unison, "did you bother to buy that old steel bed and bring it all the way from Athens? We all have old beds like that in our store rooms we don't ever use."

"But would you have sold one to us?" asked Alec.

"Oh no," they replied.

There were no tables or chairs for sale on Ithaca, so we searched in Kefalonia where, in a dusty corner of a warehouse full of complicated carved dark brown furniture, we finally discovered some simple old-style upright Greek chairs with tensioning cross-wires between their legs. The salesman couldn't imagine why we wanted them, as he told us several times. We carried four chairs off proudly to our taxi. The following day, just in time, we rescued a table from Captain John's bonfire and cut off the rotten bottoms of its legs. It had been too tall anyway.

To organise our building work Alec often used to go along to Costa's shop to use the telephone. Keen to get things moving he sometimes even went to use the phone when there was a slight drizzle of rain. Ever optimistic, Alec hoped the telephone might work if it wasn't raining hard, but it never did. The Chorus, watching his every move, were puzzled.

"The telephone won't be working," they said. "Can't you see it's raining?"

Six years after we first looked at the house, we finally moved in. First, we went to Costa's shop to buy what we thought we would need. He sold us a tall besom broom and a twig brush to go with a tin dustpan with a zigzag crinkled edge. We bought a small plastic washing up bowl to hold our precious sterna water and we agonised over the colour. Should we have bright blue or bright red? We chose bright blue, and Costa filled us another Coca Cola bottle of wine he had made himself.

Later, as the light faded over the harbour below us, we watched as the moon rose huge and yellow and the stars lit up. We ate spaghetti and raised our glasses to the new house, to Captain John, to the Greek Chorus and to our future in Kioni. The Milky Way glimmered across the centre of the sky like a sparkly scarf through which we looked deeper and deeper into the universe. Then, just as some dark clouds began to blow up over the mountains behind Costa's shop, we carried our table into the house and settled down for our first night on our new bed. We were just in time as during that night the autumn rains began.

The next morning, as we looked forward to a happy day in our new house, a massive figure loomed in the doorway. I was reminded of a passage from *The Odyssey*.

'I had an instant foreboding that we were going to find ourselves face to face with some barbarous being of colossal strength and ferocity, uncivilized and unprincipled.'

(9: 212-14 Rieu)

"Everything out!" he said.

The man's bulging muscles glistened in the rain as he stood blocking our doorway. Beside him on our front terrace stood a machine like an industrial sized lawn mower. It was a machine for polishing our marble floor. Captain John had told us our floor needed one more grinding and polishing session and we had been trying for months, to no avail, to get it done. Finally, just when we had decided to accept the floor as it was, he had turned up. Because the earth path from the road was now muddy from the rain he had carried his massive machine all the way along it, cradling it in his oak-like arms. We couldn't get him to go away so we resigned ourselves and moved our furniture out onto our rain-swept terrace. We called him the Marble Monster but when Alec complained to the Chorus he got no sympathy. Physical strength was greatly admired in this village.

"His father was the strong man of the island," they said. "He could lie on his back and lift up a lorry by its axle. His son takes after him."

Two days later, we swept the marble dust from our newly polished floor and moved in again. Immediately we had our first visitor, Adrianna from the Chorus. She opened our front door without knocking and walked straight in. She brought with her a gift of bright green peppermint liqueur tied up with a fancy bow, but declined very firmly when we offered her a glass of it. We offered her a glass of Costa's wine from the Coca-Cola bottle, olives, or a glass of water, but she turned it all down as she looked thoroughly into every part and corner of the house.

"It's very nice," she said. "We on this island don't like fine furniture or expensive carpets. We like our houses to be simple. We are not impressed by pomp or ceremony as the thing we value lies within. We like a person with a good heart."

It was praise indeed and we were delighted. After she had gone Alec told me about a play he had seen in London, by the fifth century BC playwright Aeschylus. While the great king Agamemnon, leader of the Greek forces in the Trojan War, was away fighting, his wife Clytemnestra had an affair with Aegisthus, a contestant for the throne of Mycenae. When Agamemnon returned from the war his wife gave him a grand welcome. In the play Alec had seen, she laid out a red carpet up the steps to the entrance of his palace. The Chorus, who were watching everything, suspected her motives. They instinctively distrusted Clytemnestra's grand display and said, "We are not impressed by pomp or ceremony as the thing we value lies within." It was exactly what today's chorus member had said. King Agamemnon's people were correct in their values. In the very next scene, blood began to ooze from below the front door and to flow on down the red carpet step-by-step. They looked on in horror. His wife and her lover had murdered the great King Agamemnon, leader of the Greek troops in Troy, on his return, in his own home in Mycenae.

4
Back in Ithaca

We lay in the dark in bed and listened to our neighbour Maria trudging by with her donkey on her way to the vineyards. It was 5am. Spurred on by her industry we got up ourselves.

We watched the red ball of sun creep out of the sea next to the dark shadow of Atokos Island. For a few minutes the rosy-fingered dawn shafted in through our double-leafed front door and into the living room, before turning golden as it rose higher in the sky. By eleven, when Maria made her way back with her heavily laden donkey, it was too hot for grape picking. If we were outside, and we usually were, she paused by our house. She pulled long bunches of glistening grapes from the donkey's pannier and insisted we take as many as we could carry. We often asked her up onto our terrace but she usually said she had work to do and passed on down the track.

Maria was in her seventies and, although her clothes were ragged, her face was beautiful and she had a lovely smile. As we passed her house we often saw her pulling her bucket up from her water sterna by hand. She had a small electric pump but we never saw her use it. Perhaps she wanted to save electricity, or maybe she was just used to drawing her water by hand. One day she asked us both into her simple kitchen. She served us glasses of cool sterna water on a table covered with a flowered plastic cloth.

"Sterna water is much better than the stuff you buy in bottles from the shop," she said.

She fetched down a jar of sticky homemade grape jam from a flimsy sideboard. Its shelves were decorated on their front edges with lacy perforated paper fixed up with drawing pins. She served us each a saucer of jam to eat with a teaspoon.

Maria never sat with the Chorus on the benches at the end of our track. She seemed a bit isolated and we never completely understood the reason. She was always friendly to us and she seemed to like our company. We never saw her in Costa's shop either and it was hard to know what she ate. Yet she worked all day when we were there. In September she picked her grapes and made wine. Later in the season she picked her olives. She booked a turn at the communal olive press in Frikes where they crushed them into fresh, greenish, peppery oil. She sold her extra olive oil to Aphrodite in the taverna down by the harbour, which explained the sensational chips we ate there.

One March, a friend who knew about botany stayed with us. Our wild garden on the far side of the communal stone steps had not been dug in fifty years, maybe longer. Our friend was amazed by the diversity of plants growing there, including many species of orchid. The next time Maria passed by, Alec persuaded her to come up into the wild garden so she could tell us which plants were used to make the delicious 'horta' (literally greens) down at the taverna. In a flash, she picked us three full carrier bags full of weeds from a very small area. She explained that nearly every weed in our garden was edible and went through them saying, "This one is fresh and sweet, and this is delicious for pies, this is for headaches, but this one is a bit sour, we give it to the animals."

Later, we cleaned up a good load of the sweet variety, boiled them down and ate them with a squeeze of lemon juice and a slosh of olive oil, as she had instructed. They were delicious and had exactly the same authentic sharpish taste as the horta in the taverna. We felt sure they must be doing us good, but I'm afraid we didn't manage to finish them all. We had to secretly dispose of the rest where we thought Maria wouldn't find them.

Maria perfected her skill at using her weeds for food and medicine for herself and her donkey during World War Two and its long aftermath. We were beginning to find out more about the lives of the islanders at that time. Over a thousand people lived in Kioni during the war, more than six times greater that the resident population today. No food was imported and the people had to be self-sufficient. The villagers collected wood from the hillsides to fuel their cooking stoves, and to keep warm in the winter. They caught fish and octopi, and collected shellfish, sea urchins and snails. They grew vegetables, and collected weeds to eat and for medicines. They grew vines for fresh grapes and wine, dried their grapes to raisins and currents, and crushed their olives to make oil.

During World War Two, the people grew wheat and rye on every remote stone terrace and they used the old stone windmills to make flour. The mills were placed on hilltops and headlands where their cotton sails could catch the most wind. You still see their ruins standing around in windy places, three on the headland at the entrance to Kioni harbour, one up in Rachi on the high ground behind the church, and a fourth by the sea on a peninsula between Kioni harbour and Mavronas.

When we first looked at the Rachi windmill, the original thatched roof and the cotton sails had already gone. A flimsy corrugated iron cover had replaced the roof, and this still protected the original mechanism inside its tall stone tower. The circular movement of the sails was once transmitted by linked cogs to a massive horizontal wooden wheel inside the top of the tower. This, in turn, was connected, by a vertical shaft to two huge millstones at its base.

Mill machinery in Rachi

We were afraid the roof might blow off one winter and expose the mechanism to the rain. Alec offered to pay for the roof to be replaced by something more permanent, but this couldn't be arranged. We were told that twenty-three different people owned the mill, most of whom lived in Australia. It is possible they feared Alec might want to lay some claim to their property. In any case it wasn't to be. In due course, just as we had feared, the roof blew off and the huge cogged mechanism fell down to the base of the tower where it now lies rotting.

The windmills for corn, and the presses for the olives, were owned communally. Now they are no longer in use, this communal ownership makes their upkeep particularly difficult. Even when the owners have the money, they rarely agree on how it should be spent. The many local oil presses, with millstones once powered by donkeys or mules, often stand in ruins around Kioni. I only know of one, hidden inside a building up in Rachi, which survives intact. They have been replaced by a more modern communal oil press, imported from Italy and driven by electricity, in the neighbouring village of Frikes.

One September, Maria let us help her pick grapes for her wine. We were flattered as she was the most careful of all the villagers with her picking. Not a single squashy grape was permitted, although those dried to currants were allowed. As we carefully cut each bunch from the vines and rootled out the squashy ones, I chatted in English to Maria's sister Sonia who was over for the summer from South Africa, and she told me a bit about the family.

'Life was tough for our large family when my sisters and I were growing up. As time went by it only grew worse.'

She told me that Maria was seventeen in 1940 when Greece joined the Allies in World War Two, and nineteen when her country fell to the Germans. The Greek Civil War followed the occupation and then, in 1953, the earthquake.

"A friend from the village wrote to me from Africa," said Sonia. "She knew a man who needed a wife. He was older than me but he was kind. So we exchanged photographs, I agreed to marry him, and I set out on the sea journey to Africa. It took ten weeks to get there. When I arrived, I found a whole new world and a whole new life. We were happy together, and now my husband has died I live near my children in South Africa. I see them often. I have been lucky with my life."

Her whole face glowed with a broad smile as she told me her story. Meanwhile, her sister Maria had stayed home in Kioni. We sensed that things had not been so easy for Maria, though she never complained. The only problem she acknowledged was the pain of her bulgy, arthritic knees. Each year she pulled up her skirts to show us how there was no improvement.

We did not know at the time but Maria too married a man quite a bit older than herself and he too had since died. He was a local leader of the Communist Party. The communists were strong on Ithaca and the neighbouring island of Kefalonia where they led the resistance during World War Two. We never knew Maria's husband, but the villagers recalled him with respect, although they admitted he could be something of a bully: quick to enforce his rights against his neighbours as to land, animals or crops, and slow to acknowledge the rights of others. We wondered if this man could have something to do with Maria's apparent isolation in this tight community.

In Maria 's vineyard, we felt enfolded by peace and beauty. The colour of the sea, far below us, shifted from pink to indigo to ultramarine. Out across the water, the distant mountains receded, one behind the other in ever-paler layers of atmospheric perspective, to the far dim outline of mainland Greece. Behind us, the green hillsides rose up, covered with cypresses and pines and an infinite variety of bushes. Here and there, amongst them, gleamed the silver of an occasional olive not yet overwhelmed.

"It was not like this when we were girls," Sonia explained. "Then the whole of this side of the mountain was covered with olive groves, vineyards and orchards. They were all in use. If you wanted timber for cooking you had to climb over the top of the mountain to the sunless side."

As we picked and sorted the grapes the church bell began to chime down in the village with an unusual double note. Ding-ding. Ding-ding. Ding-ding. A death. It was the second that day. Nikóla, the local gravedigger, passed by with his donkey and Maria shouted up to him for news. The first had been a local lady. She had been ill for some time and her death was expected, but the second, Nikóla said, was a man who had been living in New York. He had not been back to the village for thirty years but he wanted his body to be buried there. His coffin had arrived that morning on the ferryboat. It had been brought to the village by taxi, all the way along the winding and precipitous road from Vathi. We understood how this man should want to be buried in the remote and beautiful village of his early years but Maria, the one who had stayed behind, disapproved.

"How selfish of him to make us grieve for him now. All these years he has been away he never visited us. If he had come back sooner we could have had a good time. Now we have to mourn. He should have spared us that."

In the afternoon, Maria and her sister Sonia put on their best silk dresses and went down to the village to attend the two funerals. From our terrace we looked down at the small figures. They were silhouetted against the turquoise sea as they followed the coffin past the little pebbled beaches where tourists had begun to swim, to the cemetery by the very last beach. They were buried right away, since with no refrigeration on the island they had to be quick.

We liked to sit on our terrace and watch the villagers down by the harbour. Their tiny shapes were as lively as the ancient bronze statuettes in the museum at Delphi. Sometimes we could hear every word they said. Kioni harbour forms the base of a natural amphitheatre, and the slope is such that we not only had a direct vision, but we could hear their words by direct sound. It was as if the villagers were actors in an ancient play.

Mimis the son of the priest had a friend who, like him, had a very good singing voice. The friend worked in New York as a decorator but came home to Kioni each summer. Sometimes in the evening the two men sat together on the far side of the harbour. There they sang old Greek songs and, in the clear quiet air, every word, every breath, floated up to us. No doubt the ancient Greeks also experienced this phenomenon as they looked down their steeply sloping hillsides. From this knowledge, I imagine, they formed the idea of building amphitheatres with the seating steeply angled to obtain direct sight and sound. No wonder the idea of theatre and drama, and the words for it, were conceived in Greece.

One morning, we saw bright spots of light dancing on the inside wall of our house above our kitchen sink. The light was coming through our front doors, which were open onto the terrace. Searching for the source we saw Captain John standing way below on his balcony at the front of his house. With a mirror he was directing the sunlight through our front door. We neither of us had telephones in those days but Captain John had thought of a way to attract our attention. He wanted us down by the harbour and we set off right away.

Now our house was repaired John thought we should employ someone to keep an eye on it over the winter. He told us he had appointed Thanasi Kotsis, who had done our plumbing, to do this job. Thanasi lived up in Rachi and, like John, had worked for Onassis. He had been a ship's engineer. John had known him all his life, so he knew he was strong, handy, inventive and reliable. It hadn't occurred to Alec or me that we needed anyone to look after our house over the winter, but we soon adapted to the idea.

Thanasi was about the same age as Alec but physically much stronger. Although he was short and slightly bandy-legged he had strong shoulders and bulging muscles. He was well respected by everyone in the small community of Rachi. He knew about everything but he was discreet. He was careful to keep in with everybody. Captain John had done us another big favour.

Thanasi took charge of the matters he considered essential: our water sterna, pruning the trees, and planting vines. He planted four vines in front of our house, each of a different, carefully chosen, and very ancient local variety. The grapes had thick skins and plenty of pips, but they were all very tasty, each type in its own different way. Thanasi pruned the tall almond tree in the wild garden and the two mimosas Alec had planted by the house for shade. At Easter they were covered in bright yellow flowers and in summer their long slim leaves fluttered in the slightest breeze, but they grew quickly and their soft wood made them vulnerable to winter storms. The jobs Thanasi considered less important, he sub-contracted to his friend Nikóla the gravedigger. In that too we were lucky.

Nikóla was a regular member of the Chorus who passed us often with his donkey as he went up to tend his vineyard. He had even features, twinkly brown eyes, a ready smile and a wide traditional moustache curling up at its outer ends.

He was not stocky like many of the working men in the village, but slimly built and short. He was well liked but universally patronised. Why was this? He was the only man in the village who couldn't read or write. Nikóla was taken early from his school because of a family tragedy. His father died suddenly when he was twelve years old and Nikóla, the eldest son, had to work to support his mother and younger siblings. The social stigma of not reading, in this community where education is taken so seriously, meant he had to find a wife who could not read or write either. In Chrysanthe he found the perfect match.

Chrysanthe came over from the mainland when she was seventeen to help the islanders with their olive harvest. Nikóla, a little older, had eyes for no one but the pretty young girl. He married her and brought her over the water to live on Ithaca. By the time we knew her, Chrysanthe was thin and work-worn but still striking with her blue eyes and reddish-blond hair. Her loud voice, with phrases often ending in a loud squawk, was quite a feature in the neighbourhood. We often watched her as she strode, well laden, up the steep lane to her house. When we saw them together, Nikóla and Chrysanthe's love for each other was obvious, even after all these years.

From that time onwards, Thanasi paid our Greek bills for us and his wife Eftichia kept immaculate accounts. Many years later Thanasi admitted he was not very good at reading either, and explained the reason. He left school at thirteen when the island was occupied during World War Two. The Italian occupying force renamed the Kioni school the Scuola Italiana and ruled that all lessons must be conducted in Italian, but the schoolteacher didn't speak Italian and neither did any of the children. So, in effect, the school closed down.

"The schoolmaster never was much good. He was more interested in using the cane than teaching lessons," said Thanasi. "I don't think he knew much himself."

When we first moved into the house, the tall dry-stone retaining wall to the 'wild garden' had fallen down in places. Ithaca can have spectacular storms and, from our terrace, we had panoramic views of forked lightning, followed by deafening claps of thunder and stair rods of rain. Sometimes the whole width of the sky was lit up with violent electric flashes. In ancient days the great god Zeus was said to orchestrate these storms and, watching them, I could believe it myself.

In Greece, we had often seen retaining walls washed away by the winter rains and we didn't want to be held responsible for blocking the donkey track up to the vineyards. I felt it would be safer to rebuild this wall in the same traditional manner without mortar, so the rainwater would pass through and the pressure wouldn't build up behind it. With some difficulty Alec managed to persuade Nikóla to re-build it for us, and he was really skilful. He carefully chose each stone and chipped it with a hammer to perfectly fit its allocated space. It was a knowledge passed down through generations, so Nicola thought nothing of it. He was not encouraged when I told him how difficult it would be in England to find a man who could build a dry-stone retaining wall four metres high. He assumed my words were idle flattery. He probably also thought this was a man's job and a woman wouldn't know anything about it. He did suspect, however, that only he would agree to build a dry-stone garden wall for a foreigner. A genuine stonemason would be much too busy for that menial job.

As it turned out, I was right and Nikóla's wall stood for twenty-five years. However, the retaining wall built by the Papalexis brothers with cement mortar in front of the house began to sink and split almost immediately. Our newly built little stone house was surrounded by huge old stone retaining walls, many of them bulging and falling. It wasn't long before the newly mended water sterna mysteriously emptied as well.

When Nikóla had finished his wall, we began to plant up the wild garden on the far side of the communal steps and many of our conversations with the Chorus at that time were concerned with this. Our water supply was unreliable from the start, so we decided that we would plant only local plants which could survive through the summer, if needs be, without any watering at all. This turned out to be a good strategy.

One spring we made a trip to the Mani, a peninsula in the southern Peloponnese. There we were stunned by the brilliant mauve blossom on the leafless branches of the Judas trees, which grew on some of the driest and most inhospitable slopes. We hadn't seen a Judas tree on Ithaca but we decided that this was the answer on a particularly difficult bit of sloping scree in our wild garden. So when we next went to Kefalonia we bought some bulbs, three bougainvilleas, and (our most triumphant purchase) a couple of Judas trees. A valiant taxi driver stuffed them into the boot of his car, from where branches kept springing out, and lashed down the boot with a rope in seamanlike fashion. Finally, we carried our purchases proudly up the track past the Chorus. Their first reaction was astonishment that we should think of paying good money for plants from a plant nursery.

"Why did you do that when you could simply have fetched some plants from up the hillside?" They asked.

However, they admitted the bougainvilleas were fine specimens and they agreed that it was sometimes difficult to grow them from a cutting, especially as we wouldn't be here to water them, but when they saw our Judas trees their admiration turned instantly to laughter.

"Those are carob trees," they chorused.

A carob is a very large tree, with long beans that can be used to make a type of chocolate.

"Where are you going to put them?"

"They will grow to 20 meters high."

"What will you do with the crop of carobs?"

"Do you have enough donkeys to eat all those carobs each year?"

"Don't you know that a carob will kill every other plant in the vicinity?"

Alec had looked up the word for a Judas tree in a book of Greek trees and shrubs to be sure he got it right. Now he wondered if the word for a Judas tree in Athens might be different to the one they used in Ithaca and Kefalonia. He tried to bluff his way out of it by explaining that the tree he was after was the tree on which Judas hanged himself, but the eyes of his audience glazed over. He could see that he was not getting through and eventually he confessed he had made a mistake. Immediately the Chorus agreed, saying,

"We all make mistakes."

Later, we threw the two carob trees down the hillside in a discreet spot, but I've no doubt that one of the Chorus discovered them and they all had another good laugh at our expense.

We aimed to keep our lives simple in our tiny Greek house with its fabulous view, sunny weather and sparkling sea. Yet the 'simple life' was not always so simple in practice. Our most difficult problem by far was the water supply. Our water sterna, theoretically mended by the Papalexis brothers, was never reliable. We patched it up. It leaked again. Alec was reluctant to spend much money on it and I was reluctant to spend my precious holiday time dealing with it. The situation went on for years.

The system in Kioni was that each household collected rainwater from their roofs over the winter and used it frugally throughout the summer. The first time we discovered our water sterna was empty we told George Papalexis the builder, but he didn't come up. So we went to Stavros where we bought ourselves a 2½ cubic metre plastic tank. Thanasi found a couple of local lads to help us haul it along the path from the road, up the communal steps, and to place it behind the water sterna. From there he ran a pipe down to the house to serve our kitchen, basin and WC. Then we had to fill our new tank with water. This wasn't easy. The only water delivery tanker on the island was the fire engine 24km away in Vathi. It took several phone calls in Greek from the newly installed telephone at Costa's shop and a great deal of persuasion to get the fireman to come up. When he arrived he gave us a thorough ticking off.

"You people from Kioni don't seem to realise this is the only fire engine on the island. What would happen if there was a fire in Vathi when I was twenty-four kilometres away up here? You Kioni people don't even pay taxes towards the fire engine and we have to provide you with a service. You didn't tell me you don't even live in the village, and now I find you are out in the woods."

His twelve-year-old son Hector and I had to drag the heavy fire hose as we scrambled up one-hundred yards of steep and prickly un-cleared slope from the recently built by-pass road down into Kioni. Finally, we pulled the head of the hose across the track then on up the communal steps to the new tank up by the water sterna. The fireman stood grandly down below in his water lorry waiting to turn on the tap. Alec tried to help us but his encouragement was often more useful than his physical help. When the water was turned on, the heavy pipe thrashed about like an enraged python, and we struggled to hold it as the tank filled.

George Papalexis finally arrived two weeks after we had filled the new tank and just as we were packing up to leave for the winter. He insisted we went with him up to the paved 'aloni' around the top of the water sterna, where he spent over an hour lamenting the fact that the sterna had leaks. Our house was good enough and we loved it. George didn't offer any solution to our sterna problem and he was holding us up with our packing. We were too busy to share his lamentations and we were relieved when, at last, he went off down the track.

Our children grew up and, as the house was so small, they began to come out on their own or with resourceful friends. They loved to stay outside late into the night on the terrace lit only by the waxing and waning moon and the brilliant stars. Pine martens ran up and down our track and bats flitted around making high thin cries as if they were entering the underworld.

I wrote a little book of instructions, which included a few unusual suggestions. Some members of the Chorus were inclined to walk straight into the main living room of our house without even a shout or a knock at the door. On these occasions, I suggested, even if our friends or children were half-dressed or in a bikini, they should cover up quickly and offer the guest a drink of water, tea, ouzo, wine, or whatever they had, with a few olives, as that is the custom in Kioni. The Chorus were probably just being nosey but we liked to be welcoming.

Then there were the cats. Year after year the polite old cat Grizoula, whose owners up the track had died, came and stood at our open door with one paw raised asking for food. After the winter when we first arrived, we found her so thin you could see her whole skeleton, but year-after-year she survived, and year-after-year she had kittens. My mother, who sometimes came out with us, thought we shouldn't feed the wild cats, as they would get to depend on it and give up hunting. But these Greek cats were very hungry. They would leap on any piece of dry bread or stale biscuit we gave them and gobble it up. Sometimes we bought tinned dog food, or hideous multi-coloured dried cat food ladled from a sack, from Aleka's shop down by the harbour. They ate it ravenously. Alec and I felt the cats needed every morsel of food they could get. When sadly, one spring, Grizoula was no longer there, her place was taken by her many children and grandchildren. We usually managed to keep them out of the house, where we hoped they would catch rats.

Aleka's grocery shop down by the harbour kept a remarkable range of provisions but, in those days, nothing fresh. When we first came to Kioni there was a bakery with a large wood-fired bread oven in a stone shed down by the harbour. This closed in the late 1980s and then we relied on white bread cooked in a similar old oven in Stavros. The bread was delivered to Kioni in a little red van and, as we were a few hundred yards from the nearest road, it wasn't always easy to catch it. The van passed through Rachi on its way down to the harbour around 8.00 am and again on the way back around 9.30 am. You just had to watch out and run down the track to catch the bread-man as he passed.

Vegetables were another difficulty. Many people in Rachi grew their own vegetables but visitors like us relied on travelling greengrocers who came to the village in vans or lorries. They shouted their wares over a loudspeaker. Sometimes it was gypsies with colourful costumes selling melons. Some greengrocers only sold potatoes, onions and garlic. Philippos had the best selection. He came over to Frikes by the small ferry from fertile Lefkas and drove around the village shouting, "Patates, domates, kremythia, scortha, limonia." (Potatoes, tomatoes, onions, garlic, lemons) through his loudspeaker. We rushed to the end of the track to catch him before he vanished again to catch the ferryboat back home. As soon as the weather played up these small ferries, which the locals call 'slippers', stopped. Then the village could go many days without a supply of vegetables.

Another problem was rubbish. We accumulated much less rubbish in Ithaca than in London, but still it was a problem. It was hard to know what to do with it. In those early years, the villagers had a couple of places where they just threw their rubbish down the hillside. We ourselves, early on, once made a tiny bonfire of our discarded paper and old vegetable peelings out on our front terrace. It was a terrible mistake. It blazed up in a flash in the dry weather and we were shocked by how quickly the sparks flew up and blew away on the wind. Almost immediately our neighbours Vasso and Ilias were down on our terrace with buckets of water, which they poured on top of our little fire. They told us that to start a fire in the open at that time of year carried an automatic prison sentence and no bail was considered. In Greece there is a very real danger of starting a forest fire. We had been very stupid indeed and we never did it again.

But we still had a problem. We bought our drinking water in plastic water bottles and occasionally we ate food from tins. We dug pits to bury some of our rubbish. We thought our compost heap might attract rats and, in any case, our vegetable peelings didn't rot down in the dry Greek summers. We only knew of one rubbish bin on the island and that was 24km away in Vathi. Now there is a rubbish collection from large plastic bins placed around the village and they take lorry-loads of smelly rubbish over to Kefalonia on the ferryboat. I don't know what they do with it there. On a larger island, they may have an un-used valley where they can dump it. It's not ideal.

On the whole our guests managed these constraints with ease and aplomb and left us, or the next guests, welcoming notes about the dead lizards they had cleared from the water tanks and similar good deeds.

Thanasi and Eftichia live higher up the hill above Costa's shop. We often sat with them outside on their vine-sheltered terrace with its long, wide view over the sea to Lefkas and the mainland. In cooler weather, they move into their sitting room inside. They keep their house and garden perfectly organised in the old-fashioned way. Below the house is the workshop Thanasi uses for carpentry. His tools hang neatly in rows from nails along the walls. Another workshop is used for grape crushing and winemaking. Their year's supply of wine is stored there in barrels. A few flowers are planted around their house but, further on behind their outside loo, is a perfectly laid-out kitchen garden. There various types of greens, onions, garlic, tomatoes, artichokes, peppers, aubergines and courgettes grow in neat rows. At the end of the kitchen garden are the sheds where their two donkeys live. Beyond that the terraced hillside is lined with fruit trees: apple, wild pear, and figs and beyond that again are his olive trees. Thanasis' metalworking workshop is further from his house near the end of our track. Some years later, when he bought a van, he also used it as a garage. Their vineyard is along the track that runs past our house. It is a perfectly self-sufficient arrangement.

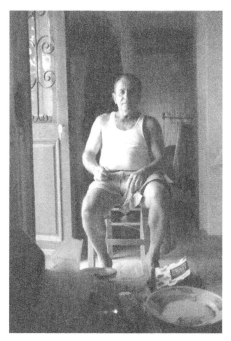

Thanasi at our house

Right at the end of Homer's *Odyssey*, Odysseus visits his father Laertes, the former king of Ithaca. He found the old king on a terraced land hoeing around a tree. Odysseus was still in disguise and his father didn't recognise him as he spoke about his garden:

> *'Old man, you keep everything so well tended here that I can see there is nothing about gardening you do not know. There is nothing, not a green thing in the whole enclosure, not a fig, olive, vine, pear, or bed that is not carefully looked after.'*
>
> (24: 245-9 Rieu)

Homer could have been describing Thanasi's garden.

Later, Odysseus owned up to his true identity but, by that time, Laertes was reluctant to believe his son had really returned. So, to prove it, he told his father about the trees and vines in his garden:

> *'Then again, I can tell you all the trees you gave me one day on this terraced garden. I was only a little boy at the time, trotting after you through the orchard, these very trees you told me all their names. You gave me thirteen pear-trees, ten apple-trees, and forty fig-trees, and at the same time you pointed out the fifty rows of vines that were to be mine. Each ripened at a different time, so that the bunches on them were at various stages of ripeness as the seasons of Zeus weighed down their branches.'*
>
> (24: 334-44 Rieu)

It could have been Thanasi describing his vines and his trees, all of which still grow on Ithaca today.

5

Denis comes home

DENIS
SIKIOTIS

Towards the end of the 1980s, some charter flights began to fly directly
from England to Kefalonia. This was much more convenient than coming
via Athens. We were first off the plane. We couldn't wait to soak up the
warmth of the air, and breath in the smell of the mountain herbs. We
strode across the tarmac way ahead of the little queue of people still struggling down the steps from the plane. They stood blinking in the bright
Greek sunlight as the airhostess hurried them on. We waited impatiently
outside the small wooden hut that served as an airport terminal back in
those days, for the men to unload the suitcases and bring them over in
a handcart. We took ours quickly, and found a taxi to drive us across to
the port of Sami on the eastern coast of Kefalonia. From there we caught
a boat round to the deep harbour of Vathi. The ferryboat continued on
to Patras on the mainland, but we took another taxi up the precipitous
coastal road to Kioni, where it dropped us off at the end of our track. Then
we greeted the Greek Chorus, and dragged our cases three hundred yards

further along the track to our house. We climbed up onto the terrace and, before we opened the front door, Alec insisted we did a little Greek circle dance, the 'Kalamatiano', to celebrate our arrival. He accompanied this by singing the tune lustily, but with more enthusiasm than musical talent. We finished it off with a little jump with both feet off the ground.

In 1992, we arrived in May. Ten years had passed since our first visit to Kioni. In Rachi nothing much had changed over the years, but this time something amazing had happened. A large and strikingly beautiful house had appeared below the benches where the Chorus sit. We couldn't believe our eyes, but the Chorus told us nonchalantly that some Italians from Rome had built it. This was something very different. Who had managed to do this? And how?

When we went to the shop Costa put his arm round Alec's shoulders, drew him close, and whispered in his ear. A shopkeeper knows the price of everything and this time the price of the Italians' new house was the hot gossip of the neighbourhood. The Romans had engaged an architect from Kefalonia, who had come over every week throughout the winter to supervise the work. It was a clever move and the result was spectacular.

Soon the newcomers invited us round. They offered us drinks and antipasti on their cool wide veranda. Their view, down to the harbour and out over the sea beyond the peninsula with the three ruined mills, was almost as spectacular as our own. We discovered that Angelo Bettoja owned a chain of hotels in Italy and his wife Jo was American. They were both strikingly good looking and they both spoke English, which was nice for me, Jo with a delightful southern-states accent.

Jo explained how she first came to Europe in the 1950s with two girlfriends from Georgia. All three young women stayed on and married (we discovered later) the three most eligible bachelors in Rome. Later, when they lived in Paris, Jo walked into Dior and Balenciaga. Her looks were such that both houses immediately signed her up as a catwalk model. Angelo wore his moustache waxed to points on either side of his face. He looked like the golden mask that Schliemann thought was that of King Agamemnon of Mycenae. Jo showed us around. Their sitting room, stretching the full width of the house, had three sets of French windows opening onto the veranda. Copies of the New York Review of Books were scattered on wide sofas. Classical music was playing. Upstairs each bedroom had a metal four-poster bed, its own bathroom, and two windows each with a different view. Over the windows fine white cotton curtains billowed gently in the light breeze that came up the valley from the sea.

Our new neighbours were not only handsome and rich, but also intelligent, artistic, and not at all snobbish. They were careful and friendly towards the local people and very generous. How interesting, we thought, that these cultured people, who had travelled the world, had chosen this remote village to build a country house.

Jo and Angelo were the first other foreigners to move into the village. A few others followed, over the years, but not many. The number of yachts down in the harbour, in contrast, increased steadily. But up the top of the hill in Rachi the lives of the local people carried on much as before.

At this time we still kept our pick and spades in the house. They leaned up against the wall of our sitting room, which was also our kitchen and guest bedroom. Even alongside our country furniture this looked a bit rough and, after our visit to the Bettojas, we began to think some improvement was needed. So we asked Nikóla if he would use some stones from the half-demolished walls of the ruin next to our house to build us a 'kaliva', or donkey shed, where we could store our tools. We knew that he would know exactly how to knock up a donkey shed. He agreed to do the work, but insisted it should be done 'properly', as he put it, in the modern fashion with mortared walls.

It was fun for us to have Nikóla doing this work, but we soon realised it was quite an event for him as well. It was the first time that he had used mortar in building up a wall and been paid for it. Alec (who was much more concerned about status than me) thought that in this community using mortar for a wall marked a jump up the social scale. Nikóla was now a mason, while building dry-stone walls was a labourer's work. As a mason he was entitled to a mate to fetch and carry for him and to help mix his cement so, as no one else was available, that had to be Alec. This type of work was not really Alec's thing, but in Kioni it was expected of him. At the end of the working day, and after he had accepted a glass of our ouzo, Nikóla set off home instructing me:

"Tell Alec to wash the basin where we mixed the mortar."

My Greek was progressing bit-by-bit, and by that time I could perfectly understand Nikóla's instructions. Besides, he had been mixing his mortar in a large plastic bowl that doubled as our shower tray, and we needed it.

Later that year, there was a wedding in the Rachi Church. Alec was keen to go and watch. We hadn't been invited but we stood around with a group of local people at the end of our track to watch the fine company arriving. First, three tall young men arrived. On their heads they carried trays frothing with muslin and piled high with sugared almonds. Then the groom arrived riding a massive and sparkling clean Harley Davidson. He was dressed in a grey morning suit with a wing collar and spotted red bow tie. His hair was tied back in a ponytail, which stretched down his back. After that there was a long wait. We wondered if the bride had thought the better of it and, if so, why should she do so now as, in modern fashion, the couple had already lived together for several years.

Eventually, far off, we heard a chorus of hooting cars. At first the sound was plaintive, over the sea, then insinuating, and finally deafening as the cavalcade roared up to Rachi. The arrival of the bride was greeted with relief, admiring smiles and nods, and much chatter. Then there were photographs. The bride, blushing and pretty as she stood against the old stone wall of Thanasi's workshop, was wearing a very short white dress. Little white flowers were stuck all over her hair, which was short but puffed up. It was a wonderful occasion.

Alec's own parents had an arranged marriage. They both came from Kastoria in Northern Greece. Before World War I, his father left his Greek school in Smyrna, which is now in Turkey, and came to work for an uncle who was a furrier in London. The business flourished. In his thirties Alec's father, and his younger brother who had joined him, wrote back from London to their relations in Kastoria to send them two brides. They sent photographs. Alec's mother and a friend of hers sent photographs back, but there was something Alec's mother and her friend could not see from these photographs. Although Alec's father was good-looking he was quite short. His younger brother was tall. Alec's mother was small, but her friend was smaller still; tiny in fact.

The two young women arrived by boat at Portsmouth and made their way up to London by steam train. They had arranged to meet the brothers at Victoria Station, where they were waiting on the platform. Alec's mother immediately spotted the tall brother and hoped he was for her, but unfortunately it was the other way around. Her tiny friend had been allotted the tall brother and she was to be married to the smaller of the two. Alec used to say his mother never really forgave his father (who I never met but he sounded like a delightful man) for being the smaller brother. Her tiny friend and the taller one got on famously, but Alec's parents argued endlessly.

"That is why I became an arbitrator," he said. "I am a compulsive arbitrator. Some of my earliest memories are of arbitrating in my parents' arguments."

The family spoke Greek at home but Alec rarely used it outside the house until, aged seventeen in the early 1950s, he first went to Greece with his father. He was enchanted. First, they went to Kastoria to meet his Greek relations, and then they made their way down to Athens.

Alec and his father in Athens on a later visit

On the evening of the wedding in Rachi, Alec remembered a wedding in Metsovo, an old-fashioned place high in the mountains.

"The young bride was slim and pretty. No doubt she's a stout matron by now," he said. "She was brought to the church by her friends and relations walking in procession. They all wore national dress, the men in white or brown kilts. Bagpipes whined and clarinets and drums mingled. It was a raucous sound. Friendly hands pulled me and my father into the procession. We watched the service and later joined the party round a campfire on the hillside. Dancing went on late into the night. Men and women were vying with each other to show their pace. The girls were extraordinarily graceful, gliding in a circle, the men agile and inexhaustible. I remember my father said, 'They twist like snakes.' He thought snakes were magical as well as dangerous."

The day after the Rachi wedding, in the evening, we went down the hill to see Captain John and Loula. We set off from our house along the track towards the road. As usual the Chorus were at the end of the track but, instead of sitting on the bench, they were standing around in a tight group facing the sea. There were a few extra people there as well. We were met by silence. They looked the other way. The atmosphere was strange and, as we turned the corner to walk down to Kioni, I looked back. There, lying at the foot of the same stone wall where the previous day wedding photos had been taken, lay a donkey. We walked back. The donkey was large, very large. He seemed perfect, but his eyes were glazed.

"He's dead," they said, as they stood around, gloomy, embarrassed.

He had had a heart attack, suddenly falling where he stood. A van arrived to take him away. Those downcast faces and shuffling feet were his funeral rites. As we walked down the hill we looked back and saw the first unsuccessful efforts to get the body into the van. More muscle power would be needed.

When we reached his house Captain John told us the death of a donkey would be known throughout the village within minutes.

"It is a matter for sadness, not just because a donkey is expensive and a donkey burial weary work, but because a donkey is as much a member of the family as a well-loved dog. When a donkey gets too old to work, they are normally tethered up by the vineyards so when they die they can be buried right there, without the need to move them."

This donkey had caused a problem by dying suddenly and unexpectedly in his shed.

One morning, late that September, Alec and I came out of our front door. A sea mist, unusual at that time of year, had enveloped our garden. Then, on the far end of the terrace, a pale form emerged. A large white donkey was standing under our mimosa tree, but with no sign of an owner. Round his neck was a small woven halter with a bell on it. When Alec approached him, the donkey swerved, shied past him, and rushed on up the steps to the paved area round the water sterna. He had reached a dead end and he stood there frightened. I went up slowly with a handful of grass and managed to catch hold of the strap around his neck. With Alec looking on I coaxed him down the steps and led him along the track to the Chorus. We assumed they would tell us immediately who owned him, but we were wrong.

"We have never seen that donkey in Rachi before," said Adrianna and her friend from the Chorus. "It must live down by the harbour. Why don't you take it down the road to the harbour and then up the cobbled track behind the coffee bar up the other side of the village? There someone is sure to recognise and claim him."

When we didn't look convinced by her suggestion she made another.

"You don't need to take the donkey down the hill. Just set him off on the road, give him a whack on his bottom, and he will find his own way home."

Then she had another thought.

"Don't send him off on the old road, where he might eat the flowers out of people's gardens, but on the new road."

We still weren't convinced. The new road was used by all sorts of traffic and this didn't seem like good advice. I led the animal along to Costa's shop in the hope that Costa or his wife Panayiota would recognise him. But they didn't, they said.

"Can you lend us a rope to tether him to a post up by the crossroads until someone comes to claim him?" asked Alec.

Costa, normally so helpful, wouldn't lend us a rope. He said we could buy one, but as we had no other use for it we didn't want to do that. I stood at the crossroads and held the animal by his little homemade halter with the bell while Alec went in to see if he could borrow a rope from Maria. As soon as he was out of sight Marika, wife of Andreas Cominos keeper of the hairy goats, came bustling down the hill from her house. The donkey was hers. She took him by the halter and led him away. By the time Alec got back, proudly carrying a rope, the mystery was solved. He was a very local donkey. As local as the Chorus themselves.

The local people must all have known the donkey belonged to Andreas and Marika. Did they think it would have eaten our plants and we might be angry? Did they feel guilty it had strayed into our garden? We enjoyed the donkey episode, but we noticed that sometimes the local people felt the need to group together to protect each other. In this tight-knit community we, and our new Italian neighbours, were welcomed warmly, yet we were also outsiders. It was a fine line.

On Ithaca the first grandson in each family is given the Christian name of his grandfather, thus the Christian names alternate through the generations, Gianni, George, Gianni, George, Gianni, for instance. If a man has several sons, who each also have a son this can result in several grandsons all with the same Christian and surname, and all living in the same village.

This could lead to problems as we discovered one time when we went to the small town of Stavros to see our friend the environmentalist Denis (short for Dionysis) Sikiotis. We had only once before been to his house and both Alec and I had forgotten exactly where it was. We walked about in the village till we found some people in their garden, but when I asked them if they knew where Dionysis Sikiotis lived they replied, "He's dead."

When we eventually found Denis' house, with Denis fully alive inside it, he explained he had two first cousins in the same village also called Dionysis Sikiotis and one had recently died.

Whether it is to distinguish between first cousins, or for other reasons, the men on Ithaca usually have nicknames. When he was a child, Costas Raftopoulos, who lived down by Kioni harbour, loved sweet vanilla spooned from a jar. He left the village aged seventeen and spent his whole working life in South Africa. After fifty years he retired and returned home. Everyone recognised him.

"Welcome home Costas Vanilias," they said.

The nicknames can also be ironic. A builder who is teetotal is called 'kanas' meaning a 'wine tankard', and Philippos the travelling greengrocer from Lefkas is called 'koukla', meaning 'little doll', because he is deemed to be ugly.

We first met Denis walking down the track past our house with a small team of men. We discovered he had managed to get funding to open up, clear and preserve many of the ancient footpaths on the island. He was marking them with fresh spots and targets painted on the rocks. As well as helping the local people he wanted to extend the short tourist season into the cooler months by suggesting walks the tourists might take. Denis' family came from Stavros in North Ithaca but he had lived and travelled the world. He had a wife and children in Australia but, as with so many others, a feeling of 'nostos' has drawn him home to Ithaca. When he retired from his career as Professor of Chemistry at the University of Melbourne, and his post as Professor of Environmental Studies for the University of the Aegean, he retired to Stavros. He tackled several important local issues in Ithaca, where his Australian family visited from time-to-time.

As a chemist, Denis was concerned about a free government scheme to spray the olive trees with insecticide. The spraying was carried out by helicopter and, in an island where most people collect their drinking water from their roofs, this was clearly a dangerous practice. There was a high incidence of cancer on the island and Denis thought there was a connection. He campaigned tirelessly for a more scientific approach and eventually he won the battle. The helicopter spraying stopped. As a result, Nikóla's youngest son was given a new job for which he was paid a small but regular wage. On every 1000th olive tree he now hangs an insect trapping bottle and pins a chart. Every week he visits the chosen trees and counts, identifies and records any insects in the traps. He then sprays with an appropriate spray only the olives in the areas where damaging insects are found. This more focussed method appears to be working well.

Back in Ithaca Denis tackled many important problems with impressive tenacity and Alec used him as a sounding board for serious island problems. He tended to discuss these quickly, fairly, and concisely before turning to some amusing or scurrilous story from his hobby, the ancient history of Greece.

In 1994, some new archaeological excavations began near Stavros, where Denis lived, in the northern part of Ithaca. The archaeologists from the University of Ioannina in Central Greece looked at several sites. They thought they might locate the remains of the Palace of Odysseus and Penelope at a site known by the cumbersome name of Agios Athanassios/School of Homer. But neither name is any help in our search for the palace. Agios Athanassios (literally 'St Deathless' and a clear reference back to previous Greek gods who never died) was the name of the Christian church built on the site in the eighteenth century AD, already some 3000 years after the time of Odysseus. Its ruins still stand on the site. The name 'School of Homer' is said to come from a joke made by a local priest to an early Homerist William Gell at the beginning of the nineteenth century. As far as anybody knows Homer never went to school, or taught at a school, on Ithaca. He is said (but even that is uncertain) to have come from the faraway island of Chios, or from the nearby mainland now in Turkey.

We had some good discussions with Denis, who was following the excavations closely. He took this task seriously, yet he was always quick to de-bunk any silly or pretentious ideas. As soon as he felt his fellow Ithacans were puffing things out of proportion, he wrote articles in the local newspaper.

"At primary school," he explained to us, "the children of Ithaca were brainwashed with a simplified, expurgated version of Homer's *Odyssey* and we all felt proud of our association with a man so famous for his deeds. We could bask in all this glory without ever having to lift a finger."

Alec trained as a barrister. In his work as a maritime arbitrator, he often cross-questioned his witnesses. Now he was interested to know Denis' view on the existence of Odysseus as a historical figure, so he asked him what he thought. Denis' reply was surprisingly unequivocal.

"Yes, I suspect that womanising, plundering chieftain existed," he said, "and it seems likely he once lived here on Ithaca very near my own house in Stavros."

The historian Michael Wood had given us some background information on this subject as well. When, around the time of Shakespeare, scholars in England began to read Homer's poetry, the general assumption was that his brilliant stories were entirely fictional. A few scholars suggested his stories were based on true history but the tales of sphinxes, of cannibal Laestrygonians, and of the one-eyed giant Cyclopes didn't help their cause.

By the second half of the nineteenth century AD, when Heinrich Schliemann began to excavate, scholars in Western Europe were still discussing whether the kings Agamemnon, Menelaus, Nestor and Odysseus really went to war with King Priam of Troy, as Homer described in the Iliad, or if his stories were purely mythological. But, as time went by, studies and excavations were showing that many of Homer's stories were built on a basis of historical fact.

In 1995, Maria's son Manolis came back from South Africa to live with her. We were relieved. She worked so long and hard in her vineyard and we hoped her son would help her with the grape harvest in the summer and the olives in the winter. Manolis was in his early forties. He looked strong and fit. Many an Englishman, we thought, would give his back teeth to quit his stressful desk job in grey, rainy London for the opportunity to live such a peaceful and satisfying life on this idyllic island.

Quite soon Manolis dropped by. He had been living for many years in South Africa and spoke very good English. He had been a storekeeper there, he told us, but his shop had twice been robbed. Once the robbers had beaten him up and left him unconscious. He still owned three shops and some land in South Africa, but now he hoped to sell it all and settle back in Greece. Unfortunately, he said, he was no longer living with his wife and son.

Manolis said he owned some land through the gate at the top of the communal steps beside our house and one day he took us up there to show us. We followed him through the gate and along a narrow track past the ruin of an old house. We finally reached a paved area round an ancient water sterna. Manolis let down a metal bucket into the sterna and drew it up full of clear water. If only ours would hold water like that, we thought. We gazed out over two magnificent views; to the east over Kioni harbour and over the blue, blue sea to the mysterious island of Atokos. To the north we looked over Frikes to the purple mountains of Lefkas and the faded outline of the mainland beyond. It was Heaven.

"How lovely!" I exclaimed.

"It's marvellous!" said Alec.

"I am going to build myself a house up here," said Manolis.

"You are a lucky man," we replied.

That year, it rained a lot in August and early September. The Chorus were concerned about the grape harvest. The grapes had swollen but they failed to ripen and many were rotten inside the bunch. The people hesitated about picking, weighing up the risk that further rain would cause more damage against the chances of a stretch of sunshine ripening the grapes till they were perfect.

It was Thanasi who picked the right moment for the harvest. Maybe he was the wisest man in the village, or perhaps he was the most impatient and least capable of waiting. With his muscly thighs bulging from faded blue shorts he was a picture of coiled-up energy. On September 5, he strode through the village heading up a team of three donkeys, one for each picker, which gives an idea of the size and speed of his operation.

I suggested we join them and Alec agreed. But in his mid sixties, after a lifetime of deskwork, his back was beginning to play up. The luscious bunches of grapes were at an awkward height so he had to stoop or squat to cut them free. This year, because of the weather, there were plenty of rotten or unripe grapes and sometimes whole bunches had to be discarded. Some bunches that looked good at first had rotten grapes right through the middle.

After a couple of hours of this work in the hot sun I was all right, but Alec was envying the donkeys who stood, well watered, in a nearby grassy glade. By the time Thanasi called a halt Alec was complaining that his knees and back were creaking, but honour was satisfied, and we were flattered when Manolis invited us to join the grape treading with him and his mother.

The ground floor of Maria's farmhouse was walled off at one end to form a grape treading area where the grapes were now heaped high. The barrels were already prepared. They had been rinsed out the previous day using a specially prepared mixture made with aniseed and other herbs. Alec asked if it would make any difference if aniseed were not used.

"Of course," was the reply.

In this traditional society this was a silly question. It seemed that on Ithaca no-one in his right mind would prepare a barrel for the grape harvest without using aniseed, so we never got to know whether it had some chemical function, whether it enhanced the taste of the wine in any way, or if it had no function at all.

We sat on the doorstep of Maria's katoï to wash our feet, then clambered over the low wall into the grape-treading area. Takis, a member of the Chorus who had come to help, was already standing there and explained what we should do. We climbed up onto the heap of grapes and stood in a row of three across the treading area. Takis got up an elaborate dance-rhythm. One, two, three, four, five and a scraping-in movement from the side. One, two, three... he set a cracking pace and Alec and I struggled to keep up. Takis was a skinny type, not much musclier than Alec but, unlike him, not scared to put his back wholly into any job for fear of aches and pains. Our feet crushed the shiny soft fruit and the juice oozed out between our toes and crept up our legs. It poured out through the carved stone spout at the base of the wall into a circular pit in the floor. Then Maria took a jug and ladled it out from the pit, sieved it, and poured it carefully into her barrels.

Manolis stood and watched. He seemed tense.

Takis with the upright hand press

When we had extracted as much as we could with our feet Takis shovelled the remaining skins and stalks into an upright hand press to squeeze out the last of the juice. Later, the yellowish, stalky remains would be fed to the donkeys, but they never liked it. All over the village we saw donkeys standing in their fields as far away as possible from steaming heaps of grape squashings.

When the grape harvest was finally in, and the wine was made, there was a sense of ease in Rachi. Gloomy forecasts about the size of the harvest were put to rest. Things had turned out better than expected.

The weather was dark and windy with gusts of rain on the evening Alec went up to see Thanasi. He found him crouched by his wine barrels in shorts and a torn vest. He had just been to Athens to have his must analysed and now, following the chemist's instructions, he was weighing out some sugar to increase the fermentation. He needed to shake the wine about too, he said, to raise the specific gravity from 11.6 up to 12.8.

Maria supplied Aphrodite's taverna with wine as well as with olive oil and we wondered if Manolis, who seemed ambitious, might build up his mother's business into something more profitable, but he made sure that we knew his interests lay elsewhere.

"I am involved with property and business," he informed us. "I am starting an import/export business here in Kioni."

Alec and I mused together about his chances of success. The island was very remote. The only telephone in Rachi was in Costa's shop where it still went dead with the slightest drop of rain. We kept our fingers crossed that things would work out for Manolis' brave venture.

6
Immigrants

In September 1997, Alec came back from a visit to a neighbour who had built a house on the new road down to the harbour.

"I've got some very good news," he announced. "I've taken on three Albanians and they're starting work tomorrow."

Our neighbour Christos worked as a building contractor in Australia. He had been employing the three Albanians to build a driveway up to his house. He had been paying them a very low rate which included the provision of lunch, and Alec had agreed to take them over on the same basis.

"I want them to rebuild the retaining wall at the back of the ruin."

This was one of several huge, old, dangerous, sagging, pregnant-bellied retaining walls remaining in our garden. But now our house was habitable I really wanted to spend my time on Ithaca on holiday from building work. I had been hoping for a peaceful time swimming and painting.

That year I had brought out some lovely handmade paper, a big fat sable brush which shook to a perfect point and six carefully chosen tubes of watercolour from Cornelissons, a posh artists' suppliers in Central London. I was not pleased, and Alec felt he had to justify his decision.

"It is a bargain and I'm afraid I couldn't resist it," he admitted.

Builders, like agricultural workers, start work early in Greece to avoid the heat of the midday sun, and the following morning the Albanians turned up at our house at 7am. They were a ragged little group with only one pick between them and they wanted to start right away. Our neighbour Christos had found them sleeping rough below the olive trees on the edge of the village. Only one of them, their leader Luli, spoke rudimentary Greek. He had taught himself by watching Greek television. Of course, they spoke no English.

Alec immediately started asking me difficult questions.

"What mortar mix should we use? How many bags of cement do we need? How deep do the foundations need to be? Where can they pile the stones?"

Worse still.

"They say they need to have vertical reinforced concrete columns in the wall. You say these are not necessary. Can you give me your reasons precisely so I can explain to them?"

This was not shaping up into the holiday I had planned.

"These are very difficult questions," I said, "especially as I have no reference books and also the materials here are rather different to those we have in England."

As they took down the sagging old wall they revealed two large bundles of chewed up plastic bags interspersed with pages from a 1950s magazine showing capacious brassieres. How could these possibly have got to be there? We worked out that rats had taken them down their burrows to line their nests.

I provided the daily lunch and our workmen ate it ravenously.

"We Albanians work hard but we like to eat," said Luli, the ringleader. "Throw it on. Throw it on!"

I reluctantly ladled out the rest of the bean stew, which I had intended for Alec and myself, onto their plates. It took me several days to adjust to the size of their appetites. Day-after-day the three of them would eat for lunch a huge casserole of bean stew, spaghetti or risotto and a whole loaf of bread washed down with a large bottle of water.

We had read in the English newspapers about the problems in Albania following the death of the communist leader Enver Hoxha, but this was the first time we had actually seen Albanians in Ithaca. We knew they had been coming over the Pindos Mountains into Greece and some years earlier we had even been mistaken for Albanian refugees ourselves.

Alec, my mother and I were staying at Kalambaka, a village in central Greece very near Meteora where medieval monasteries are perched high up on the top of rocks. We decided to walk from Kalambaka to the monasteries and took a straight line as the crow flies to where we could see them perched up high. Our unorthodox route led us along beside a vineyard where two old ladies were pruning their vines. My mother and I were a few paces behind Alec when he stopped to talk to them. After exchanging a few words one of the ladies, who might have been puzzled by his old-fashioned Northern Greek accent, asked him, "Are you Albanian?"

My mother looked the very epitome of a respectable English country lady. Only Alec looked the slightest bit Albanian, so he was amused by this rather obvious mistake. Out of devilry he answered.

"Yes, we are. We have been walking for days across the mountains."

The dear ladies were very concerned and, after discussing it for a bit between themselves, they offered us their barn for the night. There was even a hint that we might like something to eat for supper. At this point

Alec's conscience began to prick him. He owned up to not being Albanian and they took his admission in good part. But we were impressed by their kindness and generosity. After that time, the trickle of Albanians increased to a massive flow. Five years later there were half a million Albanians in Greece. We wondered, as the total population of Greece was only ten million, if those ladies would still respond to them so kindly.

The new capitalist rulers in Albania, more corrupt even than those who went before, endorsed a fraudulent investment scheme from which only they, and a few close friends, would benefit. The people, already desperately poor, were promised huge returns on their investments. They sold everything, in some cases even their houses and clothes, to invest in this get-rich-quick scheme. Then they lost everything when it collapsed.

In 1997, the government, police and army were overcome by the mob, who grabbed their weapons. The prisoners were let free from the jails. There is a tradition in Albania of firing celebratory bullets into the air, and some people were killed or wounded by stray bullets falling from the sky. In summer, the Greek army policed the long and mountainous boundary between Greece and Albania, but in the depths of winter, when dried up rivulets turn into swirling torrents and the snow was thick on the ground, the army went home. Then young Albanians made their desperate journey into Greece; the land of milk and honey.

In our little group, the leader Luli was lithe and nervous. He leapt up the freestanding gable walls of a ruin near our house and ran along them like a pine marten. His cousin Astrit crouched silently in the shadows. Vassili was the strong man. His back muscles rippled as he trundled the huge old barrow we had borrowed from Christos, piled high with sand, up and down the long track from the road, day after day, ten hours a day and seven days a week, in the baking sun.

I had to admit that this was just the type of building operation for which we had searched in vain in Ithaca. In the past, various Greek building contractors had looked at our cracking and bellying retaining walls. They had suggested replacing our old stone walls with reinforced concrete. They sometimes wanted to use bulldozers and compressors.

"How," I asked, "would they get this machinery along the narrow track to our house?"

They admitted it was impossible. Captain John suggested a hundred metre long hoist coming up from the road. Before the Albanians came nobody had been prepared to dig out the earth with a pick, or quietly barrow the materials along our track.

As demolition progressed, I cudgelled my brains to remember my student lessons in the engineering theory of retaining walls. I had never thought I might one day need this knowledge in a situation like this, with no reference books and such obvious pressure of time. And there was another problem. Even when I knew exactly what I wanted, the old-fashioned builders on Ithaca would say, "And what does a woman know about these things?"

But help was at hand. We had asked some friends to stay with us. As the old wall was almost demolished and the unsupported earth face towered three and a half metres above our uninsured and possibly illegal workers, Victoria and Richard Gibson walked quietly up the track towards our house. They had hitched a lift across from Lefkas to Ithaca with some friends in a yacht.

I had known Victoria and Richard since I was a student lodger with Victoria's mother, the artist Peggy Angus. It was Peggy who, many years later, had introduced me and Alec. Never has a competent and experienced architect from the stony Shetlands been more urgently needed than Richard was that day. He also had another attribute, one that was probably more important, he looked the part. His 6'6" height commanded a respect I could never hope to achieve.

Alec introduced Richard as 'the professor'. Each day he and I together planned the work, Alec translated our instructions, and amazingly our ragged trio built the wall more or less exactly as we asked. From deep foundations it curved and sloped back into the cliff of earth towering above it. Depending on compression for its strength the wall was nearly a metre thick of solid stone at its base and had weep holes, an innovation on the island, to let through any water caught behind it. Luli was a skilful stonemason and Astrit and Vassili provided the labouring backup.

The finished wall was superb. It commanded immediate admiration and Luli became known as 'the master' down at Costa's shop. Only the 'Cyclopean' walls of ancient times were anything like as strong. Ancient walls made with massive stones were called Cyclopean, as it was assumed that no human but only members of the mythical race of giants called Cyclops could have moved them.

It was only after our gang of Albanians had left that Alec and I ventured for the first time up into their encampment in the olive grove beyond our garden. The hillside was unbelievably romantic with its ruined stone houses, gigantic twisted olive trees with elbowing branches, and huge view over the ever-changing sea. Under an olive tree we found an old door they had used as a table. On it they had left a battered frying pan and saucepan. Inside a ruin we found a single bedstead with an assortment of rough cloths and a few pieces of foam rubber. The sheet of plastic over the top was weighed down with stones, hardly a satisfactory protection against the Greek winter to come. In every crevice were clusters of empty plastic bottles. In every bush and tree were discarded Peter Stuyvesant cigarette packets and blue plastic carrier bags. We collected four black bin-bags of rubbish. Luckily the village had recently introduced a rubbish collection system from big green bins by the side of the main road. The Albanians had fixed for a friend to help finish off some building work after they left and Alec said to him, "Their campsite was left in a terrible mess, do you live like that in Albania?"

"Oh no," the friend replied, looking genuinely shocked by the suggestion. "In Albania the women would beat us with sticks if we left the place like that. The women keep our houses spotless. When we come in from the fields we take off our shoes at the door. We change out of our work clothes and then we wash."

When they were on their own in Greece it seemed that different standards applied.

During the following winter, an English couple were murdered in their retirement home on neighbouring Kefalonia. It was the first murder in Kefalonia since the 1940s and both the Greek and English newspapers were full of it. The man had been killed with a pick and his wife with a scythe. Some money was stolen. The victims' red car, which the murderers used as a getaway, was dumped at the Kefalonian port of Sami where we catch the ferry to Ithaca. A couple of weeks later two Albanians, who had been helping the English couple with building work on their house, were arrested on neighbouring Lefkas and charged with their murder.

When we arrived in Ithaca the following April our taxi-driver told us that these same Albanians had spent time in Ithaca before going on to Kefalonia. The Greeks were upset by the affair and they feared it would discourage tourists. The timing was unfortunate, as we had decided to ask Luli and his gang to rebuild another wall for us, this time the wall in front of the house adjacent to the track.

For years I had measured the cracks and bulges as they enlarged on the four metre high wall the Papalexis Brothers had built in front of the house. It was built, I had discovered, with no foundations at all. At first, the wall was battered inwards, but year-by-year it became more upright until finally it leaned outward over the track. This track was used by nearly all the local people with their donkeys, goats and sheep. We knew we could never return to the island if anyone was hurt by the collapse of the front wall to our terrace, so we wanted the Albanians, who we had trained to build a strong, thick-based, well-battered, weep-holed stone retaining wall on deep, strong foundations, to re-build our front wall in the same way.

But we worried that we, as foreigners employing unpopular and possibly illegal building workers on a public track, might get both ourselves, and them, into trouble. We became very aware of our own vulnerability as foreigners, and of their much greater vulnerability as immigrant workers. In the end, we decided to ask the most respected builder in the north of Ithaca, George Mavrokephalos from Frikes, to take charge of the wall building and rubbish-clearance. We asked him in turn to employ our carefully trained Albanians.

Mavrokephalos was the teetotal builder whose ironic nickname was 'Kanas', the wine tankard. He sat on our front terrace sipping a glass of water, his solid figure tightly encased in grey flannel trousers and a navy blazer. His worker's hands were wide and his fingers thick and strong, but on the little finger of each hand he had grown a scrupulously clean nail to over an inch long. He was impressed by the wall we had built, and he couldn't understand why his services were needed, but finally he agreed. He made certain alterations to our proposals (no Greek builder will ever agree to do exactly as he is asked) and said he would ring us with a price on the new telephone we had recently installed.

I have since read that in old-fashioned communities a nail is sometimes grown long to demonstrate its owner no longer does manual work and no doubt this was the case with Kanas. He quoted us a very high price, but we agreed it and fixed for the work to be done over the following winter. This arrangement avoided potential problems with the neighbours, and by the following spring an excellent new wall had been built. Mitso the 'Proedros' (the president who also happened to be the only taxi-driver in the village) approved and the Chorus were quite relaxed about it.

I wonder if it was over this same winter that our closest neighbours the banker Ilias and his wife Vasso had a quarrel with Maria's son Manolis. We got on well with Ilias and Vasso. Ilias was a kindly man, but emotional. His wife Vasso, who came from the village, was warm and generous. She was an excellent cook and, if she cooked more than she and Ilias could eat, she often came down the communal steps to share it with us. Their argument with Manolis concerned the old stone steps that ran between our house and water sterna on the right and our wild garden with an almond tree and a huge old olive on the left. They went on past Ilias and Vasso's house above to the left, and lead finally up to Manolis' fields at the top. For some reason, Ilias and Vasso opened up a second gateway onto the steps from their garden, and Manolis objected to it. Manolis then erected a metal gate across the communal steps, so they couldn't reach their new gate, and said the entire length of the communal steps were his own private property.

Ilias rang us in London to tell us what had happened. He was enraged. I could hear him shouting over the phone from the other end of the room. Alec came away from the conversation looking concerned. He told me what had happened and commented, "Ilias is so worked up I'm scared he'll have a heart attack."

The people on Ithaca are surprisingly litigious. Ilias immediately took Manolis to court to get him to move the gate he had erected across the communal steps. The judge decided Manolis' gate must be taken down. When we arrived in Ithaca the following spring Manolis himself sat down on the steps and told us about it in great detail.

"How could the court decide that these steps were communal?" he asked us. "I gave evidence that the steps belonged to me and so did my mother. The judge ignored what we said and never even came to look at the steps."

Alec was sizing up the situation. "Did Ilias have any witnesses apart from himself and his wife?" he asked.

"Yes, he had five stupid people from the village, all liars," said Manolis. "I am going to have them prosecuted for perjury and they will be fined seventy-five thousand drachma each."

Because he owned the land at the top of the steps Manolis, like us, had a right to use them. Now it appeared he had convinced himself, and his mother Maria, that he personally owned the stone steps themselves. Soon he was in full swing. He told us how he had threatened Ilias saying, "If anyone carries out the court order to take down my gate, I will smash up your house, pile branches from your olive trees around it, and burn it to the ground."

A few days after the court hearing, Manolis told us, there was a knock on his door. Outside a policeman, a bailiff, Ilias and Vasso stood together in a group. They had come to get him to take down his gate. Manolis refused, so they said they would have to do it themselves. But a policeman, a bailiff, a bank manager and his wife were too dignified to carry out this task. Luckily, although we weren't there ourselves, we had employed Luli the Albanian to do some work on our house, and he was working there when they arrived. The quick-witted Luli quoted a stupendously large price, but since nobody else would do the work they had to accept it. The job was done in a second and the bailiff tried to restore amity.

"Tomorrow is the feast of St. Papoulaki in Stavros," he said to Manolis. "Let's go together and afterwards I'll buy you a drink."

Papoulaki is a local saint, said to have rescued the people of Ithaca from a tempestuous and destructive forty-year Turkish rule in the fifteenth century. His recent beatification was an excuse for annual festivities. But Manolis didn't want to make up his quarrel.

"St. Papoulaki is a fraud," he told us. "They say they have his bones in Stavros but what they have are the bones of St. Papoulaki's donkey. It's true. His arm bone was flat like a donkey's. They just broke off the muzzle from the skull to make it look like a man's."

Later, Alekaki of the Chorus gave us a different account of the court hearing. Like his wife Adrianna, who had admired the simplicity of our house, Alekaki was a neatly dressed man; slim and good-looking. His clothes were ironed and his socks were white as a Persil advertisement. He and Adrianna gave evidence that the steps were communal, along with Andreas and his wife Marika, owners of the billy goat who had surprised me, and the white donkey. The witnesses had all lived their entire lives in Rachi. Maria told the judge her family had owned those steps for 3000 years.

"And where, Granny, were you 3000 years ago?" asked the judge.

The failure of his case affected Manolis badly. His large blue eyes always lacked the sparkle of his mother's but now his legs looked more wasted and ineffectual, his voice developed a low, monotonous intonation, and his soft moustache flopped further over his full lips. Later that year my mother came out with a friend to stay in our house. When she got back to England she told us Manolis was behaving strangely while they were there. Though we didn't know it at the time, this was a premonition of a much greater problem to come.

"I didn't speak to him," she said, "but the whole time we were there he was fetching stones and carrying them up the communal steps. He did it obsessively, from dawn to dusk."

By the time we arrived later that year Manolis' had made a stone pile about four foot high, six foot wide and fifteen foot long to block Ilias' second gate. It also blocked Manolis' own entrance to his beautiful fields on the higher ground.

The following year, when we arrived, Manolis rushed up to Alec to tell him the steps were his exclusive private property and he intended to set up a gate at the bottom to stop us using them.

"So how would we get to our house?"

"I will give you a key to the gate for a period of six months to give you time to find some other way in."

Alec refused to be intimidated.

"When you show me the court papers to say the steps are your private property we will discuss it again. Until then we must consider that the decision of the court is correct and the steps are communal."

"I don't recognise the decision which the court has made against me," Manolis went on. "The judge cheated me by refusing to come and see the steps. I am going to appeal to a higher court. I shall appeal first to Kefalonia. If that fails, I will go to the court in Patras. If that fails I will go to Athens. And if that fails I will go to the Areopagus."

The Areopagus is the highest Greek court. Alec advised him he couldn't possibly win such a case and, even if he did, such a course of action would be financially disastrous for everyone concerned.

"So what," Alec asked, "will you do if the case fails at the Areopagus?"

"If that fails, I will appeal to the South African courts as I am a South African citizen."

"And if that fails?"

"If that fails, I will appeal to Nelson Mandela to come here and tell the Greeks to treat me fairly."

"But Mandela has a lot to do in his own country," said Alec. "How will he find the time to come to a small Greek island and intervene in a private dispute?"

"I know the way to Mandela's heart. I will cook him sun-dried bungey kop. It is Mandela's favourite dish and he finds it irresistible."

Manolis explained that 'bungey kop' was nasty looking, dried beef often mistaken for elephant steak. A type of biltong, I suppose. He went on to explain to us exactly how he would make and cook it.

"You must be mad if you think Nelson Mandela would come," said Alec.

It was unlike Alec to be so forthright. I was amused, but later Alec regretted it. He was always very careful with the things he said.

We were still struggling to get our sterna to hold water so now we had discovered Luli and his team of Albanians, we thought we'd have another go at it.

Alec climbing down into the empty water sterna

Together with an engineer friend in London, I devised a scheme to reinforce the top of the sterna by tying it back with steel reinforcement rods in a concrete slab to the rock face behind it. I also wanted to lower the top of its paved surround so the front retaining wall didn't loom so menacingly above the back of our house.

Back in Kioni, we asked around to find the local sterna expert and discovered it was someone we knew rather well. Andrikos was the second son of Nikóla and Chrysanthe. He was taller and looked stronger than his father. He seemed confident and rather bossy. He got down inside the sterna and tapped its walls all over with a hammer, before making his pronouncement.

"All the inside render, every scrap of it, and the concrete base, and all the crack-filling materials you have used, must be removed entirely. When that is done I will come back to re-render the inside in the correct traditional materials."

Encouraged by the success of our retaining wall in front of the house we first arranged for Luli to do the work to tie the top of the water sterna back to the rock face behind it. This time we could do without Kanas (the builder with long nails on his little fingers) as the sterna was behind the house, well away from the public track. Luli and his cousin Astrit started work immediately but the atmosphere wasn't good. We sat down to eat our breakfast in a shady patch in the courtyard below them. Their voices rose higher and higher. They seemed angry. They were throwing rocks. As we listened apprehensively a boulder crashed down from above and missed us by inches.

"Hang on, hang on," we shouted.

We lifted our table, breakfast and all, and carried it quickly into the house. From a safer place we listened to the thuds and bumps and continuous high-pitched chatter from the sterna behind.

As days went by, we began to worry about the Albanians' uncharacteristic late starts, many stops, and long lunch breaks. We wondered if they would get the work done before the grape harvest, before Luli's visa expired, and before our flight back to England. We knew they were angry but we weren't quite sure why.

I urged Alec to fix a day rate but Luli didn't want that. Finally we discovered the problem. Luli had seen how Kanas fixed a sum with us for whole work (and perhaps he had also discovered the size of it) and he wanted to work on the same basis. This was more difficult for the sterna work than it had been for the front walls as I needed them to do some preliminary excavation before I could precisely assess the best way forward. I needed to know what was under the ground before I could make the next decision.

On the morning of their tenth day, I heard Alec, Luli and Astrit in a heated discussion on the side terrace. Luli was gesticulating and shouting and even Astrit was joining in quite aggressively. I went to check if Alec was all right.

"Can you stay?" he asked. The Albanians were trying to strike a deal. Suddenly Alec said, "Shh. shh. We must go inside."

He was conscious that, in this theatre-shaped landscape, their every word could be heard right across the valley. They moved inside around the little kitchen table once salvaged from Captain John's rubbish dump. Alec insisted that all the windows and doors were shut. The room was vibrating with heat. Luli wanted a million drachma. Alec had worked out that the number of days they had agreed to work would come to half a million on a day rate, but at this speed the two of them would never finish the job at all. Luli's voice went up and up and he stared fiercely at Alec with his wild black eyes. Astrit followed up behind and he was shouting too. The sun beat down on the roof, the windows were tightly shut, and sweat ran down our faces.

At last Alec said, "OK. I'll give you a million drachma but you must take on as many men as you need and finish the whole job before we leave."

He extended his hand to Luli to shake on the deal.

Luli and Astrit were both staggered and thrilled. Alec's decision had instant effect and the following morning the position was transformed. No more peaceful watercolour painting for me. Now the deal was struck the Albanians worked ten hours a day, seven days a week, and right through the August midday sun. A new muscular helper called Leonidas was sent down the sterna to hack out the cement inside. More work was done in the next two days than in the previous ten. So these are the benefits of capitalism, I thought.

When we looked at Astrit and Luli that year, neatly dressed, muscular, confident and so fluent in Greek it put me to shame, it was hard to remember the bedraggled and furtive Albanians we first knew. They were still sleeping rough this year but they now had new shirts, wristwatches and a transistor radio.

Luli told us shyly he was going back to Albania to get married. He spent last winter studying and managed in that short time to pass his first-year university exams to qualify as a teacher in Albania. His father was both a teacher and a stonemason and Luli was wondering if he too would be able to make out in this way without coming to Greece. But he was keeping his options open and when he spotted a little sketch I had done for an extra room on the side of our house he immediately stopped work to talk about it and asked if we might be building it next year.

"If I come next year, I might bring my wife," he said. He explained he was one of nine children in his family. "My father is strong," he told us proudly.

"I think your mother must be strong too," said Alec.

The Albanians chattered continuously in voices with a special high-pitched tone. It was extraordinary to see how Luli, a small delicately boned man, could throw and catch the largest rocks as if they were balloons. Astrit had completely lost his hang-dog look. He was larger than Luli, fit and handsome. They had bought themselves a cement mixer, which they placed on the track below our house next to their sand pile. Astrit ran up and down the steps, taking one homemade hod after another full of excavated 'baza' (the stuff they were digging out) down to the wheelbarrow. They made the hods themselves from large olive oil cans with a chunk of wood nailed to one side of the rim. When they were full Astrit tossed them onto his shoulder, although I could hardly shift a full hod from the ground. Normally, he worked with complete good humour but one time when I pressed him to take back more rock than he wanted from behind the sterna (I wanted to be sure to get a firm hold for the bolts to attach the reinforcement) Astrit got angry and attacked the rock with enormous force with his pick and I closed my eyes to avoid the flying rock chips.

Poor Leonidas lived like a miner down inside the sterna's great bottle, where it took him eight full days of hand hammering and hacking to remove all the cement and concrete to reveal the bare stones. From inside the house we could hear his constant tapping as from a man buried by an earthquake. With his steady look and bandy legs we thought him a real workhorse.

One evening, we were just about to leave to have supper with Denis the Environmentalist in Stavros, leaving our Albanian workers on the water sterna behind our house, when Luli rushed up to Alec to ask him a question:

"Can you pay me 1,000 drachma tomorrow?" The next day was a Saturday. "I want to try sending money from the post office in Stavros to a bank in Albania to see if the system works. If we take money home to Albania on the bus the road may be blocked. Then men with kalashnikovs climb into the bus and rob us. We can only take our bus fares on the bus."

"Does this happen just up in the mountains?" Alec asked.

"No, everywhere," replied Luli.

Alec had hidden quite a large amount of money to pay the Albanians in a jar of macaroni, but he remembered the English couple so recently murdered in Kefalonia and said, "I don't keep that sort of money in the house. I would have to go to Vathi to get it."

Then Luli asked Alec a 'very Albanian question': "How much money have you got?"

"Only what I have in my pockets," replied Alec.

So Luli had to wait for his money.

Was Alec right to be suspicious? He was right to be cautious, I think.

We left the Albanians working on our water sterna and set out by taxi to Stavros to meet up with Denis. He was carefully watching the excavation work at Agios Athanassios/School of Homer where the archaeological professors from Ioannina were making progress, albeit slow. They were always short of money so excavations only took place for a month each year. Stavros, where Denis lived, was close to the site, so he kept a good eye on it and often wrote articles about the excavation for the local newspaper. We took the opportunity to get an update on the progress of the archaeologists' work. Alec had heard about some claims that the true Homeric Ithaca lay not on the modern island of Ithaca but elsewhere. He asked Denis,

"Is the present day Ithaca the same island where Odysseus once lived?"

"In recent years, our neighbours on the island of Kefalonia have realised that the glory attached to Odysseus can increase the inflow of tourist dollars," replied Denis, "and as a result there have been no less than seven different theories placing Homeric Ithaca at seven different parts of the relatively large island of Kefalonia."

We feared Denis' suspicions might have some foundation. Ithaca isn't suitable for mass tourism and the island isn't geared up for it. The beaches are narrow and pebbly. There are no large hotels to accommodate tour groups. There is no airport. We wondered if Denis was right to believe the Kefalonians were stealing the Ithacans' local hero simply to increase tourism on their much bigger and richer neighbouring island. He said there were seven such theories and that number, no doubt correct at the time, was soon to rise.

So, we wondered, how could the archaeologists from the University of Ioannina prove Homeric Ithaca was the same island as modern Ithaca by locating the palace of Odysseus? Denis, as a scientist, was thinking about proof.

"In my non-expert opinion," he said, "even archaeological research cannot produce conclusive evidence that this was where the actual Palace of Odysseus once stood."

Of course, any palace of the Mycenaean Era found on Ithaca won't have 'Odysseus and Penelope lived here' carved in stone in the Linear B writing of their time and placed adjacent to their front entrance. We joked about this, but Denis was making a serious point. How were the new archaeologists on Ithaca to prove conclusively that the Agios Athanassios/ School of Homer site was the actual place where his faithful wife Penelope waited twenty years for the return of her husband? Pottery from the Mycenaean age of Odysseus had already been found there, as well as at several other sites in the north of Ithaca. We wondered if the archaeologists could compare the ancient foundations they uncovered with other known palace structures from the time of Odysseus? Or perhaps they could compare their discoveries with Homer's descriptions of the palace?

Meanwhile Denis was waiting for his neighbours on Kefalonia to produce proof of their theories, but he hadn't seen any yet. He gave us a copy of an article he had written for the local Ithacan quarterly 'Τα Νέα της Ιθάκης' (Ithaca News) where he explained that there is no reason to doubt that Homeric Ithaca is the same as Classical Ithaca, which is the same as present day Ithaca, until archaeological evidence proves otherwise. It seemed to us that this was a proper scientific approach. We too waited for the Kefalonians to come up with archaeological proof before we took their claims seriously.

7
Conflict

Back at the house we were delighted with the way our building work on the water sterna was going, but Manolis was getting more and more agitated. He visited several times each day and hovered around watching Luli and his team. With the winter storms the overflow from our water sterna had, presumably from the time it was first built in the 1730s, run down onto the communal steps. We had no plans to alter this, but Manolis had decided the steps were his, and the water should no longer run that way. Then he began to build a barricade, two low dry stone walls filled in between with earth and rubble across the entrance from the steps to our water sterna.

"You must stop the water running down my steps," he said.

The barricade was very inconvenient, especially for Astrit who had to step over it each time he went up or down the steps. He had finished bringing rubbish down the steps. Now he was taking hods full of wet concrete up them. To build his dam higher Manolis even took our own bucket and walked to and fro across our front terrace filling and refilling it from our own pile of earth the other side of our house. Alec seemed transfixed by his unbelievable cheek and said nothing. Finally, I couldn't bear it any more so I went out and shouted,

"Put down our bucket and get off our land!"

To my surprise Manolis dropped the bucket and slunk off down the track looking sheepish. He even looked a bit scared. But unfortunately, that wasn't the end of the matter.

My mother and I were inside the house at eight o'clock the following morning when we heard crashing sounds from above. One followed another, again and again. Was it an earthquake? Had the Albanians allowed a pile of stones to fall down onto the house? At last the noise stopped and we heard the sound of shouting outside and the monotonous drone of Manolis' voice. Manolis was picking stones from the pile he had made to block Ilias and Vasso's new gate and hurling them through our roof. Fortunately our flimsy matchboard ceiling held or the situation would have been much worse. Alec heard the noise too. He rushed over from the wild garden and came running up the steps from below.

"Get away," Manolis shouted at Alec, "or you'll get one on your head."

He swung a huge stone up above his head and Alec scuttled away down the steps. But Luli and Astrit rushed forward and seized Manolis, holding him until Alec felt safe enough to come up.

Manolis was raving. He tore free and waved his arms around his head, shouting threats. Luli, lithe as a cat and fearless, leapt onto ridge of our broken roof saying,

"If you want to throw stones at the roof you will have to throw them at me."

"Yes I will," said Manolis picking up a large stone.

Astrit seized him, took away his stone, and held his arms in a lock behind his back.

"If you kill Luli," he said, "I'll tie the heaviest stone in your pile around your neck and I'll drop you into the sea."

Luli's black eyes were flaming. He was standing up on the roof above them all and shouting back at Manolis.

"Get off the roof, Luli, get off the roof!" hissed Alec through his teeth. "Can you hold on to Manolis while I go and see his mother?" he asked Astrit.

Manolis continued to shout and wave his arms but eventually he sat down. I sat beside him, and the Albanians stood watchfully over us.

Alec found Maria in her garden, sitting beside her donkey and sorting a little pile of grapes. She had a basin beside her with a few almonds she had collected. It was a pathetic sight and Alec's heart was wrung by what he had to tell her. As he explained what had happened her arms went limp, her face sagged and her head wobbled on her shoulders. Alec took her by the arm and sat her on a chair. She looked as if she was about to faint. She couldn't come to talk to Manolis, so Astrit frog-marched him down the steps and along the track to their house. At last Manolis was silent, and it was his mother who croaked her distress:

"What have you done, my son, my son, what have you done?"

Back at the house Luli and I surveyed the damage. Twelve large and four smaller stones were lodged in our roof, the longest about 60cm long. Even the smallest, a round stone about 15cm diameter, had smashed through the roof tiles. Sixty big tiles were broken. Thanks to the Albanians we had had a lucky escape. We were glad to be alive and unhurt.

Later that day, I took some photographs of our broken roof and Alec used the new telephone we had installed to ring Kandiolotis, our lawyer in Vathi. He had spent his entire working life on the island and knew everyone.

"Manolis has mental health problems," he advised. "If you prosecute he will be put in gaol for a few weeks and then he will emerge ready to smash up the rest of your house. You must make a statement to the police, of course, and you should ask them to give him a warning."

When later that day Alec went again to see Maria she burst into tears and begged him not to send Manolis to gaol.

"That it should happen to you, of all people," she said, "who I love like my own family. I get so lonely here and I so look forward to your visits."

Then the lamentations began and it all came out like a river in flood.

"The sea swallowed my son-in-law just three years ago outside Alexandria my brother had just finished building himself a new house in South Africa and came back to fit the front door key on the way home his van collided with a broken down bus on a bridge over a dried-up river bed there were five people in the van and none had a scratch except for my brother who was killed instantly my husband too was building a house down by the beach when he was struck down by a stroke like a blow to the head his mates carried his body home to me in a blanket my father went the same way too Charon took two of my sisters he took them by the heart."

In Greek mythology it was Charon, who carried the souls of the newly deceased across the river Styx, which divided the land of the living from that of the dead.

Maria told Alec about Manolis's life. For a long time he had worked as a shop assistant in South Africa earning almost nothing, but eventually he borrowed the money and set up his own rented shop. Alec noticed that Manolis had claimed he owned three shops in South Africa, a bit different from his mother's account.

"He was robbed the first day it opened. Then something worse happened. One evening three men broke into his shop, tied him up, and beat him about the head. A man working in a garage nearby heard the noise and roused Manolis' wife, who screamed so loudly that the robbers ran away. Manolis was unconscious for days and he has never been the same since that time. His business failed and his wife left him taking their son. He rarely sees him any more."

Alec was touched by these stories. He promised Maria that he wouldn't prosecute Manolis unless, of course, he attacked him again. But when he told Luli and Astrit we weren't going to take him to court, but only going to report him to the police, they were scornful. Alec had difficulty preventing them from going to Manolis' house right away to beat him up.

"In Albania, the police and courts aren't interested in private matters like this," explained Luli. "We have to deal with them ourselves."

Albanians are descended from the ancient Illyrians who were the crack troops of the Roman Empire. We watched these tough and fit young men and decided the Romans had had good reason for their choice.

At dawn the following morning, Alec and I set off on the daily bus for Vathi. Already sitting in the bus as we climbed in was Manolis. He was smartly dressed in an ironed white shirt and fawn trousers and carrying a little red A4 file. He was not the slightest bit remorseful about the damage to our roof and greeted us with a cheery, "Good morning."

"I'm going to see my lawyer," he told us.

We were going to see our lawyer too, and the police.

In Vathi, old Kandiolotis explained the reason for the advice he had given the previous evening on the phone. He told us that Manolis' ex-wife, who he used to beat, had taken him to court and obtained an order granting her the rent from a flat they owned in Athens in order to bring up their child. After the case, Manolis went to see his wife's lawyer, a woman, and tried to strangle her. She had him forcibly put into a mental hospital for many months.

We made our statement to a pleasant policeman, one of only three on the island, and suggested they give Manolis a caution. They asked Alec to pick Manolis off the bus for them. The bus, which only goes back to Kioni once a day, waited for Manolis to return. I felt the bus should have left at the scheduled time; it would have served Manolis right if he had had to spend his money on a taxi, or had to walk, but the whole busload of people waited patiently for his return. They made no comment as he climbed into the bus to come home with them.

Meanwhile, Luli and Astrit were racing to finish the work on our water sterna before their visas expired. Leonidas finished up his work down inside the sterna but promised to come back one extra day to help us to barrow some sand to replace some we had borrowed. The following morning, Luli waved goodbye as he rode off down the track on a tiny scooter with a Calor gas bottle tied on the back next to a small bundle of clothes wrapped in a cloth.

As he was now on his own, we offered Leonidas a share of our lunch. He sat with us at our little table stuffing his mouth with food, chewing and talking all at once. As he chatted he leaned backwards on his chair and I realised he was taller and more good-looking than he had seemed when he emerged at the end of a day down our sterna. He began to tell us about his family.

"In Berat, where I live in Central Albania, I live within a stone's throw of Astrit's family," like from our house to where Ilias and Vasso live, he indicated, "and Luli's family live a little further away," like down by the harbour he showed with his hand. "There is a big river running through Berat. I live with my mother and father, my wife, my son of eight and my daughter of four. My father has worked hard in the fields all his life but now he can't work any more and we all live on the wage I earn here in Greece. I can't earn enough to feed us if I work in Albania. Two full days' wages for a man doesn't bring in enough to buy a chicken. But we have a cow, and vineyards, and some olives there."

We asked him if he ate rye bread in Albania (we could now sometimes get very delicious rye bread from Vathi) and he said:

"We had to eat brown bread for a couple of years after the communists were overthrown. Under the communists, bread was very cheap, almost free, and everyone had enough. Now there is a new factory in Berat which makes white bread, like this," he picked up the whitish Greek loaf from our table, "but it is expensive. After the communists fell we reached the bottom in Albania." He reached down from his blue painted wooden chair to touch the stones of our terrace. "Now things are a tiny little bit better... about here," he said, raising his hand to a point about two centimetres from the ground. "The present government is better than the one before. Our new president has agreed with the Greek Government that if we have no criminal record we can buy a work permit to work in Greece. It lasts one year."

We only had a couple of days left before we had to leave. We still had huge holes in our roof but luckily the September rains held off. We gave our situation some thought. We decided we'd better go along to Costa's shop to tell him about our roof. That would ensure that our side of the story would get to all the villagers, in case they only got it from Manolis. At the shop, only Mimis, the son of the old priest who used to work the communal telephone down by the harbour, admitted he had known about Manolis' previous time in mental hospital. Alec managed to get Mitso the taxi driver, who was also the 'Proedros' or President of the community, to come along the track and look at our roof. He was shocked, but he too may have known of Manolis' past history as he said,

"I had no idea he had got so bad."

Then other stories came out. Nikóla's son Andrikos the sterna expert had caught Manolis putting his own initials on a rock on land that belonged to him. He had seized Manolis by the arm and said,

"You see this arm? This is your arm. If I ever catch you putting your initials on my land again, I will cut it off!"

Another strong local man had made a similar threat when he caught Manolis fencing off an area of his land and threatened to cut off his ears and nose. That threat had an Odyssean ring to it. Penelope's chief suitor Antinous threatened a beggar at her court:

'I'll throw you into a black ship and send you over to the mainland to King Echetus the Destroyer, who'll have your nose and ears off with his cruel knife and rip away your privy parts to give them as raw meat to the dogs.'

(18: 83-7 Rieu)

We ourselves had discovered by chance in Vathi that a surveyor had drawn up a plan of his land for Manolis, which included our water sterna. When we told the surveyor the actual position of our boundary he adjusted his plan and admitted he had discovered Manolis doing this elsewhere as well.

In the 1990s, as Costa often told us, land values and house prices on Ithaca were rising. With no central land registration, and many owners abroad, Manolis' activities could obviously lead to serious problems.

Costa recommended a local roofer called Scoros, who lived down by the harbour, to mend our roof. We ordered seventy tiles from Stavros and had them delivered to the end of the track where the Chorus sat. It was our last day when Scoros rang to say he hadn't been able to find a labourer to help him. That meant only one thing, he wanted Alec to mix his cement and carry and fetch his tiles for him. Like Nikóla, he wanted an assistant.

We also had to pack and clear up for the winter. Things didn't look good.

"There is only one thing to do," I said to Alec. "You had better ask Manolis to come and skivvy for Scoros. It is only just. He did the damage."

Alec was reading Dostoyevsky's *Brothers Karamazov* at that time, and something about the discussion of morality in the novel made my suggestion seem appropriate. He put it to Manolis who came like a lamb. Then Alec explained the situation to Scoros, who took it in good part. As he followed Manolis, who was carrying a hod full of mortar up the steps, I mouthed to Scoros,

"Is it all right?"

Behind Manolis' back he threw back his head with a sharp intake of breath and rotated his hand, palm upwards, to show his acceptance of an unavoidable arrangement. That evening, when we went down to the harbour to eat our last supper at Aphrodite's taverna, we found Scoros seated at a table surrounded by a large crowd. They had all gathered to hear the latest news and when we arrived they rushed up to us, cracking roof jokes. Even Aphrodite and her sons, who were normally working too hard to share much gossip, came up to us especially to tell us they had heard the story. We had our meagre revenge and the roof was mended for the winter.

Leonidas the Albanian had taken out every scrap of hard cement and cheese-like concrete from the inside of our water sterna, and we hoped we might finally be able to solve our water problems the following year. In England, over the winter, the television news showed pictures of the mob overthrowing the new leader in Tirana, capital of Albania. Civilians were setting fire to cars and firing their guns into the air outside the parliament building. To make matters worse, refugees from the war in Kosovo were pouring over the border into Northern Albania.

We had to leave our water sterna empty over the winter but the following spring, Nikóla's second son, Andrikos the 'sterna expert', came to re-line it. He made a reinforced concrete base. Then he made a mix of volcanic ash with fine black sand and a small amount of cement to render the walls and floor. This time we had done everything according to best local practice and supervised every step ourselves. Again, we ordered seven cubic metres of water from the fireman in Vathi and again he ticked us off for calling him out. We crossed our fingers we would never have to do it again. Finally, Thanasi's son, who had taken over his plumbing business, installed a smart new water pump.

All that summer our sterna held, the new pump gave us power showers, and when the rains came that autumn the sterna filled with rainwater as planned.

Around Christmas, Alec rang Thanasi from England and he answered on the new telephone he had now installed in his house. The news was good. The sterna was full of water and everything was working perfectly.

In February Alec rang again.

"It's empty," said Thanasi.

And he wasn't joking. Our newly repaired water sterna had sprung a leak and every drop of water had drained out.

Now I had a new idea. We could buy a few more plastic tanks and give up our attempts to make our old sterna hold water.

"We can convert the large stone bottle-shaped cistern into a spare bedroom," I suggested. "We can knock a doorway through into the base from the small courtyard at the back of the house, and put a round Perspex roof light on top of its stone ring to keep the rain out."

Alec didn't look convinced so I carried on:

"The sterna has given us enough grief now. We've struggled with it for fifteen years and I've had enough of it."

Finally, only after I had given up, Alec decided to throw money at it. He wanted the water sterna mended. I did some research and discovered the product the Water Board in England use for leaks to reservoirs and to their concrete water towers on tall legs. When I rang the suppliers, they assured me their product would work, that it wouldn't asphyxiate the person who applied it, that the lining would be flexible, and suitable for drinking water. There was only one problem, they said, it had to be applied by a specially trained operative, and there were none in Greece.

It was difficult to persuade the manufacturers to work with us to find a way to use this wonderful modern flexible paint in Greece. I explained the whole saga of our efforts to mend our water sterna, and how there was really no alternative source of water in the village. Eventually they were sufficiently intrigued by our unusual predicament that they agreed that Alec and I should go up to Northamptonshire for the day to be specially trained. The rubberised paint they supplied came with a catalyst. The two parts had to be stirred together with a huge spiral stainless-steel mixing paddle, powered by a strong electric drill. Half an hour later the paint would set to a stretchy rubber finish. Only seven square metres could be applied with a roller before the rubber set and the roller had to be thrown away. The huge chamber of our water cistern needed two coats. We ordered 30 five-litre cans of the product and had it shipped out to Vathi, from where we brought it to Kioni in a taxi. We barrowed the boxes up the track, unpacked the cans, and arranged them in a row under the olive tree in our wild garden.

Luli hadn't returned, but we found another Albanian called Dino. He and a colleague helped us buy thirty paint rollers, every one on the island. I marked out the inside of our water sterna with chalk, in segments like an orange. All four of us worked together for four days to mix and apply the paint, but the Chorus were nowhere to be seen. They showed no interest. Nobody came up the track to look. It was very unusual. Were they scared we might ask them to help? Alec, with his experience as a maritime arbitrator, thought some of them might have experienced poisonous paint fumes in the holds of ships.

When we had finished, I pulled a flexible plastic skin out of a paint bucket and took it along to Costa' shop. I showed everyone and they were impressed. It was an expensive solution but it worked. If it ever cracks in a future earthquake there is a simple way to mend it by covering the new crack with masking tape and painting over it to create a wider flexible joint.

The very next year, the eldest son of Aleka who runs the grocery shop down in Kioni obtained an EU grant to install a German desalination plant down by the harbour at Mavronas. It is the size of a Portakabin and makes a continuous swishing noise like a filling tank. It pushes super-salty water back into the sea. Desalinated water is then pumped up the hill to a large holding tank and pipes run down from there to every house in the village.

We installed a metered standpipe on the far side of the communal steps. It was ironic that piped water should arrive the moment we finally managed to mend our water sterna but I was glad we had done it. We now had a secure water system. If the water sterna runs dry we can refill it from the tap. If the tap only works spasmodically, or on certain days, we can rely on the sterna, which I prefer. The desalinated system is modern, but probably not an ecologically sound solution.

The issues with Manolis and the communal steps had another unfortunate consequence. Our Athenian neighbours Vasso and Ilias were so unnerved by his threats and actions that they decided to sell their house up the steps behind our own. Alexandros, a charming Greek solicitor from Vathi, bought it as a weekend cottage. He told us that no lawyer on the island would work with Manolis any more and that as he hadn't paid the interest on his loan on his land at the top of the communal steps, that land had been reclaimed. Alexandros moved Manolis' huge pile of rubbish from the communal steps and made some very good repairs and alterations to his house.

A couple of years after the rock-throwing incident we had a message from the Chorus that a motorbike courier was searching for us. Manolis had carried out his threat to bring a case against us for discharging our water down the communal steps, which he still claimed he owned. Alec prepared carefully for the case. He consulted a lawyer in Vathi and took a great deal of time and trouble to prepare his statement. He was particularly worried that the Greek court might favour a local person over a foreigner.

The court started as soon as the judges arrived on the ferry from Kefalonia, and at 8.30 am Alec and I had arrived in Vathi by taxi. The courtroom, the upper floor of a balconied building in white-painted clapboard construction, was already full. Windows on either side of the room were open onto wide balconies. Men were sitting astride the window sills. They sat half in and half out. Some were smoking.

At the far end of the room three women judges sat behind a table on a wooden platform, their documents laid out neatly in front of them. At the front of the room people were explaining their problems to the judges, one by one. Alec and I looked at the printed list of cases pinned to the wall. There were hundreds to get through and ours was way down the list.

All day we hung around in Vathi, dropping by at the court from time to time to see how things were progressing. At 4.30 pm on the dot, the three judges packed up their papers and rushed off to catch the ferry-boat back to Kefalonia. They had only managed to get through fifty cases and the next court hearing would be the following March, when we had no plans to be in Ithaca. Alec was quite fed up about the precious holiday time he had wasted, but I was quite intrigued to see the local court in operation.

Our case was eventually heard a year later in September 2002. Three women judges were seated, as before, in a dais at the far end of the hall, but the room they used as a court was different. This time the court was held in a gloomy brick-built hall with closed windows high up in the walls. Smoking wasn't allowed. The room was tightly packed with people, but we managed to get a couple of chairs while we waited for our case, which was quite near the top of the list this time. Several people we knew from Kioni were there, including Manolis.

Eventually it was our turn. First Manolis stood up at the front of the room and made his case. He was ranting and waving his arms. Then our lawyer stood up and introduced Alec, who explained to the judges what had happened. Alec then showed them the photographs I had taken of our steps, our water sterna, and our broken roof and explained that this court had previously decided these steps were communal. He told the judges about the rock-throwing incident and explained why he had not taken action at the time: first because he didn't want to cause further pain to his neighbour Manolis' elderly and frail mother, and secondly, because of Manolis' psychological state, he was advised he was not responsible for his actions. Finally he told the court what Manolis had said to him the previous evening;

"Whatever the result of the court case, I will block the entrance to your water sterna with stones and stakes and put a gate across the lower part of the steps to block access to your house. And if you remove my stones and my gate, I will drive a gate post through your body and smash the whole of your roof with stones."

We won the case but Manolis continued to threaten Alec with lawyers and court cases whenever we met him on the track. Alec always greeted him civilly in response, but I cut him dead. My response was more honest and, I thought, more effective. But who can be sure?

"I have seventeen cases in the courts," Manolis boasted to us.

"Surely," I said to Alec, "there must be a way to prevent such a waste of court time?"

Manolis didn't often visit Costa's shop but, when he did, the people there listened politely to his complaints. But, the following winter Alekaki, an elderly member of the Chorus, argued with him about some point or other, and Manolis lifted a chair and hit the old man over the head. Alekaki didn't take any action over this, probably for the same reason as us. If Manolis went to jail for a bit he would come out more violent than ever, and the local community would still have to live with him.

It was hard for us to know what to do about the rickety stone communal steps. When Alec was around seventy his back began to hurt him quite a lot. His doctor didn't know the cause. He found the steps increasingly difficult and dangerous but a few more years passed before he and our new neighbour, the lawyer Alexandros, decided to go ahead and mend them. We got a price from Dino, the Albanian who had helped us with the rubberised paint on the inside of the water sterna, and arranged to split the cost with Alexandros. Dino said he would do the work over the winter. So far so good.

Around Christmas time Alexandros rang us in London to tell us what had happened. Dino gathered together a group of four Albanians and they did a full day's work, but that evening, before the mortar had set, Manolis came and tore all their work apart, throwing the stones in all directions. Alexandros immediately had him arrested and taken to Kefalonia where he was put into the police cells.

Alexandros managed to get a court hearing in Kefalonia only three days later. The judge ruled that if Manolis set foot on the communal steps ever again he would be put in prison immediately for six months. Dino repaired the steps while Alexandros and Manolis were away. By then Alexandros reckoned he had contributed enough to this project so we paid for the extra work Dino had to do. After this, Manolis stopped threatening Alec when he met him up the track and so far he has never mentioned the steps to us again. It is a great relief. But, to finish this story, I have jumped forward in time.

8

Others plan to come home

Thanasi, in his faded blue shorts and sandals, walked up the track past our house. He carried a large trunk on his shoulder. The new arrivals strolled behind him. They were smartly dressed; she in a straw hat, he in a cream-coloured jacket.

"They are relations," explained Thanasi afterwards, "I had to help them."

Tina and Panayiotis ("Call me Peter") had been living for thirty years in Australia. He was the son of the original owners of the polite cat Grizoula, and of the last house on our track before it meanders on through the vineyards and on up the mountain. The next day, when we walked along to greet them, Peter and Tina invited us down onto their terrace. We sat with them under thick-trunked vines.

"We had to leave after the earthquake in 1953. There was nothing for us here. The place was destroyed. The earthquake was terrible," Peter said. "Terrible," he repeated quietly.

He shook his head and, after all these years, a look of shock and despair crept over his face. Tina listened attentively although she must have heard the story many times. She had been a teenager with her family in Corfu at the time.

"This house never fell," Peter explained, "as it is built on a single great rock. The first quake began on Sunday 9 August with a noise like an explosion of dynamite. Luckily it was about ten in the morning and most people were outside their houses. Buildings cracked open like eggs and boulders came crashing down the mountain on top of us. A huge crack opened all along the coast road, as wide as this." He stretched his arm out to its full length.

"Every day there were smaller quakes until, early in the morning on Tuesday 11, there was a second massive quake. On the morning of Wednesday 12 came the third quake, and this was the strongest of all. It started around half past eleven in the morning. The earth shook from side to side, and up and down, like a stormy sea. That afternoon it got worse again. It went on and on. We were standing out in front of our house by the water sterna looking down at the harbour below. The houses were falling down and, as each one fell, a cloud of dust rose up into the air. By the time the shaking stopped only thirty houses in Kioni were still habitable and, luckily for us, this was one. Most of the houses in Anoghi were in ruins. No one could bring help by road as all the roads were cracked. The boats in the harbour pulled away from their moorings with the rough sea. The British and the US sent their navies to help. Most of us were living in tents right through the following winter."

Peter and Tina were not keen to show us inside their house because they hadn't tidied up, they said, but we persuaded them to take us round. Their furniture had been spoiled by the occasional tenants who had used the house in the fifteen years since Peter's father died, Tina told us, but we thought it was lovely. We were fascinated by its traditional Greek style.

There was an enviable collection of framed damp-spotted sepia photographs of whiskered old gentlemen, ladies in headdresses, and bewildered children staring wide-eyed into the camera. They were hanging on the tall walls in absolutely correct Ithaca-fashion, well above eye level with the top of the picture leaning forward at an angle. The ceilings were painted a faded blue-grey. The carved oak furniture appeared unscathed and an old washstand was carefully painted to imitate marble. Alec found the washstand particularly charming but it was not to Tina's taste.

"We'll get rid of this and put in a proper marble one," she said. She complained about the broad-planked cypress-wood floors. "We'll have to clear these out. There are too many gaps between the planks."

Alec bossily told her how valuable these floors are, and how treasured, in England. He was apprehensive about the work they were about to do. Their house was just as he would have liked ours to be. They were starting at the point he would have loved to arrive, but couldn't hope to achieve. Peter was determined to replace his stupendous front door as, he said, it let in the rain. This was the door I had photographed to show the carpenter what we wanted for our house, but I admit I had altered the level of the floor behind it to keep out the rain. In the event, Alec had no need to be apprehensive as they did up their house very nicely, but now Tina wanted Peter to show her the old family vineyards and olive trees.

"We will have to climb," said Peter. "It's a rough path and I don't even know if I will find the way after thirty years."

We showed an interest and they invited us to join them.

"We will start early in the morning," they said, "before the sun gets too hot."

At 5.30 am the following day we set off up the mountainside on a small track opposite their house. We passed a roofless ruin with a fig tree inside it. We had picked those figs with Christos, the Australian building contractor who first employed our Albanians Luli and Astrit. He had told us it was the house where he was born but Peter had a different family connection:

"My auntie lived here," said Peter, "and over there, by that pile of stones, is where we kept our pigs. Further up the hill, if I can find it, I'll show you my dad's goat house."

Peter was beginning to move like a goat himself, darting up a steep path we had never noticed. The rising sun was filtering through the taller pines and cypresses. Prickly holm oak had grown shoulder high on either side of the path. Peter need not have doubted his memory. Wherever the path forked he knew immediately which way to go. The path was steep. Peter had to hang on to a tree root to haul himself over a projecting rock. Suddenly, we came out into a sunlit clearing that Alec and I had never seen before. Great old olive trees rose on neatly tended terraces up the hillside. Every olive had its owner and Peter knew them all.

"I spent a lot of time on these mountains as a boy," he explained. "You could put a blindfold on me and lead me up any of these paths and I would know where I was. Funny that I've not been up here since I left so many years ago, although I've been home for short stays a good many times. It is Tina who got me going this time."

"I want my children to know their land," said Tina.

We had a clear view now. Looking inland, on the far side of the valley and somewhere over the skyline, the mountains rose up to Anoghi. For once the sea seemed far away. Silvery green olives shimmered pale amongst the darker woodland trees.

"It has all gone wild," said Peter. "I had a lot of land over the other side, but when the government tried to charge me death duties I told them to take it. Do you see that big patch of cypress trees half way to the skyline? You can't really see it from here, but over on the right there is a shallow valley. That is where the people made their first settlement when they began to come down from Anoghi. That would be 300 years ago now. Of course, pirates were still a danger and they had to hide their houses as best they could. Later they moved down to Rachi. Your house was built about 250 years ago. Later still, they felt safe enough to build down by the harbour. Shall we go on and try to find the path from here to my vineyard? Or shall we go back to where we started and take an easier route?"

"Press on," said Tina, and we agreed.

We walked through more dense woodland. Suddenly we were out in the sunshine once more in another valley. It was a secret garden with vineyards on either slope, the vines were beautifully pruned with clusters of grapes catching the sun. There were gates made with old metal bed-ends still complete with round brass knobs. A couple of donkeys stood under the olive trees with bowed heads. Through a doorway in a stone shed we glimpsed donkey saddles, hoes and brightly coloured plastic containers. We followed the path across the valley. The vineyards lay, jewel-like, between the thickly wooded slopes on every side. This was a closed and silent world with no sense of an opening to the sea, unusual for Ithaca. On the other side of the valley the path rose again and disappeared into the undergrowth. For the first time Peter hesitated. Would we have to walk all the way back the way we had come?

As we scanned the vineyards we saw we were not alone. A woman with a kerchief on her head was stooping between the rows.

"Ehhh," shouted Peter.

The woman looked up. She was far away but she recognised him immediately. "Is that you Panayiotis?" She called.

As we walked towards her I saw it was Ioanna, a familiar figure from the Chorus. She showed us a path that skirted the wood for a short distance before rising into a well-trodden track between the trees.

"I know where I am now," said Peter. "Behind these bushes there is a cave where my uncle hid from the Germans during the war. There were three andartes hiding here, and we brought them food. Nobody has ever explored these caves properly, but once we put a cat down and eventually, four days later, it came out at Frikes."

The first purple colchicums of autumn were pushing, leafless, through the stony soil with delicate veined petals on juicy pale green stalks. We saw the sea peeping through the trees and at last we recognised where we were. We had reached Nikóla's vineyard.

"It's mine," said Peter. "Nikóla looks after it for me and takes the produce. He has never given me a single grape."

But Nikóla had often given us juicy bunches of grapes and even a carrier bag of figs from this vineyard. How could he have done the same for Peter when he was never here? Peter set to work dismantling Nikóla's gate, a rustic work of art composed of innumerable boughs and occasional bits of wire. The centrepiece looked like the skull of a goat but proved to be the gnarled and twisted root of a vine with eye sockets of earth. A headdress of brushwood topped it off. Soon we were through.

The light of the sea and the sky filled the vineyard. Far away beyond Atokos the blue mountains of Lefkas and the mainland lined the horizon.

"This corner was a beast," Peter pointed to the patch where we were standing, "stony soil and a lot of weeds. It was on this spot," he said, "that I told my dad I was leaving. I was twenty-three. He didn't say much. He knew I would go. I'd been away before. I'd worked at sea since I was fourteen, then I did my National Service in Corfu, where I met Tina, and we married. I brought Tina back here and we stayed for a year before we went off to Australia. There was nothing for me here, and I didn't want to leave Tina and go to sea again."

Atokos hung motionless in the air between the sky and the sea.

"Out in Australia did you ever think of this place?" Alec asked.

"All the time," Peter said. "We will come back to live here as soon as I retire."

They did up their house beautifully and they had plans for the garden when disaster struck. One winter in Australia Peter died suddenly of a heart attack. Tina came back to hold a funeral service and to bury his ashes. Their children still come occasionally but more often the house is empty and locked.

Now we had a reliable water supply in our little house in Rachi Alec wanted to buy a washing machine, but I resisted the idea.

"I want to keep our life in Ithaca simple. It is good for us to do our washing by hand."

My idea was probably naïve. In any case Alec won. We bought a washing machine, a better oven, and installed a solar panel to heat water. I admit I very quickly began to enjoy these wonderful amenities of the modern age.

This change was reflected in the village as a whole, especially down by the harbour. Joining the EU had brought financial benefits to Greece. Around the year 2000, a larger and stronger stone pier in the same position replaced the little stone pier where we had arrived. The new pier was twenty or thirty meters long and about four meters wide. Immediately more yachts came in from outside to spend the night in the sheltered water behind it. We watched from our terrace high up on the hillside as flotillas of yachts arrived. Large private yachts came and moored. Tour boats came in from Lefkas and Kefalonia and disgorged hundreds of people at a time. The tourists walked around to Aphrodite's taverna for lunch. Some went to a second taverna, where they once only served bean soup. Some went to the new taverna run by the sons of the old man who once ran the mint-green hut with the telephone, where Mimis later worked.

They went into the new tourist shop run by the daughter of Aleka, who runs the grocery shop down by the harbour.

Once, a motor yacht of extraordinary grandeur sailed into the harbour and dinghies of white-uniformed sailors came ashore for supplies from Aleka's shop. We went down to Aphrodite's taverna to see who had come, but she and her two sons said they didn't know. We didn't believe them and assumed they had been sworn to secrecy. The generator on board throbbed all night keeping the lights glowing brightly, but by dawn the yacht had vanished like a dream. It could have been Prince Charles and Diana, we thought, and we were sorry they didn't feel able to eat at the taverna with the rest of us. We were glad we didn't have to live like that.

Aleka's daughter with the tourist shop built a new house with two small flats to let, Captain John helped his sister build some pretty tourist apartments, and another taverna set up on the ground floor and in front of it. The couple whose wedding we had watched set up an excellent coffee bar which stayed open late at night. Young men no longer had to leave the village to work in the merchant navy, and the number of children in the village increased. In summer, everyone, whatever their profession, worked in the tavernas. No use trying to get Thanasi's son, now the electrician and plumber for the whole village, to come in the summer. He was down by the harbour roasting lamb on a spit for the tourists.

Sitting barefoot on our front doorstep in the cool evening breeze I looked out over the sea towards Atokos as I peeled vegetables for our supper. Out of the blue, I remembered something I had long forgotten. As a teenager my aim and ambition in life was to live in a warm place with a long view over the sea and the dry dusty earth between my toes. I had wanted time to paint. Seemingly by mistake I had achieved my life's goal. I was doing architectural work free-lance from home and my time was more flexible. I had always fitted in life drawing and now I could paint as well. In Ithaca I was surrounded by clear light, intense colour and astonishing beauty. If I could capture the essence of this, I thought, I might discover something uniquely special. This was my best chance. If I couldn't paint anything worthwhile here on Ithaca I might as well give up.

Around this time, Alec and I began to spend longer periods in Kioni. He had completed a two-year session as President of the London Maritime Arbitration Association, and now he had more time. In London he had an efficient legally trained assistant who sent out his papers by fax, and he found he could manage much of his work from afar. The quiet of the island helped his thinking, he said, as well as giving him time to take long walks and swim in the clear blue sea. We came twice a year staying for a month in the early summer and returning for six to eight weeks from late August till October. We wondered whether to spend a winter in Kioni, but our family in England was growing. My children had found partners and now they had children themselves. Soon we had five grandchildren. They brought their families to Ithaca, but the house wasn't big enough to house us all together, so they came out separately. Alec's two children came to the house with friends. In London, they all lived near us. We missed them all when we were in Greece, so we never stayed for the winter.

In London I set up a painting group, which met regularly at our house. One year a small group came out to paint in Kioni.

"But what shall I do while you are all painting?" Alec asked.

"You must join in."

"Oh no," he said. "I couldn't do that."

But when the group came out and started painting Alec surprised us all. He picked up a brush and his paintings were wonderful.

"You old devil," I said. "You never told me you could paint."

Alec pretended he had forgotten that as a young man he had done quite a bit of painting. He had even thought of taking it up professionally, he admitted, but knew it was more practical to train as a lawyer. Now our house and our water sterna were stable Alec often joined me in my painting.

"O psarás!"

Oddly, it isn't easy to buy fresh fish in Kioni but that distant cry meant that a fisherman from Stavros had come to sell off his surplus. I rushed along the track to intercept him on his way down to the harbour, but he had already passed over the top of the hill where our track meets the road. I managed to overtake his little white van by taking a short cut down the stepped footpath and bought a beautiful large and very fresh bream. Alec was thrilled. Later that day, he met Mimis. His father, the old priest, had recently died, and now he lived alone down by the harbour. Since we had a fish Alec asked him if he'd come up to share it with us for supper.

That evening, as the light faded and the stars came out, Mimis sat with us on the terrace in front of the house. I put some candles in glass jars onto the table and we sat quietly watching the moon rise over the sea. Out of solidarity we were drinking water. Twice so far Mimis has reached a point when the doctor told him that if he wanted to live he must give up alcohol entirely. If he wanted to die he should carry straight on the way he was going. The first time he gave up he lapsed after only a few months, but the community got together to send him to a specialist clinic and now he was fighting his demons again.

The temperature dropped and Alec and I put on jerseys and long trousers, but Mimis didn't seem to notice. He sat serenely in his usual short-sleeved striped tee shirt. I had made some pungent aïoli but he seemed hardly to notice that either, or even the handsome fish on its large plate surrounded by wedges of lemon. He was absorbed in his thoughts. Then he began to talk.

"My very first memory was a scary one. I must have been only two or three and I was staying with my uncle and aunt. I was playing on the floor, and when I looked up I saw a monster with a terrible twisted face looking in at me through the window. Its huge unblinking eyes were looking straight at me. Would it get in and eat me? I screamed in terror and ran shivering to my aunt. But she didn't comfort me. First, she told me I hadn't seen anything at all. Then she told me to forget it. My uncle playfully took up a stick and went out of the house, pretending to chase it away. For years I found it hard to sleep at night. I saw that face in my dreams and even by day it was hard for me to keep it out of my thoughts."

Years later, he told us, he understood that it was a mentally defective neighbour with a strange-looking face, who wandered about staring at people. Then Mimis started on another story. One time when he was about five he was sent on an errand to another uncle:

"He lived in this house," Mimis glanced behind him at our front door, "and I came up on my own from the harbour."

Was Mimis' uncle the father of old Panayiotis Paizïs who had sold us the house? Mimis seemed lost in his memories and I didn't want to break into his story to find out. Nearly all the people in the village are related to each other.

"When I arrived my uncle was drinking wine. He gave me a little glass too. It is the custom in Greek families for children to drink a little wine like everyone else. My uncle was in a relaxed mood. He played with me and chatted and, as he did it, he absent-mindedly filled my glass from time-to-time. I forgot about my errand and when I finally left the house to go home I felt dizzy and I didn't seem to be able to walk straight. I had been away from home rather a long time and my mother came up the hill to find me, which was lucky. Otherwise I might never have found my way back, or I might have fallen over the edge of one of these precipitous tracks. My mother put me to bed in the middle of the day, the sunlight was coming in through the window, and my brother was laughing at me. I didn't know why".

A thin cloud was drifting over the moon and the slender branches of our mimosa tree were whipping in the wind.

Mimis started on a story about life in the village during World War Two. It was the same story he had told us years earlier but we were happy to hear it again. He concluded with a comment:

"Ever since that time, as soon as I feel stressed, I dream of that grim column of soldiers with their heavy helmets pulled right down above their eyes."

Mimis had recently had a breakthrough in his life. When he reached a certain age, he began to receive a pension from America for all the years he had worked there. He bought a little boat, and a small red van with which he made deliveries. Now he could travel, he was also able to go and sing in other churches outside Kioni.

A few days after his visit I went down to the harbour and did a painting of his new boat. It was bobbing on the water, its turquoise body and red and yellow trim reflecting on the ripples. I threw a little biscuit, which came with my coffee from a new bar, into the clear water around the hull and a swarm of small fish clustered and fought for it. A modern rubber dinghy with a Toyota engine drove in and moored alongside. Mimis' boat, by contrast, was a picturesque craft with old-fashioned good looks and clean curves. A surprisingly large blue and white Greek flag blew from the roof of its jaunty white cabin. Mimis told me about the trips he intended to make in his new boat as soon as the tourist season ended. The boat is a triumphant symbol of the new Mimis and recognised as such by the whole village.

For years they have held their breath and prayed for Mimis, who everyone loves, as they watched and empathised with his struggle to gain control of his drinking and his life. Upsetting thoughts from the past still came back to him by day as well as by night.

At first Rachi, in the upper part of the village, was not much altered by the new wealth in Greece. Donkeys still passed our house on the way to the vineyards but, when we went to the shop, Costa told us how house prices were rising and gave us precise figures of sales. Coaches full of tourists from Kefalonia negotiated the tight bit of road outside his shop before they carried on down to Kioni harbour. The local shepherd built up a herd of fifty sheep and his mother made cheese from their milk. Once a week she took it for sale in Kefalonia. Islanders who had left to work elsewhere wondered if they might be able to come back to eke out a living in their home village, and in one case this caused a problem.

Gerasimos was an officer from the merchant navy married to a pretty lady from Patras. Now their daughter was two years old he was keen to settle ashore and he decided to develop a summer bar and restaurant at his family home in Rachi. It was on the road right opposite Costa's shop. Gerasimos threw out the old wine barrels, pitchforks and donkey harness from his ground floor storeroom. The room was dark and cavernous and backed onto the rock face, but he and his wife scrubbed it clean and painted the rocks with several coats of glutinous yellow varnish. Fishing nets and shells were hung on the walls and a sign outside announced the name of the bar as Remenzo, the landing place.

Scotch whisky and other exotic drinks were served and a few simple dishes; fresh whitebait, chips fried in local olive oil, and Greek salad. Friends and relations, and the few summer visitors up in Rachi, began to use the bar. Some people even came up from the harbour to give it a try.

It was a real asset. Things were going well, but it didn't last.

When we arrived the following year we found Costa outside his shop. He was reaching up, holding a bucket of water above his head, and pouring it into a new water tank cantilevered from his outside wall. The process was laborious. First, Costa brought a heavy stepladder up from the katoï, the basement workshop below his shop, and then he went down again to pull up a bucket of water from his water sterna inside the katoï. He climbed the ladder and filled his tank bit by bit, bucket by bucket. It took a dozen full buckets to complete the task. Finally, he returned the bucket and ladder to the katoï.

Alec watching Costa fill his tank

Later he fixed up a pump and a hose pipe which made his task a little easier. The tank was there to service Costa's new loo cistern. Luckily his customers nearly all live within a few hundred yards of the shop, and at home they have loos of their own. The loo in the shop was only for show. The few foreign tourists who ventured in never felt sufficiently at home to sit inside amongst the Chorus. A tourist would never use the loo, whose flimsy door led straight off the sitting area. The loo is there to comply with the authorities, 'tis arches' as Costa calls them. Perhaps ultimately it is there to impress the EU Commission in Brussels who, it is said, have made all kinds of rules that affect the people of Rachi. Costa doesn't talk of Brussels. The doings of the authorities in Vathi, twenty-four kilometres away along a precipitous road, seem almost as remote. The regional capital Corfu, at least ten hours away, is hardly ever mentioned. Athens is another world. It was against this background that Costa fought his epic battle with young Gerasimos across the road.

Costa was a reluctant combatant. He had looked after his shop for thirty years, ever since he took over from his father, and he was friendly with everyone. His shop served as the local pub, post office and telephone exchange, and he listened to every scrap of local gossip. What he heard he tested for consistency, and filtered clean of every trace of malice. He passed it on only if it reflected no ill on anyone.

Tassos the postman called twice a week. He left the post in Costa's shop. Costa knew which envelopes contained cheques and he knew from the foreign stamps where the few Rachi sailors had anchored to discharge their cargoes. Everyone in Rachi went into Costa's shop so there was no need for a postal delivery. We had a letter once and a neighbour was soon knocking at our door to tell us it had arrived, so we knew the system worked. Once a week, Tassos brought the pensions. The pensioners of Rachi gathered in the shop to wait for his arrival. He dealt out the pensions in cash onto Costa's tables. He knew, from his book, how much each pensioner was owed.

It was a big step forward for Rachi when a public phone was installed in Costa's shop. Then, as long as it wasn't raining, the pensioners of Rachi could phone whenever the shop was open. Anyone in the shop could listen in. Costa was thus at the hub of the community, and he took his responsibilities extremely seriously. He knew of every emergency and he was always ready to help.

Costa told us how, one day over the winter, a policeman from Vathi walked into his shop.

"We have received a complaint that you are selling drinks without a licence. Is there any truth in this?"

The policeman looked round the assembled drinkers.

"I have always served drinks," Costa explained, "and my father before me. Nobody has ever suggested that I should have a licence. But, if I need one, do you have an application form I can fill in? And how much will it cost?"

"Unfortunately," the policeman explained, "it isn't that easy to get a licence. You will need to have a sink in your shop to wash the glasses, a refrigerator and a WC with a washbasin. Until you have complied with all the regulations you must stop serving drinks. I will be back in two weeks to check you have taken the chairs and tables out of your shop, and that drinks are no longer served."

When Alec and I came out we saw at once that things had changed. Half the old wooden counter had been removed, and in its place was a new bar counter with a marble top. There was a large display fridge with a funky handle shaped like a Coca-Cola bottle. Two brands of beer were displayed: Fix and Amstel. There were bottles of spring water, and one or two plastic screw-top bottles filled with Costa's own wine from the barrels in his katoï below. To make it legal there was also a small notice giving the prices of coffee, brandy and other drinks.

Yet Costa looked glum and the Chorus were puzzled. Who could have reported Costa to the authorities in Vathi? Only one person stood to benefit and that was Gerasimos, so they decided he must have made the complaint. When we arrived, Costa leant confidentially towards Alec and, in a low voice straight into his ear, he told him the story.

"What was I to do?" he asked. "Could I take my chairs down to my cellar and lock them up for ever? The night after the police came from Vathi I went to bed but I couldn't sleep. I felt defeated. At last I fell asleep, but not for long. I woke up at 4 am and I knew what I had to do. I couldn't let that devil Gerasimos shut my shop. I had some money saved and I decided I would spend every last cent if I had to. Thanasi put in the WC in the corner and made a door with a latch. There was no room for a cistern so he put a tank on the wall outside. Thanasi thinks of everything. He didn't charge me much. He is very kind. Here behind the bar is my sink with running water. But the thing that cost me most was the big refrigerator, although I managed to get it second hand."

The new fridge with the Coca-Cola bottle handle must have been ex-display. Costa told Alec exactly how much the alterations had cost and it did seem quite a lot. His savings were not enough and he had to borrow from his brother, which he didn't like to do.

"It was that devil who did it," said Costa, pointing at Gerasimos's bar across the road. "The police showed me his signed statement. They said they would use it to prosecute if I sold drinks without a licence. When they came back they were surprised to see I had done all they asked. They gave me the go-ahead, but a few weeks later they were back again."

Someone had spotted he had no hot water in his sink. Another offence. So Costa had to go back to Thanasi who improvised a hot water system from on extended payment terms. By now every member of the Chorus was furious with Gerasimos. His bar was empty. Only Adrianna, a close relative, still sat there, and this confirmed the general village view that she was a person of poor judgement. The other locals sat solidly in Costa's shop, glaring occasionally at the empty bar across the way. Gerasimos had looked forward to a division of labour, where Costa would run the local shop and he would run the bar. But what would the locals have done for a bar in the winter when Gerasimos went back to Patras?

The battle was soon over. Gerasimos took his wife and daughter back to Patras. We wondered if Costa would ever be able to repay his debts, or build up his savings, as he charges much less than the coffee bars down by the harbour.

"Up here they can't afford more," he explained.

He had also bought a television and now he felt he had to stay open until his last customer had gone home. This was sometimes not until 2 am as people came into his shop to watch the late programmes. Now he had to work for others too, helping prune their olive trees, to eke out the family budget. His wife Panayiota took over the shop when Costa looked after their vines and olives. Their charming children had also reached the age of maximum financial strain. Their son was in Italy learning to be a PE instructor and their eldest daughter had passed her exams for Athens University. Soon their youngest would be leaving school. They were good children and they did their best. In the summer, they all worked in the tavernas down by the harbour. Costa and Panayiota were thrilled their children were doing so well, but never-the-less their college fees were expensive.

Panayiota took the threat of these looming expenses calmly. Her tactic was to bake cakes and yet more cakes. She appeared in the shop with great pans of home made baklavas stuffed with honey and nuts, more delicious than any baklavas we had ever eaten elsewhere. She made karydopita (walnut cake) in large slabs sliced into rhomboid shapes in traditional fashion. Her sweets were made to local recipes, one with semolina and one with rice. They were sold not only in Costa's shop but also in coffee shops down by the harbour, and in the neighbouring village of Frikes. She had cemented her reputation as a good cook.

Sitting in the shop with half an eye on the new television I remembered how the shop had been when we first came to Kioni. The rat traps and donkey harness had now vanished, though the donkey and rat population remained unchanged. Sickles were no longer to be seen, nor picks for the stony soil, or those shovels the locals use, set at right angles to their handles. Costa still kept red-lead primer for metal, white wood-primer, and several bright shades of translucent glossy boat paint, used in several coats over a white undercoat for windows and doors as well as for boats. You could still buy sacks of lime putty for mortar and lime wash, but for the blue, green and ochre pigments you now had to go to Vathi. You could still buy the blue school notebooks, and flowered plastic tablecloth from a roll but the blocks of hard green washing soap had given way to washing powder shovelled from a sack into a plastic bag. Best of all there was yoghurt, one type of cheese, and eggs from a local supplier. But I was shocked to find Costa had run out of dried beans.

"They're not poor enough now to eat dried beans," said Costa. "It used to be all they ate."

The moment of plenty showed itself in the insect and animal world too. As Alec and I walked down the road from Kioni to Frikes, a multitude of furry caterpillars were walking down the mountainside, over the rocks, down the road, and into the sea. They were so thick on the ground we could hardly find spaces between them for our feet. The road was encrusted with their flattened bodies. Yet those who survived marched grimly onwards towards the sea, where a mass of writhing bodies were drowning by the shoreline. The Chorus seemed unconcerned. They were glad the caterpillars chose to walk downhill to a death by drowning. Yet where did they come from and what drove them on?

"They drown themselves because they have fulfilled their biological function," said Kanas, the builder with a long nail on each hand, when we got to Frikes. For a second I was convinced by his suggestion. Then I remembered the silkworms I kept as a child which spun silky cocoons from which they later emerged as moths. It was the moths, not the worms, which laid neat rows of eggs on the small rectangles of blotting paper I put into their boxes. It seemed unlikely that the life cycle of a furry caterpillar would differ in any radical way from that of a silk worm.

As the insects walked over the hills, they ate the leaves from the holm oak trees and left them bare, and we wondered if the damaged trees would survive the hot Greek summer to come. We puzzled to find a reason for the invasion. Had Denis the environmentalist got any ideas? We rang him in Stavros but he was nowhere to be found. He had gone to Australia to visit his family. Since he managed to stop the spraying of the island's olive trees by helicopter there were noticeably more birds in the village, but not nearly enough to eat their way through such a glut of caterpillars.

In August, we met up with Denis, but he didn't know about the caterpillars. The trees had been brown for a bit, the Chorus told us, but now they had recovered. Over the years, we noticed these gluts of insects are a cyclical phenomenon in Ithaca. Sometimes it is caterpillars, sometimes mosquitoes, or wasps, or grasshoppers, or small shiny black beetles.

Years later our eldest grandson did a degree in Biology. He explained that many creatures have population booms from time to time. These surges in number can be caused by a change in the weather, a temporary abundance of food, a lack of predators, or a combination of these things. When numbers get too great this sometimes leads to migratory behaviour.

"Although this may look like mass suicide," he said, "it is not the case. It is a myth that lemmings commit suicide by walking over the edge of a cliff."

The many descendants of our dear old cat Grizoula fluctuated in numbers, politeness, and beauty. Some years only a few came to the house, but other years they came in crowds. We tried to keep the cats and kittens outside the house and we asked our visitors to do this too. I don't think our children or grandchildren invited them in, but others may have done so and the kittens learned quickly. It caused some problems for us, and probably for our Greek neighbours as well.

The September after the caterpillar event, a new cat came up to the house. She was a lithe and beautiful small-headed, long-eared tabby with touches of orange. She looked skinny. Not pregnant, at least, we thought. Then we noticed her dangly sucking tits. Two days later she brought her brood along to see us, and they began as they intended to go on. They chased and danced and leaped and scrambled and hugged and boxed and bit each other. It soon became obvious our new cat had had enough of breast-feeding and she vanished for a couple of days.

"She has dumped them with us," said Alec. "She saw us as likely suckers who'd take them on so she could go off with some rough diamond and get herself pregnant again before the winter begins. If she does that now she'll put herself in danger of starving."

This seems to be the pattern with our female cats. They have such poor taste in men. This one took no notice of the handsome and gentlemanly deep grey tomcat we encouraged. He was so polite. He never pushed, fought, or came into the house. But the second some raffish, torn-eared, dirty, beaten-up black and white tomcat stuck his head around the wall she was off.

"There she goes," we said.

And off she went, wiggling her hips, her long thin tail up stiffly straight in anticipation.

Our children wanted to know about the cats. They weren't interested we were trying to paint like Bonnard. We were working at it all day long, striving to capture the brilliance of the light, the dancing colours, the morning blues and the violet hills in the distance. They rang up and sent messages aimed at me.

"Please do us some drawings of cats."

"We loved the watercolours you did of cats last year."

"All your grandchildren want drawings of cats"

"Could you put me on the list for drawings of cats?"

And so on.

"They don't stay still for a second," I explained.

"Oh, but you can manage."

"Do you know what happened to Edward Lear?" I asked. "He did the most beautiful paintings of Corfu. He was really good. But people were more interested in his nonsense rhymes and drawings."

I suspected it was ever thus.

"But they're brilliant," my daughter exclaimed.

"I like them too."

"I'll collect your cat drawings into a book."

Now that is really pushing it, I thought. She's trying to flatter me now.

"I'll draw the cats as soon as the weather breaks," I said.

You don't need perfect light for cats, but that year the weather stayed resolutely beautiful day after day after day. The landscape shimmered around us. Meanwhile the kittens got bigger and stronger and cheekier by the day. They slipped into the house the second we opened any door or window. All our windows and doors were shut and, although it was autumn, it was still really hot. We were barricaded in. Outside the view was stupendous but we couldn't see it. We were shut inside in the gloom. Somehow a kitten got in and headed straight for my palette of oil paints. In a flash it had viridian green, cadmium red and chrome yellow paint on its feet and it was climbing around the house.

"Jackson Pollock would probably have made something of this," I said to Alec as I chased after it, "but it's not the effect I'm after."

The kitten hid under the bed before I could get the broom to sweep it out. At last I pushed it out of the window and bolted the shutters behind it. That evening when I spoke to my mother on the phone, she suggested we put wire fencing three foot high across our doorways. She did this to keep her chickens out of her kitchen in England. But as soon as she rang off I knew it wouldn't work.

"She's not thinking of this kind of cat," I explained to Alec. "They'd be up and over any wire mesh you can think of in a flash. She's imagining English kittens. Fat complacent ones. Not these. But we must teach them not to come in. If they get used to coming into the house, they'll drive our Greek neighbours mad in the winter. Then they won't feed them. They might even drown them. When we go home these cats will have to manage outside on their own."

The kittens thought about us from dawn till dusk. They wanted to be as near as possible to us all the time.

"Why can't they go off and chase rats?" I asked.

Alec thought I was being too tough on the kittens. Now he was defending them.

"I've found four dead rats in the shed in the last few days," he said, "so I know their mother is teaching them."

I was glad they were learning their trade. Come the winter they would have to learn to eat rats too, not just leave them for Alec to clear up. But for now we were providing food and they knew it.

Every morning we woke up to little mewing sounds. One day they found their way onto the roof. We lay in bed and looked up at our bedroom skylight from inside our mosquito net. A row of sleek little heads along the lower edge were silhouetted against the sky. I was afraid they might try jumping down onto our mosquito net. It would make awful holes, and if they missed and fell onto the floor they'd really hurt themselves.

Anyway, their strategy worked. They got their way and we got out of bed to get them their breakfast. Another day had begun.

The following year we had a glut of cats. One evening, twenty-seven cats followed us as we walked back along our track from the road. A visitor, who was staying in Kioni with our South African friends Piers and Lynda, came up to the house to look at my paintings. She took a great interest in my landscapes and said she loved them; but obviously something else caught her eye. After she left she wrote a poem about cats. She wittily called it Cat Walk and she has kindly allowed me to include it here.

> CAT WALK
> *By Frances Wilson.*
>
> *Thin to the point of skin and bone,*
> *they lope down the steps, disdainful*
> *and hungry. Every pause is a pose,*
> *every swivel, every lift of hip*
> *and flank is elegant and easy.*
> *They are so loose-limbed you wonder*
> *how the bag of their fur can hold them*
> *together. It's impossible*
> *not to watch them: those huge ears,*
> *those sharp faces, that eyeliner.*
> *And they read our attention,*
> *Every gesture, whether it's a fish*

ODYSSEUS' ISLAND

Or a stone we'll hurl at them,
even our cold shoulder, so they turn
in a movement as low and fluid
as water and streak off, back
to the shadows which belong to them.

9

A threat from outside

The archaeologists from Ioannina were making progress on Ithaca but clouds were coming up over the horizon. Denis had counted seven claims that Odysseus came from the larger neighbouring island of Kefalonia then, all of a sudden over four years, there were three more. The most recent, put forward in 2005 by an English marketing consultant Robert Bittlestone, was widely promoted internationally.

Back in England, a lawyer friend of ours, knowing of our association with Ithaca, went to a lecture given by Bittlestone at Kings College, London. He was excited by what he heard. Bittlestone claimed that the Paliki Peninsula in the northwest of Kefalonia fitted the words of Homer much better than Ithaca itself. He had followed every incident from the relevant texts of *The Odyssey* and found their exact locations in Paliki. He claimed that in Homer's day Paliki was almost certainly a separate island from the rest of Kefalonia.

"He has found exactly where the sea channel used to run between Paliki and Kefalonia," our friend explained. "Later an earthquake lifted the seabed and rocks tumbled in from nearby hills, so now it is only a valley, but from a satellite it is obvious where the original channel used to be."

In response, we told him about the Greek archaeologists' excavations at Agios Athanassios/School of Homer near Denis' house in Stavros in the north of Ithaca. But, although our friend was polite, I'm not sure we made much headway.

Bittlestone was a specialist in marketing. I put this in the past tense, as unfortunately he died in his early sixties quite a short time later. He was not an expert in geology, or philology, but he had some impressive support. His book *Odysseus Unbound* was co-authored by two specialist academics: James Diggle, a Classics professor at Cambridge University, and John Underhill, a professor in Stratigraphy at Edinburgh University. It was published by the Cambridge University Press, one of the oldest and most respected publishing houses in the world.

Alec and I discussed the problem. The Ithacans are proud of their association with Odysseus. The younger Ithacans are relying on tourism to survive and, although they may not have made the connection, Odysseus was an asset. Young men like Thanasi's son could live with his family in their island home without going to sea with the Greek merchant navy. The number of children in Kioni was rising. Now there were around twenty. The village was coming to life again. Yet the money the local people earned from tourism during the summer months had to last them all the year round. Their economy was fragile and vulnerable.

The neighbouring island of Kefalonia is much larger, more modern, and more accessible. The Kefalonians were aiming for the mass tourist market. Holiday companies were bringing groups of tourists to enjoy the wide sandy beaches in the west and south of their island. The little wooden hut we first knew as the airport building had been replaced by a modern concrete structure with a rubber conveyor belt to deliver the luggage. We couldn't imagine how they would ever fill it. No doubt the Kefalonians had also noticed that their Ithacan neighbours weren't making much of their ancient association with the Homeric hero Odysseus.

On Ithaca, Denis was trying to extend the holiday season by clearing the footpaths to encourage walkers. He was waiting for the archaeologists at Agios Athanassios to come up with evidence that this was the real site of Odysseus' palace. But Robert Bittlestone's campaign was on a different level. Supported by the two professors he visited over a hundred European universities to make his case. The latest developments in his work were advertised breathlessly on a well designed website. We crossed our fingers and hoped the threat would go away, but it didn't. In fact, it grew worse.

When Bittlestone's book *Odysseus Unbound* was published in 2005, it generated more than one hundred newspaper stories around the world. In the USA, the History Channel broadcast a programme *Digging for Truth*, based on his theory. He gave a lecture to the Anglo-Hellenic League in London in the presence of the Greek Ambassador and Consul General. Jon Snow described the new theory on a Channel 4 news broadcast, and a recording was immediately posted on the *Odysseus Unbound* website. Bittlestone may not have been a specialist academic but he was a charismatic enthusiast, a talented linguist, rich, and, most importantly, extremely good at marketing.

Back in Ithaca, few people had telephones, let alone access to the internet. The threat seemed a long way away. It seemed curious to us that anyone should suggest that Odysseus had come from Kefalonia and we couldn't imagine how such a view might have arisen. When we next went to Vathi we visited the Archaeological Museum. One of the glass-topped showcases contained silver and bronze coins dating from centuries before

Christ showing the head of Odysseus. On several, he was wearing a 'pilos', a typical pointed travellers cap. On the backs of the coins were a rooster, the symbol of Ithaca, or the head of the goddess Athena, or a standing male figure also thought to be Odysseus. Some had the head of Odysseus and the word IΘAKΩN (of the Ithacans) on the same side.

'IΘA' can be seen to the left of Odysseus' head

Bittlestone, we were told, had suggested that the names of the islands had changed at some time in the distant past. But these coins from fourth and third centuries BC had all been found on Ithaca and they had the island's name on them. It seemed to us that, back then, Ithaca was called Ithaca just as it is today. These coins indicated a direct and ancient connection between the hero Odysseus and this particular island.

It was puzzling.

We mentioned Bittlestone's challenge to a few local people in Kioni. The man behind the bar, whose wedding we had watched, gave a typical response.

"The Kefalonians can say what they like but it doesn't change anything. Odysseus came from Ithaca and this is Ithaca."

So we concerned ourselves with local matters, which were, in any case, more amusing. Alec went down the hill to see Captain John and Loula. As he left, they told him how much they loved us and asked us to supper. Alec in turn asked them to supper with us, but there was a problem. We knew that they both found the walk up the hill a bit difficult, but the problem was different. John agreed to come but suggested we ask Costa's wife Panayiota to cook a chicken for us with plenty of roast potatoes. Panayiota is known throughout Kioni as a good cook, but I too quite fancy myself as a cook. On the last occasion they came, I remembered, I cooked them a vegetarian moussaka. Perhaps John felt deprived that I didn't cook him meat? Did he think a moussaka made with meat was beyond me? Alec tactfully suggested it was quite natural that John should want to savour the full gastronomic delights that Rachi had to offer, and no doubt he too fancied roast chicken.

Alec went to the shop to see if he could make a deal with Panayiota to cook us a roast chicken and potatoes, but there he found a further complication. Costa said that if Panayiota cooked a meal for us, Aphrodite, who ran the taverna down by the harbour, must never find out about it. If she thought Panayiota was competing with her family business she would pursue her mercilessly, we were told. We shuddered at the thought of Aphrodite's angry screeching, which we had witnessed more than once. Finally, Alec came to an arrangement with Panayiota. She would roast the chicken and potatoes then Alec would somehow smuggle the meal secretly back into our house. And this is what happened.

On August 20, 2010, five years after Robert Bittlestone's book *Odysseus Unbound* came out in England, the archaeological professors from Ioannina University, Athanassios Papadopoulos and Litsa Kontorli-Papadopoulou, made an announcement at a 'Conference of the Odyssey' held in

Vathi. They had identified a megaron, or great hall, of a Mycenaean palace from the time of Odysseus at Agios Athanassios/School of Homer near Denis' home in Stavros.

Were the archaeologists finally certain that this was the site of the great hall of the Palace of Odysseus? Was this the place where Homer envisaged the horrific slaughter of Penelope's suitors while she was asleep upstairs? Was this the place where, after the slaughter, Penelope came downstairs from her upstairs bedroom to the hall, or megaron, to meet Odysseus, who was still disguised as a beggar? Where Homer portrayed, so sensitively, the long-awaited meeting between husband and wife? Where finally, after twenty long years, they sat together in the flickering light of the fire? Where, on either side of the central fireplace below a columned wooden superstructure, Penelope tested her long-lost husband?

We looked up the passage in our copy of *The Odyssey*.

'She left her room and made her way downstairs, a prey to indecision. Should she remain aloof as she questioned her husband, or go straight up to him and kiss his head and hands? When she had crossed the stone threshold into the hall, she sat down in the firelight by the wall, on the opposite side to Odysseus. He was sitting by one of the great columns with his eyes on the ground, waiting to see whether his good wife would say anything to him when she set eyes on him. For a long while Penelope sat there without a word, with bewilderment in her heart. As she gazed into his face, at times she saw a likeness to Odysseus, at others she failed to recognise him because of the vile clothes he was wearing.'

(23: 84-97 Rieu)

On the evening of the 'Conference of the Odyssey' where the announcement was made we had supper with Denis, who had spent the day there. Alec and I were delighted to hear that the archaeologists from Ioannina had excavated the foundations of a megaron, or palace hall, from the time of Odysseus at Agios Athanassios. Although Denis didn't doubt the sincerity of their claim he didn't seem elated. As he himself had pointed out years earlier, it was one thing to find convincing remains from the right pre-historic era, quite another to prove that Odysseus and Penelope had actually lived in any particular place. He seemed a bit fed up. He wanted a peaceful supper, and he was disinclined to discuss the matter in much detail.

After the announcement, two foreign women living full-time on Ithaca began to take groups of tourists on walks to Agios Athanassios/ School of Homer to show them around the palace site. Alec wanted to check it out but, now he was eighty, he was getting frail. He was walking with a stick like the three-legged man in the Oedipus riddle and he didn't feel he could manage a longish walk over rough ground. So I said I would go with two grandchildren who were staying and report back.

Our guide stopped at the ever-flowing fountains at Kalamos, where we all had a drink of fresh water then, as we took a left turn up an old donkey track, she explained that the mountain of Exoghi, which we were climbing, is full of water lying just below the ground. The track, with its wide ancient steps, lead finally up to the high village of Exoghi, and the site of Agios Athanassios was half way up the mountain from a fertile plain. As we emerged into a clearing a rocky outcrop appeared before us, its massive ruined walls stood high on the top of a cliff. At the base of the cliff, according to our guide, were the foundations of the hall, or megaron, of Odysseus.

I climbed up to the citadel with my grandchildren. There, the ruins of the eighteenth century church had clearly been built up from more ancient walls at its base, built in massive cut stone blocks. Many were over two metres long and not much less than a metre in height and depth. The corner stones had once been fixed together at the top with huge metal connectors shaped like double axe heads. How could men have moved these stones to build these walls? We discussed block and tackle, rollers, and other methods.

"Were those huge old stones built back in the time of Odysseus?" I asked.

Our guide seemed unsure.

We stood inside the ruins of the Byzantine church of St Athanassios. This was where, our guide told us, Penelope's bedroom once stood. But what remained of it? We could clearly see a flight of stone steps carved into the rock leading down to the position of the hall below.

"Were these the actual steps where Homer envisaged Penelope descending from her bedroom 3000 years ago?"

"The archaeologists believe so," our guide replied.

From the summit, my grandchildren and I looked northwards down to Afales Bay and, further away to the east, through a gap in two hillsides, to the Bay of Frikes. We looked out over the fertile plain below us and decided that, if we were kings in ancient times, we would be happy to live in a place like this. We would have fresh water within easy reach and good land to grow our olives, vines, and fruit trees. In our fortified citadel on this high ground we would be safe from pirates. We would have a choice of easily accessible harbours facing onto different seas for travel and trade. If pirates attacked, we would choose the best of three harbours to make our escape.

The archaeologists had cleared the site and dug deep rectangular pits, each about ten feet deep, leaving a great heap of sifted soil to be moved later. They had labelled their finds carefully and packed them into boxes, we were told. We walked down to the flatter area where, according to our guide, the great hall, or megaron, once stood. The excavation pits were covered with corrugated sheets and rough wooden structures, which our guide assured us were temporary. She lifted a cover where, she explained, the stone foundations were of the correct building type and dimensions, and the plan layout a match to the halls of other known Mycenaean palaces.

Was this where, according to Homer, the returning hero shouted to the suitors:

> 'You dogs. *You never thought to see me back from Troy. So you fleeced my household; you raped my maids; you courted my wife behind my back though I was alive...One and all your fate is sealed.*'
>
> (22: 34-40 Rieu)

A short distance further down the hill our guide showed us a hole in the ground like the entrance to the underworld. My grandchildren climbed eagerly down through a stone shaft to look into the circular pool of dark water below. I didn't go with them, but I noticed this water source was much nearer the citadel than the fountain at Kalamos, where we had begun our walk.

The archaeologists' work was incomplete but the signs were good. The site had been compulsorily purchased from its private owner. The University of Ioannina, the Municipality of Ithaca, and the Greek Ministry of Culture had bought it jointly. The archaeologists had been promised a grant to continue the excavation, for cleaning and conservation of the finds, for photography, and to complete their records.

The people of Ithaca tried to resist the flood of new theories from Kefalonia by forming the 'Ithacan Friends of Homer Association'. An energetic retired sea captain Dimitris Païzis-Danias collated the history of the archaeological finds on Ithaca and, in 2013, he mounted a small exhibition in Stavros. He did a tremendous amount of work, yet his task was difficult. Once the seed of doubt has been sown, it is difficult to dispel it. The sheer quantity of detail in Païzis-Danias' exhibition made it complex for the average foreign tourist to understand. Even Alec and I had difficulty. In addition, compared to the large numbers of tourists visiting Kefalonia, very few reached the little town of Stavros in North Ithaca.

Alec's back was giving him trouble. At first I thought it was due to a life-time of deskwork, but later I began to wonder if it was more than that. He was finding it hard to climb up the hill from the harbour to our house so we hired a car, which I insisted on driving. The car also made it easier for us to reach other beaches so we often went to Polis Bay, the harbour below Denis' home village of Stavros, for our daily swim. A good 'kantina', or beach bar, had started up there. It sold simple food and drinks and it was a favourite both with Denis and with Liz McGrath (sometimes known by her maiden name of Elizabeth MacLennan) the playwright and poet from Exoghi who had been helping Païzis-Danias with his exhibition. We often met up there. As well as good beaches for swimming, the place has extraordinary archaeological significance; which interested us all.

When we first came to Ithaca, the long, stony beach at Polis Bay was covered with seaweed, driftwood and sea-shoes, but now it is clean. In summer, an Ithacan from Australia hires out sun beds, umbrellas, and a couple of kayaks to tourists. Many years ago, a little sign with a map was put up to show the position of 'Loïzos' Cave'. The cave was excavated, it told us, by the archaeologist Sylvia Benton in the 1930s. Alec and I walked to the far end of the long beach and searched in the groves of twisted ancient olives beyond, but we couldn't find the cave. There was no sign of it. Then we discovered it had been partially destroyed in Classical times and that the earthquake of 1953 had finished it off. In this land of earth-quakes and changing sea levels, caves near the sea are particularly vulner-able. The Ionian Islands are riddled with caves. They come and go, reveal themselves or collapse, with each of the many earthquakes suffered there.

Back in London, I went into the Library at the Society of Antiquar-ies on quiet days to discover more about the archaeology on Ithaca, then

I reported back to Alec. We discussed my discoveries with Denis and Liz. Alec had always been on the trail of the Palace of Odysseus and now I too became keen to find out about life on Ithaca in those ancient times. First, as we went there so often, I found out more about Polis Bay.

These days Polis Bay is a rural and unassuming place, yet this wasn't always the case. Its unusual name 'Polis' indicates a city once existed nearby. Polis Bay opens onto the Ithaca Channel, which runs between Ithaca and Kefalonia. In ancient times this channel was a major sea route to the west. Ships left the Gulf of Corinth, made their way up the Ithaca Channel, and sailed on up to Corfu before cutting across the Straits of Otranto to the heel of Italy.

The name of the archaeologist, Sylvia Benton, kept coming up in my searches. So I found out more about her too. Wild and remote places beckoned her, and Ithaca held a particular pull. Some of her most important work was carried out at Polis Bay where, every evening after work, she would swim across the bay and back again. Her swimming, I was told by those who knew her, showed more strength than style, but she was always athletic.

At Cambridge, where she read Classics before World War One, she played hockey and tennis for her college and university teams. Benton was a bluestocking. She shared her classical interests with her father, one time Chief Judge in the Punjab, where she was born in Lahore in 1887. In the late 1920s, she studied archaeology at the British School at Athens before reading for a Diploma in Classical Archaeology at Oxford. The title of her B. Litt. Dissertation was *The Barony of Odysseus*. In the early 1930s she was the obvious choice to assist in the excavations on Ithaca, funded by Lord Rennell of Rodd, and under the direction of William Heurtley from the British School at Athens. Her path was leading, as if pulled by a magnet, towards Polis Bay, where she excavated Loïzos' Cave.

As its name suggests, Benton wasn't the first to investigate this cave.

Back in the 1860s a local landowner, Dr. Dimitris Loïzos, had a good look into this cave and excavated two hundred ancient graves in Polis Bay. He kept no record of what he found. He took most of his treasure to Paris, where he disposed of it and lived the rest of his life in luxury. And Loïzos was by no means the only person who looted ancient artefacts from Ithaca. An enormous number of finds were removed in the early years of the nineteenth century, especially after the British took the Ionian Islands from the French in 1807. Païzis-Danias explained how Captain Guiterra, commander of the islands from 1811 to 1814, became very busy excavating the ancient sites. He made a huge collection of finds, which he later sold in Italy for more than £6,000, a very large sum at the time.

Finds from Ithaca can be found in museums all over the world; in the Archaeological Museum in Athens, the British Museum and the Society of Antiquaries in London, the Metropolitan Museum in New York, the Archaeological Museum in Brooklyn, as well as museums in Paris and Neufchatel in France, Munich in Germany, and in Switzerland. The infamous German archaeologist Heinrich Schliemann made his first brief visit to Ithaca in 1868 before he went on to excavate Troy and Mycenae. The record of his ten-day visit *Greece and the Troad*, is now on the internet. He reported that he bought from Loïzos some Egyptian scarabs, some coins, and a small statue of the goddess Athena. But he was disappointed he didn't immediately strike gold. As he left for Troy, he remarked that the island of Ithaca had been well and truly ransacked by those who came before him.

Mercifully, in the 1930s, the archaeological team from the British School at Athens under William Heurtley and Sylvia Benton found there were some things left, and they did things differently. Their extensive and careful research and excavations, made on several sites in North Ithaca, were carefully photographed and recorded and stored in the two museums on the island.

The collapse of Loïzos' Cave in Polis Bay in Classical times turned out to be a blessing in disguise. Without it, Dr. Loïzos would have taken everything, but the collapse and subsequent flooding preserved both most of the stratification of the earth and some of the objects inside. In the 1930s, Sylvia Benton brought a pump by boat from Patras on the mainland over to Ithaca and, after pumping the seawater out from the cave, she dug down through several undisturbed strata and found many things that Loïzos had missed. She excavated votive offerings to the chthonic gods of the underworld from way before the time of Odysseus. Loïzos' Cave had been used as a place of worship, certainly since 3000 BC and probably for much, much longer. In the second century BC, Benton believed, this cave was used for the hero-worship of Odysseus himself.

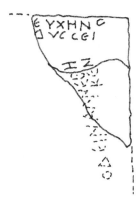

Confirmation of the hero-worship of Odysseus in Loïzos' Cave at Polis Bay is found in a small triangular-shaped sherd of pottery Benton discovered there. It sits, with little explanation, on a shelf in the one-room Stavros Museum. It doesn't look much. You could easily miss it. But amongst fragments from around a hundred clay female masks from the second century BC Benton found this one with the words ΕΥΧΗΝ ΟΔΥΣΣΕΙ (an offering to Odysseus) scratched into it. Two letters which can be seen on the edge 'H*N' probably belong to the word 'ΑΝΕΘΗΚΕΝ'

(dedicated) before which might have been the name of the person making the dedication.

This indicates that, way back before Christ, the Greek-speaking people believed Odysseus was real, and they worshipped him in Loïzos' Cave.

Alec and I often visited the one-room museum at Pilikata to the north of Stavros, where the little sherd is kept. The museum was set up by Heurtley and Benton in the 1930s. It displays finds made in North Ithaca dating from way back in prehistoric times, over the time of Odysseus, up to the time of the Roman rule of Ithaca from 180 BC to 396 AD.

In a showcase at the far end of the room are some remains of the twelve bronze tripod-lebetes also found by Benton in Loïzos' Cave. Their strange black bronze decorated legs are about a metre long, and one has a wheel at the end of it, along with round bronze handles decorated with lively figurines of horses and goats. A little picture adjacent to the showcase shows a reconstructed whole 'tripod-lebes'.

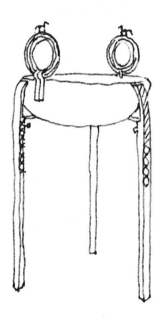

A tripod-lebes is a somewhat ungainly object with three long bronze legs (the tripod) supporting a wide, shallow cauldron (the lebes). On each side of its rim, stand two large circular handles placed vertically, topped with small bronze statuettes.

Another curiosity concerns the number of tripods found. Sylvia Benton found the remains of twelve, but a thirteenth had been found by Loïzos. When she first arrived in Ithaca Benton interviewed two local men. One had worked for Loïzos on his excavations, the other had hosted Schliemann in Vathi. Both independently told her that Loïzos had found a complete tripod-lebes in the cave at Polis Bay but that later, when the authorities got wind of it, he melted it down.

There is nothing in the small Stavros Museum to explain the extraordinary Homeric significance of the fact that thirteen of these objects were found in this cave. To understand this we have to go back to Homer's story.

Nearing the end of his ten-year journey home from Troy, Odysseus managed to struggle ashore in Phaeacia, thought to be modern Corfu. By this time, he had lost all his ships and all his men. The generous king and queen of the Phaeacians invited him to join them in a banquet they were holding. They and their guests gave Odysseus gifts of gold and sumptuous clothes. In addition, the king gave Odysseus a 'large tripod and cauldron' and he arranged for each of the twelve noblemen present at the banquet to do the same:

> 'The clothing, gold ornaments and other presents that our counsellors brought here are already packed for our guest in a polished strong-box. I now suggest that in addition we each give him a large tripod and a cauldron.'
>
> (13: 11-13 Rieu)

This made thirteen tripod-lebetes in all. The king of the Phaecians realised this was a lot to ask as he added.

'Later we will recoup ourselves by a collection from the people, since it would be hard on us singly to show such generosity with no return.'

(13: 13-15 Rieu)

Could these thirteen bronze tripods in the museum in Stavros be those actually brought back by Odysseus on his return after twenty years to the island of Ithaca? Well, no.

The tripods found in the cave at Polis Bay are thought to be from the ninth and eighth centuries BC. That is post-Odyssean but pre-Homeric. Experienced Homerists have made a different suggestion. They believe that Homer himself may have visited Ithaca to check the details of a pre-existing story sung by poet bards before his epic poem was recorded in writing. It is suggested that Homer may have based his story of a gift of thirteen tripods on the fact that he found thirteen on his visit to Ithaca. The number, thirteen, could have influenced Homer's story rather than the other way around.

And what was the use of these grand, but (to us) odd-looking, objects from the ancient past? At first they were no doubt used as cooking pots, but they also had other uses.

In *The Iliad* an 'ordinary' bronze tripod had the same value as an ox, but a 'fine' one was described as a 'twelve-ox tripod'. Coinage wasn't yet invented in Odysseus' day, but a bronze tripod was valuable. It could be given as a gift, or used as barter for trade. Grand tripods, such as those discovered by Benton in Loizos' Cave, were used as centrepieces at feasts or given as prizes for supreme athletic feats at organised competitive games.

At Polis Bay, a wire fence separates the kantina, a small car park, and the long, stony tourist beach from a wide and flattish valley running inland. Inside the fence a notice in Greek asks people not to park or camp. Next to it a large fig tree had grown up and, one hot day when we were there, a herd of sheep had packed themselves underneath it to make the most of its shade. There was one black sheep on the edge of the herd with its bottom sticking out into the sun. It amused me and I did a watercolour painting of the scene. But this scruffy valley has more significance than I realised at the time.

Sylvia Benton believed that the valley behind the fence at Polis Bay was used for athletic competitions in ancient times. This was a favourite male pastime in those ancient days. In The Iliad Homer records the hero Achilles organising competitive games at Troy and, in *The Odyssey*, he tells how King Alcinous of the Phaeacians organised racing, wrestling, chariot racing, discus throwing and boxing contests in honour of his guest Odysseus.

Benton investigated the link between these tripods and the athletic games of ancient times. Fragments of around two hundred grand bronze tripods were discovered in Olympia on the nearby mainland, where the Olympic Games were first held in 776 BC. But these Ithacan tripods are from an earlier date than those found at Olympia. Around two hundred grand bronze tripods were also found at Delphi, site of the famous Shrine of the Oracle. Twenty-three were found at the Idaean Cave on Mount Ida in Crete, where the legend says the god Zeus was born. Next on the list comes Ithaca, where thirteen bronze tripod-lebetes were discovered. Ithaca looks like an anomaly on Benton's list, as it has always been a small and relatively impoverished island. She believed that this pointed to a very important shrine on Ithaca in ancient times, at the cave she had ex-cavated at Polis Bay.

The Ithacan Games, a precedent to those in Olympia, were called the 'Odysseia'. This name clearly links them to the island's ancient hero, Odysseus. We know this as, in the second century BC, the people of Itha-ca sent a tablet to the people of Magnesia in faraway Asia Minor inviting them to their games. The tablet can be seen, I am told, in the Pergamon Museum in Berlin.

During World War Two archaeological work stopped on Ithaca. Sylvia Benton was employed by the United Kingdom Hydrographic Office to produce a Gazeteer of Greece and a Glossary of Modern Greek. She then worked on 'uncommon languages' for the Postal Censorship Department, as well as fire fighting by night.

By 1947, she was back in Ithaca excavating further and arranging the post-war restoration of the museums in Vathi and Stavros. She was not on the island at the time of the earthquake in 1953 but she managed to hitch a lift back right away on a Royal Navy destroyer carrying relief supplies. Although she was by this time in her late sixties, she couldn't bring herself to use the ladder to get into the sea for a swim, but insisted in diving from the deck.

She found the Vathi museum badly damaged and much of its contents shattered by the earthquake. The Stavros museum fared slightly better. Many of the finds were taken to Patras and Athens for conservation and, along with the islanders, she had a hard fight to get them back.

The repair and reconstruction of the two museums on Ithaca took many years and, in her eighties in the mid 1970s, Benton was still bringing groups of students from the British School at Athens to show them around the archaeological sites of Ithaca.

10

Three deaths and a miraculous escape

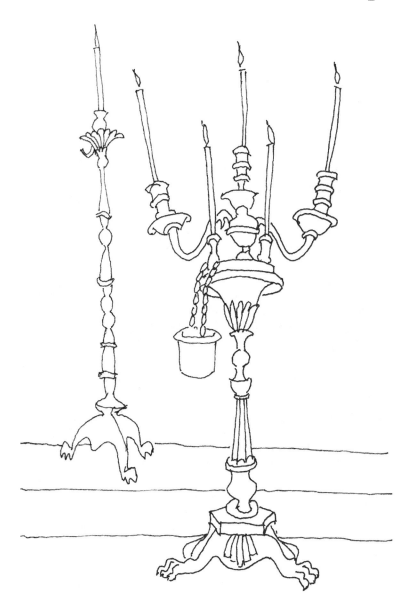

In late August 2011, the weather on Ithaca was dry and hot. As September came, the wind got up. It blew the dried leaves from our grape vines through the open front door of our house into the main room and through into our bedroom. We should have had rain by now, yet the sky was still pure, clear and blue, day after day. The smell of herbs was muted. There was an insistent dry wind, which made us apprehensive, yet as we looked down from our house over the harbour, the sea was calm and the tour boats were coming in from Kefalonia. The tavernas were doing a smart business and now, in accordance with the EU rules, they had menus with prices, and gave out paper bills on which the VAT was noted. Up in Rachi the old ways were changing more slowly, but they were changing all the same.

On Saturday 1 September Alec came back from Costa's shop with bad news. Nikóla was ill. He had had a small stroke and his wife Chrysanthe had rung for the ambulance to come from Vathi. They had taken Nikóla to the hospital in Kefalonia on the afternoon ferry.

The next day, the temperature rose again and it was humid too. We could hardly move. It is unusual to get this humidity in Greece. The new priest had built a concrete bell tower for the main church down by the harbour and its mechanical bells rang out a full joyful peal for the Sunday morning service. Then suddenly they slowed and changed their tune. They rang out a low double note. Ding-ding. Pause. Ding-ding. Pause. Ding-ding. A death.

Alec made an excuse to go along the track and down the road to Costa's shop, but I knew he wanted to be sure the bells weren't ringing for Nikóla. He came back soon to say the double bells were tolling for a lady born in the village many years ago who had died in South Africa. But, all the same, the news about Nikóla was not good. He had had a second stroke. At the hospital, they were watching over him day and night and he wasn't allowed to move.

That evening we sat out on our terrace under the stars and talked about Nikóla. We remembered how, when we first repaired our little house, it was only he who made time to work for us, the only foreigners in the village.

We remembered how he was prepared to rebuild our huge drystone retaining walls, which held up the wild part of our garden, and how he fenced round it in the old style with saplings and wire mesh to keep out the local goats. We remembered how he built us a stone donkey shed as a store for our tools and the overflow from our tiny house, and how he always stopped by our front steps on his return from the vineyards and demanded a whisky or an ouzo. We remembered how, when he eventually retired from caring for our garden, he handed over to his youngest son Nionio. Nikóla had never learned to read, or been to sea as a merchant seaman, so he thought of himself as 'only' the local gravedigger.

I remembered how, last autumn when I was painting down by the sea at Mavronas, Nikóla came to clean up an octopus he had caught on the little pier down there, and I quickly painted him into my picture. We remembered him out in Mavronas Bay in his little boat when the wind got up and the sea turned grey. He stood up and waved his arms at us landlubbers shouting "Boforia. Boforia!" It was a word he had made up based on his knowledge of the Beaufort wind force scale.

Later, Nikóla repaired and improved his old family house until he had a farmhouse with a big kitchen whose windows had a breath-taking view over the sea towards mainland Akarnania, the homeland of his wife Chrysanthe. In clear weather, the mountains rose out of the sea later to vanish like ghosts in a mist or heat haze. They were Nikóla's constant companions at the kitchen table. Recently, he had made another breakthrough; he bought a large shiny television that he placed at one end of the room. Now it didn't matter that neither he nor his wife could read or write, they could talk politics or football as well as anyone. We spoke about how close they were.

"I met Chrysanthe in the road only the day before yesterday," Alec said. "I asked her about the family and she said they were all fine, just fine. Yet that must have been only the day before Nikóla had his stroke. I guess high blood pressure is a stealthy enemy. The doctor had given him a machine to check it but he was never one to bother too much about his health."

The following day, the heat hung in the atmosphere like lead. The wind had dropped and the air was full of flies.

"I have never known it like this here," I said.

We remembered how, twenty years ago at just this time of year, we were helping our neighbour Maria pick her grapes when the double bells tolled. Back then, before the new bell tower was built, the main church down by the harbour had a simple hand-bell like ours up in Rachi. Moments later, we had seen Nikóla with his pick passing by on a higher terrace of the vineyard. As the village gravedigger he was on his way down to dig the hole.

"Who is it?" Maria had called out to him. Nikóla had shouted back the news.

Then, just as we were talking about those old days, the double bells rang out again. How odd that they should ring again so soon when they only rang yesterday. It is unusual, in this small community, to hear those death bells more than once a month. We went along to Costa's shop to check, but today the news about Nikóla was better. He was stable. The bells were for a lady from the village who had died in Australia.

But on Tuesday 4 September, it was our local bells in Rachi, in the church on the top of the hill, which rang out the double note from a large hand-bell. Ding-ding, ding-ding, ding-ding, ding-ding. The ringing went on and on and we feared the worst.

We left it an hour or so before we set out down our track towards the road to learn the news. There we met Thanasi dismounting from a small scooter. As he approached us I noticed that his sparkly brown eyes, shining out between the brown wrinkles on his face, were sincere, as always, but sad.

"Nikóla has died," he said. "Ησυχασε ο άντρας," he added (The man is at peace). Thanasi went on to say how Nikóla never picked a quarrel, was always ready to fit in, did more than his share of the work, and was always a helpful member of the community. "I must go now," he said, remounting his scooter. "They are having trouble digging the hole for his grave. There are some very big stones down there. I am going to see if I can borrow a compressor."

We wondered just how many graves Nikóla had dug by hand in a lifetime as the local gravedigger. We suspected he never once had the help of a compressor to move the large stones he encountered. Yet we never heard him complain.

"They will be bringing him back tomorrow morning on the 8.30 boat. The funeral will be around eleven," Thanasi added as he left.

The following morning Alec took a walk along the track to the road.

"Are people collecting out there by the church?" I asked him as he walked back up the stone steps onto our terrace.

"Yes. They are saying he was lucky to be taken like that, and not to survive."

The people of Kioni are practical. This remote and hilly village would be no place to be stranded with paralysed limbs. Such an outcome would have been no fun for Nikóla. But his sudden death, when last week he had seemed so well, was a terrible shock.

By 11 am the road at Rachi was crowded with cars. A row of men stood beside it with their backs to the houses. We didn't greet them, though by now we knew most of them well, but walked on up the steep path to the church on the top of the hill.

The large church was already full. A deep red carpet runner with a pattern of the double-headed eagle of the Byzantine Empire, the protector of the Greek Orthodox Church, led from the entrance doors down the centre of the nave. There Nikóla lay in a carved open coffin supported on a low table surrounded by bunches of white flowers. We found ourselves a place somewhere near the back. The new local priest was dressed in a long white gown over his black robes. He was assisted by two others from Stavros, both with magnificent long beards, and by Mimis who was dressed as usual in jeans with a striped tee shirt. They began to sing one-by-one and then in unison.

The church was steaming hot. The men wore short-sleeved shirts without ties and the women fanned themselves with zigzags of folded paper. We were standing near a tall candleholder, its tray-like top full of candles. Each person, as they squeezed into the packed church, kissed the icon of the Holy Virgin and crossed themselves, then they lit their candles and added them to the shining mass on the candelabra. Soon it was full and a man I didn't know roughly removed a handful and flung them into a bin to make room for more.

The singing went on and on. For the most part I couldn't understand the words yet I understood a few. Kyrie eleison, Christe eleison, Kyrie eleison. I picked up something about Nikóla's earthly body and about his soul, his 'pnevma'. Suddenly Chrisanthe began to cry out. She screamed "Nikóla. Nikóla!" She ran towards the coffin. Her neighbours caught her, put their arms around her and fanned her. Burly Andrikos, their middle son the water sterna expert, was sobbing too and now it set off Nikóla's youngest son Nionio, the insect-catcher. Others crowded round and comforted them.

Then the service was over. Mimis alone was singing now, on and on in his beautiful voice. I doubt this service had altered from that celebrated by the earliest Christians. Nikóla's life was probably not too different either from the lives lived in those bygone times. He had lived his whole life in this village, tending the vineyards to make wine, pruning and picking the olives to make oil, going out in his little painted rowing boat to catch fish for his family to eat, feeding his cats, sheep, goats and donkey. He was part of this solid community with roots as deep as the olive trees around his village.

As the singing went on, the congregation began to move forward. They surged around to the left of the coffin and on around it clockwise, to where his closest relations were sitting in the carved wooden seats backing on to the side wall of the church. We knew all the members of his close family but, apart from his wife and children, we hadn't known they were relations of Nikóla. We joined the crowd.

As he lay in his carved coffin Nikóla was wearing a black suit and immaculate white shirt. In life I had never seen him dressed up like this. He was tucked into his rather small coffin, fringed with scalloped white paper, under a blanket of white chrysanthemums. His hands were clasped below a huge white satin bow. His face was peaceful and natural as if he were sleeping. The lady in front of me fondled his forehead lovingly and the skin seemed to move over his skull. Only his ears were a slightly strange shade of pale mauve. I looked at his neat bone structure; the high cheekbones and curved nose, his large eyes closed, and the wide old-fashioned Greek moustache stretching right across his face. He was a good-looking man, quite slight in spite of a lifetime of manual labour. How odd that he should be dead, when he only looked asleep. And now he was dressed in his Sunday best and ready to be dropped into a pit such as he himself had dug for so many others who passed before him.

The crowd surged on past Chrysanthe and the other members of Nikóla's close family, they shook their hands and murmured words of consolation. Some of them hugged. I joined the mass of moving people. By the time I came up to Chrysanthe she seemed quite crushed and defeated, her small body pushed into the back of her seat as she shook the sea of hands extended towards her. I took her outstretched hand into both of mine and I tried to will some strength and comfort into her crumpled body.

"He was a good man," I said in Greek, and the tears welled up into her eyes and into mine as I kissed her on both cheeks.

The next day the thunder began. A dark cloud blew over the sky from the west and hung, deep grey and ominous, over the mountains behind Costa's shop. The temperature dropped. Some hours later, just as we were beginning to think it might all blow over, the rain began to fall in huge drenching droplets.

After the rain, Thanasi dropped round to see us. We all went up to look at the water sterna, but really that was an excuse. He had come round to tell us they had all known for some weeks that Nikóla was not well but they couldn't persuade him to go to the doctor.

"It was partly his drinking, I know, but his father and his grandfather both died suddenly in the same way. His family are terribly upset. We are all upset. We all loved Nikóla."

Now my Greek was better, and we had a better oven, Alec asked Thanasi and Eftichia to supper. They arrived laden with gifts. There was a half-litre plastic water bottle full of their own wine, the best in the village, and another of olive oil. A thick brown paper bag, printed with the name of the baker in Vathi, was stuffed with sweet wild plums. A plastic carrier bag contained eight juicy lemons the size of grapefruit. Courgettes with fresh flowers were in another bag, the opening carefully taped with masking tape. Three bunches of vegetables were tied with string. One bunch of assorted greens called 'horta', another of newly pulled spring onions, and a third of lettuce trimmings. The stronger leaves of the lettuce had been stripped from the outside leaving the main plant in the soil to produce more.

Thanasi talked about life when he was a child:

"Before World War Two a thousand people lived in Kioni. I was one of ninety-two children in the primary school down by the harbour. Back then the sea was full of fish, not like now. There were ten professional fishermen in the village but most men just fished for their own families. Up at the Vigla" (once a lookout place for pirates) "we grew wheat and lentils. It took an hour to get up to those high fields and when we arrived it was a hard graft. We sowed little patches of wheat under the olive trees. The vineyards had to be tended all year long and when the grapes were picked we trod them to make wine, just as we do today. The olive trees grew on terraces supported by dry stone walls. They needed constant upkeep. We kept the trees well pruned. After the harvest the olives were crushed between two huge stones driven by donkeys or mules. Everyone in the village kept chickens, turkeys, donkeys, goats and sheep. Our family kept a pig, which often came into the house," he said. "Getting material for clothes was difficult. To make them last as long as possible we patched the clothes over and over. Some people had looms and wove material, but it was expensive. They sold their cloth on the mainland where they could buy sugar and medicines, which were scarce on the island. Shoes were difficult too. We made our own shoes out of leather, or sometimes we carved clogs from wood."

The night outside was getting colder. Thanasi got up from the table, released the bolt on the front door onto the terrace, and closed it. He started talking about the draught and I noticed they used the same word as they use for an electric current, or for a current in the sea. Thanasi and Eftichia are practical people. They concern themselves with the details of everyday life.

When we arrived in Ithaca the following spring Thanasi greeted us warmly and asked us about our children, my mother, and the rest of the family. He said nothing about himself. But when we went into the shop Costa drew Alec up close and whispered in his ear,

"Have you heard about Thanasi?"

About eighteen months previously Thanasi had bought himself a small red van. Six weeks before we arrived he was driving towards Frikes with his son-in-law from Athens and an eight-week-old grandchild. He got to the point where, just before Frikes, the road bends round, and a large rock shaped like a dog's tooth stands to the right of the road. Inexplicably, when he came to the bend, Thanasi drove straight on. The car went off the road, over the cliff, and plunged down towards the sea. Elsewhere the cliff falls straight into the sea, but miraculously, several metres below that very point, there is a narrow ledge in the rock face. The van landed on its roof, but perched on the ledge. With more typical presence of mind Thanasi, who had a full tank of petrol, switched off the engine and climbed out through a window. He helped his son-in-law climb out after him, holding the baby. The baby cried a little but the adults were silent, awe-struck. All three escaped unhurt.

But how was it possible, Alec wondered, for Thanasi, a careful driver, to drive over a cliff in broad daylight? How did they all escape unharmed? They had cheated death by earth, fire and water. Impact, explosion and drowning. I pointed out that Thanasi is short for Athanassios meaning 'deathless'. It was an attribute often given to the ancient gods. Costa too had an otherworldly explanation.

"It is because he is a good man," he said, "the gods spared him."

"But why," Alec asked again, "did he drive over the cliff?"

Nobody could answer this more practical question. We searched for a scientific explanation. Did he have a blackout? Was it the first premonition of a heart attack?

Thanasi took two steps. For twenty-four hours he wore a heart monitor prescribed by the clinic in Vathi, but the doctors found nothing. Then he made an offering to the gods, or God. He built a small shrine by the road at the site of the accident. He and Eftichia keep a small oil lamp burning there.

There is now a metal guard across the gap where Thanasi drove over the cliff. As well as paying for the water desalination plant, the EU has provided money for guards on many of the more precipitous roads in Ithaca, and we are grateful.

Thanasi was spared but when Alec and I arrived in Ithaca in the spring of 2013 Costa told us Maria had died over the winter. She had been looking frail of late, so we weren't completely surprised. Alec met Manolis on the track and told him how sorry he was. Tears welled up in Manolis' eyes and flowed down his cheeks, and Alec put his arm around his shoulders. Finally, Manolis choked back his tears:

"You are not my enemy any more," he said to Alec, "Alexandros is my enemy now."

Our neighbour, the lawyer Alexandros, shares the communal steps by our house. Unfortunately, Manolis' words proved to be an omen for a future incident. A short time later, when Alexandros was sitting outside a coffee bar in Vathi, Manolis came up behind him with a heavy beam of wood and clubbed him over the head with it. Luckily a man from Kioni, who was standing nearby, managed to pull Manolis away. Blood was streaming down Alexandros' face, but mercifully his skull wasn't broken.

Manolis is a danger to the whole community but they just have to put up with him.

Manolis now spends all and every day working on his various claims and court cases. We see him strutting around Vathi wearing a suit and tie. He carries an official-looking folder under his arm. His activities are well known there and the lawyers, engineers and surveyors will no longer work for him. But I fear that, with so many Ithacans living abroad, some of his many claims to land belonging to others might be successful.

Once we marvelled at the new concrete airport in Kefalonia and wondered how it would ever be filled. Yet when we arrived in September 2013, we heard the summer visitors beside us in the queue complaining about how small and cramped it was, and how it only had one rubber conveyor belt for suitcases. Alec hobbled across the hot tarmac with his stick, last of all off the plane but quite determined to cross the water from Kefalonia and make it back to Ithaca.

Over the years, we have travelled to Ithaca via Athens, Venice, Bari, Brindisi, Corfu, Patras, and Lefkas as well as through Kefalonia. We have crossed to Ithaca by ferry, kaïki, and tour boat. The final lap onto the island now, as always, has to be by sea.

We walked the last two hundred yards of donkey track to our little house dragging our suitcases behind us, until, on the terrace in front of our house, the whole width of the sky with its dazzling light opened up and stretched out before us. Beyond the green headland sheltering Kioni harbour, the island of Atokos still floated on its pure white shoreline, surrounded by the ever-changing sea. Every time, before opening the door, Alec insisted we celebrate our arrival with a little Greek dance on the front terrace: the 'kalamatiano' ending in a jump with both feet off the ground together. Even on that last visit, with his stick, he managed it.

Alec's balance had been getting bad but nobody thought this would lead, the following spring, to such a sudden end. I had left to look after my mother who had fallen and broken her hip. That very night Alec overbalanced and fell backwards head over heels down a whole flight of our own stairs in London. Mercifully his son was in the house but, although both he and the hospital did their level best to save him, Alec died a week later on April 11, 2014 in St Mary's Hospital, Paddington.

Alec had always been reluctant to talk about death. In fact, he was rather superstitious about it. When I first knew him he told me with horror how he was in Greece when his own father died. He returned to England and went to see his father's body at the funeral parlour. His father's face had been made up with powder and lipstick so he looked quite unlike himself. Alec was spooked.

After that he would never walk past a funeral parlour, but always crossed to the other side of the road. When it came to it, however, he faced his own death with equanimity and quiet courage. He had only spoken to me once of what he wanted done in that event. I had realised this information was important and, while I had hoped I would never need it, I wrote down what he said and filed the paper in a safe place.

Although he was brought up to be Greek Orthodox, Alec didn't want an orthodox funeral or burial such as he had arranged for his own parents. A large Victorian church stands at one end of our street in London. When we first moved there, the church was very run down. Later it closed. One night a tramp got shut inside and, terrified, he broke his way out through a stained glass window. Pigeons went in to roost.

I discovered, through a contact at my work as a conservation architect, that the building was due to be sold off, and quite likely demolished. The bishops in the House of Lords at the time the listing legislation was passed made sure their many listed churches were exempt from the prohibition to demolish. Alec and I ran a campaign, obtained grants, and the church was rescued. It is now a popular church, of an evangelical persuasion, with many community activities. Alec wanted a memorial service there, after a family cremation. The excellent new vicar let me organise the service just as Alec had wished.

The church had no functioning organ, only a piano. However, we brought in the organ scholar from St Marylebone, who was also a superb pianist, and a small choir. My daughter and I went to the Nine Elms flower market and bought a carload of red, white, and silver flowers. We decorated the church and it dressed up wonderfully. An astonishing number of people came. The large church was filled with people. They came from many different walks of life. They had known Alec in many different roles.

After a rousing hymn and an opening prayer, the choir sang Thomas Tallis' four-part anthem *If ye love me*. Their red chorister's robes matched the flowers decorating the church. The beauty of the sacred song, and its formality, seemed appropriate.

Then Alec's daughter, Miranda, recited Yeats' poem *The Lake Isle of Innisfree*. "I will away and go now…"

Around the middle of the service a good friend of ours, the Guardian journalist Nick Davies, stood up and gave a tribute to Alec. He spoke without notes. Nick looked around the large congregation.

"Each one of us," he said, "probably had a slightly different relationship with Alec, at different times of his life. We knew him as a father, a colleague, a neighbour, or a friend. But probably none of us knew everything about him."

As an example, he wondered how many people there knew that Alec, during a communist phase, had studied Russian at London University, and subsidised his studies by working as a film extra at the Ealing Studios, which were near his parents' home. He obtained an Equity card and he can be seen in the background of many of the Carry On films. In historical films, with his Mediterranean features, he was often cast as a Roman soldier.

Nick explained how his own relationship with Alec began back in 1991, at a public meeting in Sussex to discuss a motorway proposal. The plan was for a six-lane highway to run right along the south coast of England, from Honiton in Devon to the head of the channel tunnel in Kent. Alec had a cottage on the South Downs, very close to the planned route, and Nick also lived nearby.

At the meeting one speaker after another said,

"Oh well, it could have been worse, better just let it happen."

Nick had come to the meeting with two friends. They were depressed by the submissive response, and a bit intimidated. Then a voice spoke up from the back of the hall.

"I was immediately struck by the beauty of the voice," Nick said. "It had the texture of velvet."

The speaker quoted Kipling's poem about the South Downs, calling them *our blunt, bow-headed, whale-backed downs*. He insisted we must protect them.

At the end of the meeting, Nick and his friends went to look for the speaker with the velvet voice, and they found Alec. Together, around Nick's kitchen table, they started up the 'A27 Action Group', and eventually, after a great deal of work, they won the fight. The road plans were adjusted from a massive motorway to a sensible dual carriageway, with roundabouts at each intersection, and trees planted on either side.

"I discovered that Alec was a man with gifts," Nick said. "Apart from his beautiful voice, I always thought that he must have been at the front of two queues when God was giving out the talents, both the one for charm and the one for wisdom. He had so much of both."

Nick wondered aloud how Alec's childhood had sown the seeds for the man he became. He mentioned how his parents had had the most terrible rows, and that this was how Alec learned, very early in life, to be an arbitrator. He spoke of how Alec's immigrant father went bankrupt in the Great Depression of the 1930s. The family were forced to burn their furniture to keep warm. Alec's taste for fish heads, which he never lost, began when his mother managed to obtain them for free to feed her family.

Nick spoke of how, during World War Two, Alec was evacuated, on his own, from Ealing to High Wycombe. The house where he was placed was quite basic, with a privy at the end of the garden, but he loved it there. He was free to roam in the woods, and he learned to love the natural world, particularly the English countryside.

Alec's childhood experiences led naturally to a career in politics. He narrowly missed election as Labour MP for Basingstoke in the 1960s and, in the 1970s as a Councillor for Camden, he managed to defeat the proposal for a 'Motorway Box', an inner ring motorway which would have demolished huge swathes of central London, including most of Camden Town, Covent Garden and Victoria. It wasn't until Alec and I had known each other for some years that we realised we both had a hand in this. It was me who had discovered the secret road plans, and made a drawing of them. Alec, as Councillor for the area, was given a copy of my drawing. This alerted him to the potential disaster in his constituency.

Alec went on to rescue the Jubilee Hall in Covent Garden from demolition. He set it up as a charity to promote health in the local community and, as chairman of the committee of trustees; he ran it for many years. At first it was a roller-skating venue before it morphed into a gym.

Nick spoke of Alec's successful career as a maritime arbitrator. He mentioned how Alec once thought he would make his fortune as a ship-owner. He bought a cargo ship, but the enterprise was not a success. The company went bankrupt and the ship was sold.

When Nick split up with his long-term partner, the mother of his three children, he seemed a bit at sea. It was out of character, and Alec and I were worried about him. We offered him a room in the basement of our house in London, and he accepted and moved in immediately. In his eulogy Nick said, "They not only gave me a bed to sleep in, but Alec did my thinking for me, usually while he was cutting up fruit to add to his porridge for breakfast."

Later, when Nick was settled back in Lewes, Alec often used to call him on a Friday evening.

"Alec here!" he would announce.

"He always sounded as though he was rather surprised to discover he was there," Nick said, "and we'd arrange to meet, the three of us, the next day. We'd go for long walks on the Downs where we would talk about politics, and life in general."

Once, Alec explained how owls are able to revolve their heads though 360 degrees. He stopped in his tracks.

"I mean," he said, "it's so unfair."

Nick wondered if Alec meant it was unfair on the mice and voles on the ground below. Then he realised he was saying it was unfair on him, as he would very much like to be able to turn his head through 360 degrees, to look all the way around like an owl.

Nick remembered how Alec explained to him that the Greeks have several different words for love. One describes a purely physical erotic arousal while another indicates a much deeper empathy. He taught Nick to say "σ'αγαπώ" (s'agapo) I love you in Greek. "And," said Nick, "that last word really spelled the core of Alec, his closeness with people. His closeness with Jane, his closeness both with his own two children, his two step-children, and with his grandchildren."

He described a photograph I had shown him. Alec was walking up to the outside of the Gate Cinema in London. We had arranged to meet there with my children and the grandchildren to see a film before Christmas. As we arrived the grandchildren were already there. They were sitting in a row inside the plate glass window at the front of the cinema, looking out. The photo caught the burst of excitement on Alec's face as he saw them, and the children, through the window, just as thrilled to see him too.

"And for me," Nick said, "although I don't know that he ever knew this, I adopted Alec as a second father."

Nick came to visit me after Alec died, and before the memorial service, to prepare for this eulogy. I showed him some of the many letters people had sent when they heard the news of Alec's death, and Nick picked out some comments from these letters.

'He had old-fashioned courtesy'.

'He could listen politely to anyone without becoming impatient or annoyed.'

'He was the most adorable, gallant, clever, funny man, and wise too.'

'He was a real Gentleman in the true sense of the word.'

'A very wise, sensitive, cultured, modest, yet gracious and honourable man.'

'A really dear, interesting fellow.'

'It was impossible not to feel close to him.'

Nick suggested that each of us would carry different images of Alec in our memory. He himself had an image in his mind of Alec turning up for parties in a natty cream-coloured suit, and dancing wildly... of lunch with us under the dappled shade of the apple tree in the garden in Sussex... of walking on the Downs... of Alec painting in Ithaca... and chatting to the Greek Chorus.

He said he didn't believe there was really such a thing as a good death, but that Alec had understood how to lead a good life. He was sure that none of us wanted to say goodbye to him. Instead, each of us might want to say to him what he would surely say to each of us, if he could: "σ'αγαπώ" (s'agapo) I love you.

Later in the service Alec's nephew, Helen's son Pip, recited a translation of Constantine Cavafy's famous poem about Ithaca.

> As you set out for Ithaca
> hope the voyage is a long one,
> full of adventure, full of discovery.
> Laistrygonians and Cyclops,
> angry Poseidon — don't be afraid of them.
> You'll never find things like that on your way
> as long as you keep your thoughts raised high,
> as long as a rare excitement
> stirs your spirit and your body.
> Laistrygonians and Cyclops,
> wild Poseidon — you won't encounter them
> unless you bring them along inside your soul,
> unless your soul sets them up in front of you.

May there be many a summer morning when,
with what pleasure, what joy,
you come into harbours seen for the first time;
may you stop at Phoenician trading stations
to buy fine things,
mother of pearl and coral, amber and ebony,
sensual perfume of every kind—
as many sensual perfumes as you can;
and may you visit many Egyptian cities
to gather stores of knowledge from their scholars.

Keep Ithaca always in your mind.
Arriving there is what you are destined for.
But do not hurry the journey at all.
Better if it lasts for years,
so you are old by the time you reach the island,
wealthy with all you have gained on the way,
not expecting Ithaca to make you rich.
Ithaca gave you the marvellous journey.
Without her you would not have set out.
She has nothing left to give you now.

And if you find her poor, Ithaca won't have fooled you.
Wise as you will have become, so full of experience,
you will have understood by then what these Ithacas mean.

After the service, when food and drinks were served at the back of the church, I was in a bit of a daze. Huge numbers of people came up to me to say how much they had admired and loved Alec. They looked at the three boards of photographs the children and I had assembled, and they were amused. There were a few formal family photographs taken in a studio in Ealing, when Alec was a child. There were some photographs from the 1950s of him looking dashing as a film extra. There were a few from the 1980s of Alec showing the Queen around the Jubilee Hall in Covent Garden, when she opened a new extension. People wondered if the Queen was a spoof look-alike, but no, those were snap-shots of our real queen. There was a photograph of Alec looking absurd with a shirt over his head in the Egyptian desert, and one of him 'driving' the totally wrecked carcass of a lorry in Libya.

They said that Nick was right. There was a lot they hadn't known about Alec, and they had learned a lot from his eulogy. They agreed we would all miss him, and that we loved him.

11

Keeping memories

After Alec died, I rang Thanasi and Eftichia to tell them the sad news. A couple of months later I went out to Greece to open up our house and, as I didn't want to go alone, our eldest grandson, the biologist, came with me. As soon as they saw me the local people rushed up to tell me how sorry they were, what a good man Alec was, and how much they loved him. They know exactly how to make me feel at home. Captain John's wife Loula (Captain John had also died a few years back) told me that the news of Alec's death had travelled all around the village in seconds. The new priest had rung the bells of the church up at Rachi. A service for Alec had been held there and a large group attended.

Back in Ithaca I maintained my usual pattern. Each morning I went down to the little working harbour below Costa's shop at Mavronas to paint boats. On one side of each boat its reflection shimmered on the surface of the sea, on the other its shadow sat way below on the seabed. I was interested in the counterbalance. This time I had left a painting down there to dry in an old shed, and I recorded my trip down the hill to fetch it.

As I passed Costa's shop the door was open and he called out, "Yassou."

A little further down the path I met Thanasi's wife Eftichia.

"The house was perfect when I arrived," I said, "clean and beautiful."

"Thanasi and I will come up and see you," she said.

"Today?"

"We'll ring and say. Not for anything, just to see you as we love you." She put her arm around my shoulders. "When you've known someone as many years as we've known you, you love them. We'll come along to the house and see you soon."

Goats were sculling about on the road. Further down the valley were the rest of the herd, a mix of sheep and goats these days, and Georgos the shepherd himself. He was dressed in classical shepherd-style with a blue cloak, the bottoms of his trousers bound, a knife pushed under his belt and a traditional shepherd's crook he had carved himself. He called out and waved to me. "Yassou."

I met Martha, whose husband Takis taught us how to tread Maria's grapes with a special dance step. She was on the road fixing her hosepipe. She rushed up, gave me a hug and a kiss on both cheeks and invited me in for a coffee. When I made an excuse she said, "Come any time and bring your grandson." But the truth is Martha not only speaks with a strong local dialect, but she slots in many Ancient Greek words. My Greek is improving, but I still miss a lot of what she says. I needed Alec to fill me in on the detail, but he wasn't here.

I picked up my painting and made my way back towards the road. I walked around the far side of the old monastery church rather than taking my usual route. There, on a low stone wall, Alec was sitting. He was sitting where I had seen him so many times before. He was leaning his skinny back against a cushion propped against the outer wall of the church. I could see every angular shape of his body. He was reading a large book. I walked up to him…but then he had gone. I was shocked. Was he ever there? Did he ever even exist? Did we really come here, together, so often?

I pulled myself together. I'm not normally someone who sees things that aren't really there. It is sometimes hard, I mused, to be sure that people really existed, or that some things really happened, even in the recent past. In ancient times, without photographs or written history, it would have been much more difficult. You would want to pin down your memories but you would only have the spoken word to remind you. You might listen to stories told by a bard. Or there might be a few small objects lying around which would confirm that past events really happened. That someone really once existed.

Back at the house, I looked for a pencil sharpener. I shuffled through a box of old pencils, pens and crayons in a drawer in our bedroom. There were no sharpeners there. But in the same drawer was a grey fake-leather spectacle case with a snap-shut top to it. I felt I was trespassing as I looked into Alec's special little hoard. There I found three soft drawing pencils, three biros without lids of the type he liked best, a well-blackened rubber crusted on the outside, and a small metal pencil-sharpener made for two alternative pencil points. I used the sharpener, then I put it back carefully in the spectacle case, and the case in the drawer. It was a small thing but it was proof. Alec really was once there.

I settled down to read in the shade under our mimosa tree, but the bells from the harbour church began to ring. Double bells. Ding-ding. Ding-ding. Ding-ding.

"Is it a death?" asked my grandson.

"Yes, but it is probably someone who was living abroad as the bells didn't go on too long."

I couldn't say anything more. The sound of those bells really gets to me.

My grandson had invited a friend to come out and stay with us and, a few days later, we went by car to meet her off the boat from Sami in Kefalonia. I am usually either arriving or leaving when I go to the isolated ferry-port at Piso Aetos but this time we weren't in a rush. So we decided on the spur of the moment to climb the nearby hill of Aetos (it means eagle) where the sign said 'to the Ancient City of Alalkomenaï' on the isthmus between the northern and southern parts of the island.

View of the Ancient City of Alalkomenaï

Alec and I had never walked up to the top of this curious conical hill and we never heard of anyone taking tourists up there. I assumed there was nothing much to be seen, but my grandson and his friend were keen to investigate. Thinking it looked steep, but not impossibly high, we impulsively (and stupidly) set out around midday in late June without a bottle of water.

After a false start ending up in a goat shed, we eventually found a path leading through some small ancient ruins with very steep stone steps. The path was rough. We clambered upwards. The painted targets on the rocks had faded and some were missing. We took a wrong turn where the path divided and came to a tumbled doorway in a massive wall. We went back and tried again, on and on, up and up. Another wrong turn took us to a defensive wall built with huge diamond-shaped stones.

The summit was much further than it had looked and the day was hot. After about an hour I sat down under a tree and said I would wait while the youngsters went on ahead. They rushed on. But some twenty minutes later they reappeared saying I simply had to come on up as the summit was amazing. So I struggled on, up and up, climbing and sliding, until finally they heaved me up onto the rocky summit.

They were right. The place is astonishing. Huge cut blocks, the remains of ancient walls, lay jumbled about. This was once a massively fortified settlement. Some of its walls still stand four metres high. We leaned against the wind as we looked westwards up and down the strait between Ithaca and Kefalonia. Any pirate in this strait would find it hard to escape our gaze. We turned and looked eastwards. There we could easily check the boats going in and out of the deep harbour of Vathi. In the event of danger, the people from this citadel had a choice of escape routes to two alternative seas, depending on the invaders' line of attack. But it was a difficult climb to get up there, and we found very little level ground at the top. The Ancient City of Alalkomenaï would not have been a convenient place to live, to say the least, and water would have been a problem. We found a large water sterna full of water a bit below the summit but this would hardly support an entire community. Water could be brought from the well at the base of the hill, but to carry it up would be a tough job, even with the help of slaves. Security must have been a paramount consideration for people to choose to live in such an inaccessible spot. They must have gone up there at a time when the seas brought extreme danger, I thought to myself. And I wasn't the first to have had these thoughts.

Later, on my return to England, I did a bit of research about Aetos/ City of Alalkomenaï and found that some early archaeologists, including William Gell and Heinrich Schliemann, were told by the people of Ithaca that this was the location of the Palace of Odysseus. But this was a mistake. The place was impressive, but it didn't fit Homer's description of Odysseus' home.

Following the leads in Paizis-Danias' exhibition in Stavros I discovered that William Gell, an English gentleman topographer, friend of Byron, and early Homerist, wrote a book on Ithaca in the early nineteenth century 'The Geography and Antiquities of Ithaca'. I ordered a reprint from the net. In the early nineteenth century, I don't know why, the people of Vathi mistakenly thought these ruins on the summit at Aetos were those of the Palace of Odysseus. Possibly, much later in medieval times, there was a gap in the habitation of the island. In any case, the local people led Gell and his party up to the top of this hill. He carefully measured the defensive walls and the position of their towers, but made precisely the same observations I had myself. This would not be a convenient place to live. [1]

Sixty years later, the infamous gold-digger Schliemann was given the same misinformation. He sweated up to the top of Aetos on two consecutive days (the second day he was wise enough to go up on a horse) but his shovel soon hit bedrock and, although he said he found several burial pots of ashes, a sword and a small statuette, he unsurprisingly failed to find the bed where Odysseus and Penelope slept all that time ago. Both Gell and Schliemann had doubts, not about whether Odysseus came from the island still known as Ithaca, but about the siting of the Palace of Odysseus at the archaeological site at Aetos/City of Alalkomenaï. [2] Although some finds from the Mycenaean Era of Odysseus have been made at the summit of Aetos, most are from a later date when the seas became more dangerous the people sought out this well-defended citadel.

Gell and Schliemann both also visited the site at Agios Athanassios/ School of Homer near Denis' hometown of Stavros in the North of Ithaca. They were told this was the Roman capital of Ithaca, and this may well have been correct. However, more recent archaeologists have confirmed that this site was in continuous use from before, during, and after the time of Odysseus right up until the time of the Roman rule. Later rebuilding on this same site has made precise dating a difficult and delicate task.

In 1900, another well-known Homerist visited Ithaca. The German architect Dörpfeld was Schliemann's assistant in his later digs at Troy. There he developed the idea of assessing the date of each layer of earth, the stratification, by comparing the finds at each level. It was he who realised that the reckless Schliemann had trenched right down through the level of the City of Troy destroyed in the Trojan War, to one from far earlier times. Schliemann and Dörpfeld planned to return together to Ithaca but, in December 1890, in the winter before their planned trip, Schliemann died suddenly of an ear infection in Naples. In 1900, Dörpfeld came to Ithaca on his own without his famous mentor, the linguist Schliemann. He aimed to locate the Palace of Odysseus.

Dörpfeld didn't repeat Schliemann's mistake, but he made a new one of his own, and this was unfortunate for future archaeology on Ithaca. He understood that the Palace of Odysseus would not be found on the top of the steep citadel of the City of Alalkomenaï at Aetos, and he began to hunt in the north of Ithaca. In this he was correct. However, after less than two months he was led astray when he discovered some very large blocks of stone from a later period on this site. He came to a radical conclusion. He decided he was on the wrong island altogether and that the elusive Palace of Odysseus would be found on neighbouring Lefkas. Dörpfeld spent the rest of his long life excavating in Lefkas. There he made plenty of wonderful finds, mostly from pre-Odyssean times, but (of course) no sign of a Mycenaean palace.

Dörpfeld's view that the Palace of Odysseus would be found on Lefkas has long been discredited, but at the time it could not be disregarded. Dörpfeld was a serious professional, the man who had seen through Schliemann's errors at Troy and a senior Homeric archaeologist of his day. The ancients had never questioned the idea that Homeric Ithaca was the same as the modern island of Ithaca but Dörpfeld's focus on Lefkas generated serious doubts, and his influence lives on to this day.

It was a visit in 2003 to Dörpfeld's grave in Lefkas that directly inspired Robert Bittlestone. He knew the Lefkas theory was incorrect but he didn't, unfortunately, then hop on a tour boat and come to Ithaca to check the latest finds there. Instead he looked up the Homeric reference that led Dörpfeld astray. He found it in Robert Fagles' English translation of the Odyssey that he had with him.

Taking this as his source he formulated three clues: Ithaca is low-lying, it is furthest out to sea, and it is to the west. So, he asked, which part of the Ionian Islands is low-lying and furthest out to sea to the west? He looked at a map. He had an 'eureka moment'. The land that is furthest out to sea to the west is the Paliki Peninsula of Kefalonia, and it is low-lying too. If only, he thought, it was an island.

In 2008, Denis had mentioned seven different theories that Homeric Ithaca would be found in one part or another of the neighbouring island of Kefalonia. By 2013, Païzis-Danias counted ten, and all in different regions. Bittlestone maintained that Homeric Ithaca was the north-west of Kefalonia, Cees Goekoop's claim supported the north-east, Metaxas the mayor of Poros claimed it was the south-west, and so on. The claimants were not bothered by this lack of consistency or by the lack of archaeological proof. The one idea they shared was that put forward by Wilhelm Dörpfeld in the early years of the twentieth century, that the modern island of Ithaca is not the same island as Homeric Ithaca. To this idea they added another exciting theory, that here lies a fascinating ancient mystery just waiting to be resolved.

Alec died suddenly and rather unexpectedly. I struggled with the probate. He still had several active cases in his maritime arbitration business, which had to be closed. The work was complicated. I needed to remember happier times so, as I mentioned in my introduction, I began to write up the stories about Ithaca I had recorded over the years in my little Greek exercise books.

This is what we do, these days. If we want to remember something we write it down. Yet as we learn how to write, our memory becomes lax and withers. Anyone who has ever known an intelligent but illiterate adult will have noticed how they can accurately remember a huge amount of detailed material without the need to write it down. It is something I could never do. When we can write, we use this skill to record our memories. Once our experiences are written we feel that they are real. It is strange, but when things are written we feel more certain that they really happened. I can read English and I can write it, but what did people do before they had a suitable script to record these memories? As the TV personality Michael Wood reminded us, they relied on poet bards to dramatize their history and to keep their memories alive.

As I wrote up my stories, I decided to add a note about my research in the library of the Society of Antiquities. I wanted to highlight the objects in the museums in Stavros and Vathi that show a direct and ancient association between Odysseus and the modern island of Ithaca. These are the coins from the fourth and third centuries BC, found at Aetos and now in the museum in Vathi, which show the head of Odysseus along with the name Ithaca, the tripods from the ninth and eighth centuries BC discovered in the cave at Polis Bay, and the small sherd from that cave dated to second century BC with its dedication to Odysseus. These objects were all found on the island of Ithaca where they can still be seen today. Like Alec's collection of biros, pencils and his sharpener in his fake-leather spectacle case these objects live on to remind us of earlier times. They are evidence of a very ancient association between the actual island of Ithaca, still known today by that name, and Odysseus hero of the Trojan War.

Yet Alec was the intellectual in our partnership. He was much more knowledgeable and better read than me, especially on the subject of ancient Greek history, and I tended to rely on him to be the expert on this. In addition, this subject is studied worldwide by erudite professors with far greater knowledge than either of us. My first instinct was not to get involved. Yet it was not only Alec who died. Over the next couple of years, the few experts on Ithaca dropped like flies.

Our dear friend the playwright Liz McGrath, who helped Païzis-Danias with some of his translations, died of leukaemia. Then Païzis-Danias himself died too. Litsa Kontorli-Papadopoulou, the main archaeological professor at the excavation at Agios Athanassios, died of a stroke. Our friend the environmental professor Denis Sikiotis became ill and his family took him back to Australia, where he later died.

All these people, all of whom were better able than me to stick up for the island, were vanishing. Robert Bittlestone also died the year after Alec, but his legacy continued. I wondered if I was being handed the torch, but I wasn't sure I could do much to help. I decided I would remind people of the work of the archaeologist Sylvia Benton on Ithaca in the 1930s, and about the objects Alec and I had seen for ourselves in the two small museums on Ithaca. That would be better than nothing.

When I had finished my first draft, I wondered who I could get to check the Odyssean parts of my manuscript. Homeric studies are a difficult subject and I was an amateur in this field. I didn't want to put my foot in it and make the situation worse. I wrote to Robin Lane Fox, Emeritus Fellow of New College and Reader in Ancient History at Oxford University. I told him about my association with Ithaca, and about the piece I had written, and asked if he could recommend someone to check it. I thought he might suggest a PhD Classics student who might read it through for me, but he did something much, much better. He advised that the person who would be best, if he would agree to do it, would be George L. Huxley, retired Professor of Greek, and a Fellow of All Souls, Oxford. He is the author of numerous books on ancient Greece and its epic poems. He is a highly respected philologist as well as being an experienced archaeologist. In some trepidation I wrote to him. And he agreed.

It was a gloomy English day in February when I arrived at Charlbury Station on the far side of Oxford. In my memory the professor, with his military bearing, pale mackintosh, shock of white hair and prominent nose, stood on the platform like a figure from a black and white Hitchcock movie from the 1930s.

As others left the train and headed off into the adjacent car park, we made eye contact. George Huxley had come to the station to meet me, something way outside what he needed to do. Already I felt heavily indebted. I realised that, if I ever came again, I must make sure the car I share with my daughter-in-law was free that day.

Huxley took me to a classic English village with a row of stone houses, a medieval church and a pub. His house, on the village street, was neat and practical. We stepped down into the book-lined hall where his archaeologist wife Davina was waiting. She was wearing a hand-knitted cardigan with colourful stripes. It showed, I thought, a proper appreciation both of colour and of good craft work. I took off the small rucksack I always carry and hung my North Face jacket on the wooden library steps with which they reached the upper bookshelves lining their hallway, and followed them through to their dining room.

There the table was covered with relevant reference books the professor had pulled from his extensive library to show me. We got straight down to work. He had read my essay, about which he was faultlessly polite. He had made careful comments, corrections and reference notes in the margins, and he guided me through his notes. He paid extraordinary attention to detail and he knew all the relevant reference books. His comments were astonishingly erudite, but he also put me straight on little points which would immediately have revealed me as an amateur and outsider in his field.

"Archaeologists normally call a fragment of pottery a sherd, not a shard," he explained.

Then we went through to the kitchen for coffee. I had brought, Ithaca-fashion, some chocolates and some honey from Kefalonia, which he and Davina accepted with good grace. The watercolour paintings on their wall were good, especially a colourful Greek landscape which, it turned out, was painted by one of their three daughters when she was only twelve years old. We chatted about Ithaca, an island they knew well, and the even more remote island of Kythera, where for many years they excavated a Minoan settlement from the Cretan Bronze Age originally also pinpointed by Sylvia Benton. These people were real experts in precisely the field I was investigating.

Invigorated by the coffee Huxley began to explain to me his own interest in the controversy stirred up by Bittlestone, whose book he had been asked to review. He was immediately disturbed by the contents. On the dust cover it claimed that 'over a century after Schliemann's discovery of Troy, this breakthrough will revolutionise our understanding of Homer's texts and of Bronze Age Greece'.

Huxley is a life-long specialist in ancient Greek texts and he questioned this claim. His disquiet only increased when he went to a lecture given in the British Museum by Bittlestone and his two co-authors. It was a great show. There was chanting of hexameters (something Huxley himself can do), and recorded croakings of ravens. Bittlestone had persuaded himself that, at the time of Odysseus, the Paliki peninsula of Kefalonia was a separate island from the rest of Kefalonia. Projected satellite maps showed the position of the sea channel delineated blue as if it was really there. There were books to be signed and sold.

George Huxley was not reassured. After Bittlestone's lecture, he expressed his misgivings to Robert McCabe, a well-known photographer and a trustee of the American School of Classical Studies at Athens. McCabe at once suggested that George and Davina Huxley should be the guests of their family on a voyage to and around Ithaca and Kefalonia to check carefully the ancient texts and landscapes against the claims made by Bittlestone. In the summer of 2007, they made their trip. They brought with them the works of Homer in ancient Greek. They checked the words of the great geographer Strabo who lived around the time of Christ. They brought books on the subject written by modern writers, and maps and charts to check the topography of the Ionian islands. They followed the texts of the Odyssey in the Ancient Greek and related it to the periplus of Pseudo-Skylax from the fourth century BC. That November, Huxley gave a lecture at Senate House to the Friends of the British School at Athens to summarise his conclusions. These can be gauged by the sub-title of his lecture 'Why the Island called Ithaki today is Homer's Ithaca'.

Huxley began his explanation with a word of advice.

"There is no shortcut to the study of texts," he said.

But Huxley didn't mean we should go away and look up an English translation made by Robert Fagles, or the Penguin classics translation made by E.V.Rieu. He meant there was no shortcut to the study of the best-authenticated Homeric texts in Ancient Greek. To get to the bottom of a philological problem, he explained, we need to go back to the most original version of the text we can find, as their history is long and complex.

The story of Odysseus and his return from the Trojan War was passed on by word of mouth by poet bards for several hundred years before they were ever recorded in writing. After they were written down, in the time of Homer, the poems were copied and re-copied by hand. Another one thousand five hundred years passed before the first printed copy in Greek was made in Florence in 1488 AD. By the late nineteenth century the texts of Homer had reached a stage where, given the passage of time and the fragmentary evidence we have of the earliest known scrolls, the Ancient Greek texts had been thoroughly analysed. Where there is a disagreement about a particular line of text Huxley considers the 'Apparatus Criticus' (Critical Apparatus) where the variant readings of primary source manuscripts are noted along with emendations proposed by scholars from antiquity onwards.

We discussed the quotation that Bittlestone had singled out 'Ithaca is low-lying and furthest to the west', from *The Odyssey* Book 9, which led him to conclude that Homeric Ithaca was really the Paliki Peninsula of Kefalonia. Bittlestone had three main clues in his search for Homeric Ithaca: Ithaca is low-lying, it is furthest out to sea, and it is to the west.

"These three clues are either right or they are wrong," Bittlestone proclaimed on his website "and if they are right, the island usually associated with Odysseus - Ithaki - simply doesn't fit. It is mountainous, not furthest out to sea, and it faces east. This could turn Classical Scholarship on its head," he continued, "simply take literally Homer's text".

The correct analysis of Homer's texts is not, however, a simple matter. So, I asked Professor Huxley, are Bittlestone's clues right or are they wrong? Huxley has put his mind to this question.

"I think they are wrong," he said. "In my view that quotation does not refer to Ithaca at all."

I left George Huxley's house late that afternoon with a large folder of papers in my rucksack. They included his typed, corrected, but unpublished notes for his lecture given to the Friends of the British School at Athens along with his paper giving details of his textual references and a great deal of other material he considered important. I was overwhelmed by his generosity and also, if I'm honest, by a sense of responsibility.

When I got back to London, I took photocopies of the papers and returned the originals to the professor. That much was easy. But I was rather daunted by the task of properly understanding all the material he had given me. The subject area was exactly what I wanted to know yet, even after his careful explanation, the reference material was difficult, and some of it was in quite technical Greek. Luckily, I am interested in the subject and I am not work-shy, so I set about working it out.

12

Some light on the subject

It took me a bit of time, over a year in fact, including three more visits to Professor Huxley and many to the British Library, to study the reference books he advised. As I read and re-read the notes of his lecture and re-searched the books he had recommended, I came to a surprising realisa-tion. I discovered that not just Robert Bittlestone's, but every single theory placing Homeric Ithaca in places other than the modern island of Ithaca (including one suggesting Odysseus may have come from Saddleworth Moor in Yorkshire, and another suggesting he came from the Caribbean) are justified by the same two lines in *The Odyssey* Book 9 that Bittlestone had singled out. These words form part of a speech where Odysseus de-scribes his home island to the King and Queen of the Phaeacians.

The professor had explained how I had to go back to the best-au-thenticated version of the original Greek. He recommended the Oxford Classical Texts edited by T W Allen. There the Greek text of *The Odyssey* Book 9 lines 21 to 26 runs as follows:

21 ναιετάω δ᾽ Ἰθάκην εὐδείελον· ἐν δ᾽ ὄρος αὐτῇ

22 Νήριτον εἰνοσίφυλλον, ἀριπρεπές· ἀμφὶ δὲ νῆσοι

23 πολλαὶ ναιετάουσι μάλα σχεδὸν ἀλλήλῃσι,

24 Δουλίχιόν τε Σάμη τε καὶ ὑλήεσσα Ζάκυνθος.

25 αὐτὴ δὲ χθαμαλὴ πανυπερτάτη εἰν ἁλὶ κεῖται

26 πρὸς ζόφον

(9: 21-6 Homeri Opera Odysseae, Second edition. Ed. Thomas W Allen. Oxford 1917. Reprinted 1965.)

This is difficult stuff, but it is necessary to explain Professor Huxley's points. I need to go through it, as briefly as I can, for those who are interested in the detail. If you don't speak any Greek, or only a little, you can just eye up this passage and read the numbers written to the left-hand side of it. These are the agreed line numbers of Homer's epic poem.

The classical philologist Thomas W Allen did not publish a translation into English with this edition, but there is no disagreement on the meaning of lines 21 to 24, which form the first part of this passage. In these lines Odysseus explains that he comes from Ithaca, which has a conspicuous landmark Mount Neriton, and that it is surrounded by other islands, which he names as Doulichion, Same and Zacynthos. It is clear that Homer is referring to Ithaca in lines 21 to 24, both because he says so and because the description is accurate. Professor Huxley translates these four lines as follows:

'I dwell in clearly-seen Ithaca. In it is a mountain with quivering foliage and conspicuous, Neriton. Around it there lie many islands very close to each other, Doulichion, Same, and wooded Zacynthos.'

(9:21-4 Huxley)

Lines 21 to 24 clearly describe the mountainous little island, surrounded by others, that Alec and I had come to know so well. The problem lies in the following lines 25 to 26. Professor Huxley translates these two lines as follows:

'It, however, is low-lying and entirely uttermost in the sea towards the gloom.'

(9:25-6 Huxley)

Huxley was very forthcoming on this matter.

"It is possible there is a line omitted at this point but we have to work with what we have," he said. "As it stands the juxtaposition of lines 21 to 24 with lines 25 to 26 makes no sense. The Phaeacian king and queen, who were listening to Odysseus' speech, would have been surprised if he now said Ithaca was low-lying and furthest out to sea as he had, just a moment earlier, said Ithaca had a conspicuous mountain and was surrounded by other islands."

In his search for Homeric Ithaca, Bittlestone chose to follow the later lines 25 to 26 but to ignore lines 21 to 24. But, as Huxley pointed out, no island, neither Ithaca nor any other, can fulfil these contradictory requirements. No island, neither Ithaca nor any other, can be both 'mountainous and surrounded by others' and also 'low-lying and furthest out' in any direction. We therefore have a philological issue that cannot be resolved by suggesting that Homeric Ithaca lies somewhere, or anywhere, else. It is no solution to say that Homeric Ithaca lies in any of the proposed locations in Kefalonia, or in Lefkas, as none of these suggestions resolve our basic problem. We have to dig deeper to discover what lies behind this conundrum.

It is true that this contradiction has puzzled scholars since ancient times, but the idea that Homeric Ithaca might attach to a different island, or another place, is an idea which was given credence only in the early years of the twentieth century when Wilhelm Dörpfeld first proposed that Homeric Ithaca lay in Lefkas.

So where did Bittlestone get the idea that Homeric Ithaca might lie in the Paliki peninsula of Kefalonia? He based it on the English translation of *The Odyssey* Book 9 lines 25 to 26 by Robert Fagles *'but mine lies low and away, the farthest out to sea, rearing into the western dusk'.* This is the translation that Bittlestone was reading when he visited Wilhelm Dörpfeld's grave in Lefkas.

You will notice that the Fagles translation of lines 25 and 26 differs from that of Huxley in certain significant ways.

Professor Huxley is a philologist. He went on to consider the translation of the confusing lines 25 and 26 in more detail. He began by explaining the first word in this second passage, which is written in the Greek as 'αὐτὴ' (now pronounced afti). Huxley translates the word 'αὐτὴ' as 'it', and anyone with an elementary understanding of Greek will see this is correct. The word 'αὐτὴ' here definitely means 'it'. Yet Fagles' translates this word as 'but mine'. He assumes this second passage also refers to Ithaca although Homer doesn't actually say this.

Huxley went on to analyse the last words in this passage, 'pros zophon'. Fagles translated these two words as 'rearing into the western dusk' and Huxley as 'towards the gloom'. The ancients discussed this passage. The great geographer Strabo thought Homer meant 'pros Arkton' meaning 'towards the Great Bear'. So northwards. Huxley agrees with Strabo and disagrees with Fagles' translation of this phrase. He concludes that 'it' must refer to some low-lying land to the north of Ithaca.

Given their long and complex history, the best Homeric texts we know inevitably still contain a few omissions and corruptions. In Huxley's view, a single stroke of the stylus could have been omitted in this case. This has altered the meaning of this one word 'αὐτὴ' meaning 'it'.

Huxley explained his theory.

Although we now work from Classical Greek texts written in lower case, in Homeric times Greek was written in one case only, the case we now call upper case, or CAPITAL LETTERS. In those days 'αὐτὴ' was written in Greek capitals as AYTH. In certain archaic Greek alphabets, a Greek Y (upsilon) could also be written as K without its lower right leg.

Thus, our problematic 'αὐτὴ' could have been written **ΑΓΤΗ**.

Huxley suggests that this lower right leg became obscured, or was obliterated, over the years from a word originally written as AKTH.

Thus **ΑΓΤΗ** would be a corruption of AKTH. As soon as we replace the word **ΑΓΤΗ** with the word AKTH we begin to see the light. We know from several ancient references exactly where AKTH (pronounced Akti and meaning shore) is to be found. AKTH is the low-lying land near the Cape of Aktion where the runway of the Aktion-Preveza airport now extends. This name is confirmed by the *Periplus of Pseudo Skylax* made in fourth century BC. We can see the remains of its ancient name still existing in the modern name Aktion. This low-lying land is on the mainland, now called Akarnania, to the north of Ithaca. (See Map 3)

This land, in Huxley's view, formed part of the mainland territory of Odysseus. To explain this view he referred to another quotation from *The Odyssey*.

"This quotation," he said, "clarifies the position of this mainland territory ruled by Odysseus."

In *The Odyssey* Book 24, after the slaughter of the suitors, Odysseus finally visits his father Laertes. Then Laertes says he wishes he had the strength he had formerly when, as king of the Kephallenians he captured the city of Nericus on the mainland cape. [3] and [4]

> 'the thoughtful Laertes replied: 'By Father Zeus, Athene and Apollo,
> if only I could have been the man I was when, as King of the
> Cephallenians I took the stronghold of Nericus on the mainland cape,
> and like that have stood by you yesterday in our palace, with armour
> on my shoulders, and beaten off those Suitors.'

(24: 375-80 Rieu)

In the ancient Greek, the mainland cape is written ἀκτὴν ἠπείροιο and any Greek speaker will recognise the word AKTH. Thus Nericus became part of the Ithacan kingdom on its mainland territory in

Akarnania. [5]

Professor Huxley has very wide experience and knowledge in precisely this field. He believes that Odysseus was saying that his home was in Ithaca, surrounded by other islands and with a conspicuous mountain called Neriton, and that this was not at all like another part of his kingdom, Akti, or Akte [6] which was low-lying and nearest to the gloom.

This philological debate will no doubt run and run, as it has from time immemorial, but meanwhile I am convinced of one thing. It is very unlikely that this single phrase in *The Odyssey* Book 9: lines 25-26, which forms the justification for all the theories locating Ithaca elsewhere, refers to the island of Ithaca at all.

Professor Huxley's explanation is fascinating, and very probably correct, but even without it the philological arguments underlying the theories that Homeric Ithaca lies anywhere else but the modern island of Ithaca have a fundamental flaw. Both in the Greek, and in every translation into English, *The Odyssey* Book 9 lines 25 to 26 directly contradict the preceding lines 21 to 24. They cannot both be correct. We know that Homer is referring to Ithaca in lines 21 to 24 because he says so. On the other hand Homer doesn't say that lines 25 to 26 refer to Ithaca at all.

Now I have considered this carefully I find Professor Huxley's argument convincing. I am persuaded that these two lines, *The Odyssey* Book 9 lines 25 to 26, do not refer to Ithaca at all.

Attentive readers will have noticed a further difficulty. In the quotation I singled out from *The Odyssey* Book 24, Odysseus' father Laertes says he wishes he still had the strength he had formerly when he was king of the Kephallenians. Does this mean that Laertes and Odysseus came from Kefalonia? I took this up with Professor Huxley. He explained that Laertes, and his son Odysseus, belonged to a race, or tribe, called Kephallenians. Their kingdom included the islands we now call Ithaca, Kefalonia, Zacynthos, a couple of other small places called Crocyleia and Aegilips, and a part of the mainland opposite. At some stage after the time of Homer, the name of the Kephallenian race attached itself solely to the island we now call Kefalonia.

"Kefalonia was indeed part of Odysseus' kingdom" Huxley explained, "which he inherited from his father Laertes, but he ruled from Ithaca. Homer referred to the island we now call Kefalonia as Samos, or Same."

The mainland territory of Odysseus was opposite the islands. In Professor Huxley's view it was called AKTH (Akti) and it was situated on the low-lying land where the runway of the Aktion/Preveza airport now stands. [6]

Amongst the reference books recommended by Professor Huxley were several that considered the *Catalogue of Ships*. Scholars believe this long passage in *The Iliad Book 2* to be pre-Homeric in origin. At the time of the Trojan War, the Mycenaean Greeks lived in small independent kingdoms or city-states. The *Catalogue of Ships* lists the kingdoms, and their contingents that went to war in Troy. Homer lists the number of ships brought by each of these rulers, including Odysseus who was king of an island kingdom on the far western fringe of the Mycenaean lands. He brought a small fleet of twelve ships to join the Greek expedition to Troy:

> 'Odysseus led the great-souled Cephallenians that held Ithaca and
> Neritum, covered with waving forests, and that dwelt in Crocyleia
> and rugged Aegilips; and them that held Zacynthus, and that dwelt
> about Samos, and held the mainland and dwelt on the shores over

against the isles.' (Iliad 2: 631-7 Murray)

Here we have another reference to Laertes' son Odysseus ruling over the Cephallenians. The name in English is spelled differently in each translation, but clearly we have the same tribe. The passage goes on to list the extent of Odysseus' kingdom. Firstly, there is Ithaca itself and Neritum (or Neriton, or Neritos, as the word endings change in Greek) which is the highest mountain of Ithaca. Then come the names Crocyleia and Aegilips. These smaller places lost their names before Classical Greek times, so we cannot be sure of their identity. Zacynthus is the existing island of Zakynthos (or Zante) to the south of Kefalonia. In the view of most scholars, including Professor Huxley, the name Samos (or Same) was, at the time of Homer, the name for the island now known as Kefalonia.

The people who say that Homeric Ithaca was based in Kefalonia suggest that the island of Ithaca could have changed its name. In theory this is possible, but in practice there is no evidence that any such name change took place. This idea presents these theorists with a further problem. There sits Ithaca, a clear-seen and obvious island across the Ithaca Channel from Kefalonia, but now it is has no name. To support their theories these people have renamed Ithaca as Sami, Samos, Small Ithaca, Anti-Ithaca and even as Doulichion, thus creating an extra layer of confusion. As far as I know the names Small Ithaca and Anti-Ithaca are just invented, but the name Doulichion once belonged to a large place near Ithaca. The name Doulichion, like those of Crocyleia and Aegilips, was lost before Classical Greek times. The *Catalogue of Ships* states that Meges, not Odysseus, ruled Doulichion. In Meges' absence at Troy, Akastos ruled it. His rule continued as poor Meges was lost at sea on his return journey from Troy. [7]

Professor Huxley commented on this:

"Homer thought of Doulichion as a large place, because more suitors came from there to woo Penelope than from any other island. It is sometimes said that because Homer calls Lefkas 'Leukas' Doulichion cannot be there. But Homer speaks only of 'Leukas Petre', the white rock at the southwestern extremity of what is now called Lefkas. Doulichion is the strongest candidate for the principal part of the realm of Meges and Akastos. Doulichion, then, is the old name of Lefkas." [8]

There is no evidence that the island of Ithaca changed its name in ancient times. The many coins found there, with the name of the island written on them, clearly indicate that Ithaca was called Ithaca in the fourth and third centuries BC, so the postulated name-change would need to have occurred before that time. Those who promote these ideas are not only robbing the true island of Ithaca of its ancient hero, of whom its people are extremely proud, but even of its name.

Robert Bittlestone decided that Ithaca was, at the time of Homer, called Doulichion. Long after he had formulated his theory basing Homeric Ithaca on the Paliki Peninsula of Kefalonia, he decided he should give the actual island of Ithaca a quick check. Chapter 21, pages 249 to 279, of his book *Odysseus Unbound* is headed 'Doulichion'. It describes his one-day trip to Ithaca.

Bittlestone arrived at Polis Bay by boat on a Monday morning. The museums on Ithaca (as everywhere in Greece) are shut on Mondays. In his book, he speaks about the bronze tripods although he didn't see them. He made a brief visit to the Agios Athanassios/School of Homer site about which he concluded: "This particular site dates from a much later period; it has never been seriously proposed as the location of Odysseus' Palace."

But this is not so.

Back in the 1930s the archaeologists from the British School of Athens discovered sherds of Mycenaean pottery and remains of Mycenaean defensive walls on this site. In 2001, four years before Bittlestone's book first came out, Professor Jost Knauss of Munich, an expert on Mycenaean hydraulics, also dated the underground well house on the Agios Athanassios/School of Homer site to c.1300-1200 BC, proving it provided plenty of water there at the time of Odysseus. This site was, and still is, seriously proposed as the location of the Palace of Odysseus.

Bittlestone never went down to the south of the island or checked any other Homeric sites on Ithaca. He left in the late afternoon of the same day on his hired boat back to Kefalonia.

I still go out to Kioni each year to paint or write, and other family members use the little house as well. Many years ago, in the early 1980s when Alec and I first came out to Ithaca, I felt we would want to go somewhere else on holiday. Later our positions reversed. When he began to earn well, it was Alec (who was always skinny and sensitive to the cold) who sometimes suggested we should fly half way around the world to somewhere warm to escape the English winter. Then I would say "Oh let's not bother. Let's just wait for Kioni to warm up and we can go back there."

I have recently made some repairs and improvements to our little house in Kioni. Astrit, the Albanian who was part of our original wall-building team, now has a wife and two children. He lives all the year round in Vathi. I found him working in Kioni with his younger brother, another excellent stonemason, and engaged them to rebuild some garden walls. Then they renewed the cracked and hollow plaster inside the house, the electrical wiring, and the bathroom. I finally abandoned the plastic bowl Alec and I had used for years as a shower tray. Astrit and his brother Marsel installed a smart new shower tray that I bought in Kefalonia. When I was back in England, they sent me daily videos of their work on WhatsApp. I speak with them in Greek. Theirs is now perfect, of course, and mine has been improving since I can no longer rely on Alec to speak for me.

"My brother is called Marsel after Marcel Proust," Astrit explained. "He is my father's favourite author."

After Alec died, I gave up painting down at Mavronas harbour. I left the brightly coloured fishing boats bobbing on the clear sea and headed inland into a dark valley to paint. Maybe it reflected my mood. Walking on past the vineyards our track passes through dense woodland until a fork to the right takes you down into a deeply shaded olive grove. At the far end the valley slopes upward to a place where two ancient olives still stand. They are huge and gnarled with hollows and splits, spreading roots, wide trunks, bulbous knots, and jostling branches. They relate to each other like humans. They have elbows, bottoms, and strange knarled lumps in unlikely places. They dance. They lean towards each other to talk. I don't know how old they might be, hundreds, perhaps even thousands, of years. Those trees have been watching the ebb and flow of life on Ithaca for a very long time.

As recently as World War Two, this side of the mountain was entirely cultivated with olives, but now the forest has crept in. Only a few clearings, like this one, remain where the olive trees are tended and the crop picked every year. The prunings from the previous year are piled under each tree, so I can see this grove is in use. Looking back from the grove towards our house the light bursts through a gap in the trees where the path leads in. The goats and sheep arrive this way. The sound of tinkling bells announces them. They are surprised to see me. Some are nervous but others are tame. One puts its nose on my arm as I paint and I scratch its head between the horns. Behind them comes Georgos the shepherd. He is dressed in traditional shepherd's clothes with his feet in sturdy boots and a woollen cloak thrown over his shoulders. He carries a canvas shoulder bag and walks with a hand-whittled shepherd's crook.

"She is called Katerina," he told me.

Georgos still has some sheep, but these days, in his herd of fifty, it is mostly goats.

"I can't afford sheep any more," he said. "Goats are cheaper."

By night he now works in the bakery at Stavros and by day he looks after his herd. He complains that he needs a woman. This is an old story. When Alec and I first met Georgos we found him sitting by the road weeping. Alec, who was always sympathetic to anyone in trouble, sat down beside him and put his arm round his shoulders. Next to him stood a single sheep. Eventually Georgos began to speak.

"I was away in the merchant navy and when I came home without warning I found my wife in bed with another man. I left her, and now I am all alone. My sheep is my only friend."

Georgos moved back with his mother, who lives on the hillside that slopes down to the harbour at Mavronas. Over the years he built up his herd until he had around fifty sheep. His mother made cheese and she sent milk and cheese over to Kefalonia for sale. His sheep often scull around me with their tinkling bells as I paint and Georgos likes it when I put them into my pictures. He once held a very fine ram by the horns, to keep it still so I could quickly paint its portrait. Ithacan sheep are not fat and woolly like English sheep. They are elegant, slim-legged, lithe and, it seems to me, more intelligent. Many have horns and they all have their tails intact. Most of them have bells around their necks.

Later, Georgos' new Albanian woman walked with him past our house with his herd.

"She stayed with me seven years and then, one day, she vanished without even leaving a note. That was six months ago now and I still haven't heard a thing," he said.

Down in the shop I discussed Georgos' problem with a neighbour. She wasn't surprised:

"He expected her to share his shepherding work, to do the milking, to make the cheese, to look after his mother, and to sleep with him too.

He'll be lucky if he finds another woman to do all that," she said. "Now the situation in Albania is a little better I suspect she decided to go home."

The next day Georgos showed me his two new goats. He is very proud of them but they look rather out of place. One is a huge shaggy white goat from Germany and the other an equally large, and particularly ugly, Austrian goat. He gave the Austrian goat a drink straight into her mouth from a large plastic water bottle as he explained that they cost a lot of money, but each gave three times as much milk as a traditional Greek goat.

I was painting one of the huge ancient olive trees on the higher ground at the far end of the grove. I sat quite close up to it. Its massive trunk nearly filled my canvas while its upper branches vanished off the top, but under its armpits, and between its neck and shoulders, visions of a brighter world were framed. On the higher land above was another sunny vineyard. I went up there to have a look and saw blue mountains over the sea beyond. I wasn't sure which way I was looking or which mountains they would be. The weaving valleys on Ithaca can be quite disorientating, but Georgos joined me.

"Those are the mountains of Lefkas," he said.

I hadn't expected to see Lefkas in that direction. I was looking directly towards the low-lying land to the east of Lefkas where the runway of the Aktion-Preveza airport now extends, the land which, in Huxley's view, once formed part of Odysseus' kingdom. Little-by-little the light is filtering back into my olive-grove paintings. It changes all the time and happens in different ways. As the day moves on, a hazy light flickers through the leafy umbrella of the forest onto the trunks and dusty ground below. Occasionally a narrow shaft pierces through onto the undergrowth.

There are two ways to make the bright part of a painting shine. One is to paint it in a light, bright, pure pigment, maybe titanium white with a dash of cadmium yellow. The second, as tones are perceived relative to their neighbours, is to darken its surroundings. The sunlit landscapes of Ithaca seemed all the more brilliant against the dark tones of the ancient olives. These landscapes, in their olive branch frames, still hide their complex secrets. Between the higher branches, above the olive's bulging shoulders, the blue light of Ithaca throws a unifying mask over distant hills, each topped with its own small ruined mill. I compare the faraway faded greens with the stronger greens of those nearby where the fresh bright green of lemon trees and vineyards contrasts with the grey-green of the olives and dark sap-green pencil pines make exclamation marks between them. It has taken me time to analyse these ancient landscapes. I am still trying to capture the essence of their delight.

Our younger grandson is a keen climber. When he recently came out to Ithaca he climbed to the top of the highest mountain, Mount Neriton, up above Ánoghi. From there, he reported back, he could see the sea all around Ithaca and most of the way around Kefalonia as well. I didn't go up with him this time, but I know he is right. Years ago, Alec and I climbed to the top of Neriton. On the lower slopes Mount Neriton is still covered with bushes and windswept trees, but the upper slopes, like those of the mountains of neighbouring Kefalonia, are now bare and eroded. The summit is no longer covered with the waving forests or quivering foliage described by Homer, but one thing is unchanged. As you look around from the summit of Neriton it is clear that Ithaca is a small sea-girt island. You arrive there by boat.

I could quote several examples from Homer where this is described. One is the example Alec found from *The Odyssey* Book 1:170-172 that I quoted at the beginning of this book. Later, in *The Odyssey* Book 16,

Telemachus asks the swineherd Eumaeus about his guest, who is in fact Odysseus in disguise:

> 'Old friend, where does this guest of yours come from? Some ship's
> crew must have brought him here. How did it happen and who did
> they claim they were? I am quite sure he didn't walk to Ithaca.'

(16:55-9 Rieu)

Later he repeats the question to his father:

> "But, my dear father, what ship can have brought you to Ithaca at this
> time, and who were the men on board? It is obvious that you did not
> come on foot."

(16: 222-4 Rieu)

Some have argued that in ancient Greek there was a word for an island, but no separate word for a peninsula. Therefore, they say, one or another Kefalonian peninsula could have been Homeric Ithaca. When Mayor Metaxas of Poros claimed that the south-eastern part of Kefalonia was Homeric Ithaca, and the Dutchman Cees Goekoop claimed the same for the north-eastern part, they were undeterred by the fact that these areas are joined to the rest Kefalonia with long land borders. But Homer clearly describes how you need a ship to reach Ithaca. You don't need a ship to reach a peninsula. You can come on foot.

To his credit, Bittlestone met this challenge head on. The Paliki Peninsula is now joined to the rest of Kefalonia, but he suggested that, in Homer's day, it was separated from the rest of Kefalonia by a sea channel, making it a small independent island. In his book *Odysseus Unbound* this was illustrated with professional-looking maps and geological diagrams. His claim was supported by John Underhill, Professor of Stratigraphy at Edinburgh University. As a result of this, several classicists who were critical of Professor Diggle's analysis of the Homeric texts, assumed that Underhill's geological theory was sound.

But was it?

I am not a geologist, but I make no geological claims. Ithaca is already, definitely, as Homer described, a 'clear-seen island'. You approach it by boat. Bittlestone was not a geologist either, but to support his theory that the Paliki Peninsula of Kefalonia was once an island his geological claim was not small, as he suggested, but very ambitious. The channel he envisaged through the Thinia Valley of Kefalonia would have been 6km long with a maximum width of 320m. At its highest point the land along that route now rises over 180 meters above sea level. If, 3000 years ago, this was a navigable sea channel, this represents an extraordinary and extreme land change.

So how did he explain this?

Bittlestone began his book with a dramatic description of the 1953 earthquake, quite similar to the description Alec and I had been given by our neighbour Peter. He suggested that a pre-existing sea channel through the Thinia Valley of Kefalonia was subsequently filled by a combination of earthquake-generated uplift and rock slippage from the surrounding hillsides. And he aimed to prove this was so.

"Boreholes are the ultimate test," said Bittlestone.

No expense was spared. The authors of *Odysseus Unbound* entered into a research partnership with the international geoscience company Fugro, based in Holland. Fugro made seventeen boreholes along the Thinia Valley, they made helicopter-mounted electromagnetic and Li-DAR surveys, ground-based resistivity and seismic refraction surveys, gravity surveys, and shallow marine seismic reflection surveys. They used side-scan sonar, sub-bottom profiling, and bathymetry. Their boreholes didn't hit bedrock but fossils of sea creatures were found where they shouldn't have been. The *Odysseus Unbound* website went quiet on the results which were, they admitted, 'complex'. More research would be needed to establish the facts, they said. Meanwhile Fugro's own website quietly dropped all mention of the investigation.

Stirred up by Bittlestone, others also investigated the possibility that a sea channel existed through the Thinia Valley at the time of Odysseus. Amongst the papers Huxley gave me was a copiously illustrated sixty-three page report on the subject written in 2006 by four distinguished Greek geologists led by Professor Maroukian, head of the Department of Geology at Athens University. The paper is written in difficult technical Greek but Classics Professor John V. Luce of Dublin University read through it. He reported his findings in a copy of Classical Association News, which Huxley had given to me. Even the title is daunting. It reads *'The Geomorphological – Palaeogeographical evolution of N.W.Kefalonia with special reference to the area between the Gulf of Argostoli and the Harbour of Hagia Kyriake in the Upper Holocene Period'*. But the study's conclusions were unequivocal. Chapter 8 is titled *'Considerations that Demolish the Channel Hypothesis put forward by R. Bittlestone, J. Diggle and J. Underhill'*. Maroukian's team were in no doubt whatsoever that Bittlestone's suggestion was not supported by geological fact. If Paliki were ever separated from the rest of Kefalonia (and this was in doubt) this was certainly not as late in geological time as the era of Odysseus through to Homer.

In 2007, Bittlestone carried on an argument on this subject with Professor Luce. On the internet I found cheap jokes calling the professor a 'Luce cannon'. But Luce knew what he was talking about. Homer was his specialism. He had published books called *Homer and the Heroic Age, Celebrating Homer's Landscapes* and, co-written with W. B. Stanford, *The Quest for Ulysses*. For many years he led archaeological tours both to Troy and to Ithaca. He spoke good Greek, both ancient and modern.

He read through Maroukian's report and summarised its geological findings, concluding that the rockfalls from surrounding mountains, which Bittlestone maintained had later filled his channel, can be seen to have been trapped by intervening steps and do not reach as far as the proposed line of the channel. The geological timescale from Homeric antiquity to the present is far too short to accommodate the massive changes proposed by Bittlestone and his colleagues, and so on.

Professor Luce also consulted the *History of the Peloponnesian War* written in the fifth century BC by Thucydides, an Athenian general in that war. There he discovered six references to Kefalonia as a single island. He picked out one example, describing a naval expedition in that area, where Thucydides states:

> 'Sailing to the island of Kephallenia they won over the inhabitants without a battle. Kephallenia lies over against Akarnania and Leukas, and consists of four city-states, controlled respectively by Paleians, Kranians, Samaians, and Pronnaians.'

Remnants of the ancient names of the four city-states of Kefalonia can still be found in modern names on that island. The Paleians lived in the area now called Paliki (Bittlestone's Paliki peninsula) and the Samaians lived in the area around the modern town of Sami (from where we catch the ferryboat to Ithaca).

Geoffrey Sampson, a Professor of Linguistics and lover of Greece, also followed Bittlestone's theories closely. He asked a different question about the proposed channel; not only how it might have been later filled by landslip or uplift, but also how such an extreme formation, more like a Norwegian fjord or a man-made canal, might have come into being in the first place. He discussed this with Bittlestone's colleague John Underhill, who was unable to explain the phenomenon. He couldn't produce an example of a single similar geological formation in a position outside the Northern icecap anywhere in the world.

I have considered the expert opinions of Professor of Geology Maroukian and his team, and of the professors Luce, Huxley, and Sampson, and I have to agree with their findings. At the same time, I have not found convincing evidence to support any of the Kefalonian claims.

You might think this is all a bit academic. You might ask why any of these alternative theories matter to Ithaca, but unfortunately, it seems, these claims have had serious consequences. A blog written in Greek by an Ithacan historian Demosthenes Syrmis tells a sad story. I cannot personally verify these allegations but, according to Syrmis, the release of the promised funds for the Agios Athanassios site in Ithaca became enmeshed in ever-increasing bureaucratic and political requirements. Although the authorities in Athens had approved the enclosure of the archaeological site, it remained unfenced. The new mayor of Ithaca decided to go ahead of his own accord, but he was prevented. As excavations on Ithaca continued, a further Mycenaean wall was discovered crossing the proposed line of the fence. Permission for the enclosure was revoked and, when the 'Ithaca Friends of Homer' wanted to take a tour of interested people around the site they were threatened with police action. The financial crash of 2008 resulted in a severe downturn in the Greek economy and, no doubt, this put a squeeze on funds available for archaeology. 2010 was the final year that excavations took place at Agios Athanassios.

Syrmis' account contains accusations of the diversion of scarce funds away from Ithaca and it is an odd coincidence that two archaeological projects started up in Kefalonia that same year. At Agios Athanassios, no replacements were made for the temporary covers to the open excavation pits and weeds quickly began to grow up over the site. To cap it all, in 2015, the lead archaeologist at Agios Athanassios Litsa Kontorli-Papadopoulou died suddenly of a stroke.

13

Odysseus and Telemachus come home

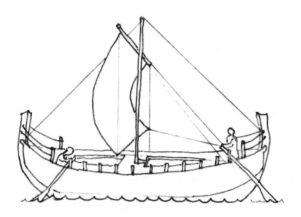

After the financial downturn of 2008 stocks ran rather low in the Rachi shop. I always went to look there before resorting to buy elsewhere but, as time went by, it became more and more difficult to find anything I wanted to buy. Costa never stocked fresh milk, but now he didn't stock UHT milk either. He only kept cans of evaporated milk called 'nou-nou', the noise a Greek cow is supposed to make. He once kept one type of cheese, but now he didn't keep cheese at all. He once kept soap powder for our washing machine in packets, then later he scooped it out of a sack into a plastic bag and weighed it, but now I had to go down to Aleka's grocery store by the harbour for washing powder. He no longer kept eggs or yoghurt or tea, although he still had bottles of water and beer.

Now that the track up to our house had been resurfaced the Chorus sat in the shop. Mimis, who previously sat around chatting or playing backgammon in the cafes near his house down by the harbour, now often joined the Chorus in Costa's shop. He didn't seem as sharp as usual and I noticed him drinking beer in the morning. I wondered if he was coming up to Rachi to drink as, knowing his vulnerability, his neighbours down by the harbour might try to stop him. Unfortunately, this was a premonition of worse to come. Later that year one of his brothers visited him in his house. He found it smelly and swarming with cats and flies. The cats were not house-trained and unwashed food bowls lay about everywhere. Mimis wasn't coping. His family took him back to Athens to look after him.

When I arrived in Kioni in 2016 there was some terrible news. Three weeks earlier Costa had died. I wondered how this could possibly have happened. Costa was a bit overweight but only in his early sixties. When I left the previous November he seemed perfectly well. The olive-picking season had begun and Costa, too, was picking his olives. This, I was told, was when the trouble began. He caught a cold and it turned into pneumonia. When it didn't improve he was sent to the hospital in Kefalonia. He stayed for a few days but he was keen to get back and he soon came home, but his health deteriorated. He was sent back to Kefalonia. They sent him back to Ithaca. Finally, when he still wasn't improving, he was sent to a hospital in Patras on the mainland, but by then it was too late to save him.

His wife Panayiota was devastated by Costa's sudden death and her grief was shared by everyone in Rachi. Costa knew everyone and everything that went on and his shop was the centre of the community. The Chorus sat in the shop, the mail was delivered to the shop, and the pensions distributed in the shop. Many old people up in Rachi couldn't walk up from Aleka's grocery store down by the harbour. Costa collected their prescriptions and kept his prices low for them. By the time I arrived Costa and Panyiota's eldest son, a PE instructor who now worked and lived in France, had returned. Their elder daughter, a schoolteacher who lived in Athens, was there too with her husband and small daughter. Their youngest daughter, who still lived at home, was also there. They were all helping their mother with arrangements and with the shop, and other local people helped as well. In an emergency they all pulled together. But could the shop survive?

Then a miracle occurred. Panayiota applied her usual solution. She cooked delicious cakes and pies for sale. She served all day in the shop and others from the community supported and helped her. Her children re-stocked the shop with all sorts of previously unobtainable goodies. They erected a canvas awning over a small outside terrace and bought new classic Greek cane-seated, blue-painted upright chairs. Tourists, who were too shy to sit inside with the chorus, began to drink coffee out on the terrace and to eat Panayiota's cakes. Over the following winter she made jars of jam to sell. She used all types of fruit and the pots weren't labelled even in Greek, let alone in English or Italian, but they sold well. The older children stayed most of the summer and when they went home the youngest daughter helped more and more in the shop. This precious community works so well.

Over the years, Alec and I had often noticed the similarities between the rugged landscape around our little house in Ithaca and Homer's descriptions of the island. We walked its long, steep, rocky paths, so clearly no use for a horse and cart, as they weave through its forested hillsides. These paths, with their dark passages and sudden exquisite sea views, still lead through shady terraced olive groves to bright secret vineyards. People work there still, just as they have since time immemorial. But in all our years on Ithaca we had never visited many of the places pinpointed by Homeric scholars. So now I needed to go by myself to check the specific

Homeric sites on Ithaca. (See Map 4) Would they stand up to scrutiny on the ground? Would I too conclude that Homeric Ithaca and Modern Ithaca are one and the same?

Professor Huxley told me where I should look, and I also made many trips to the British Library to look up the books he had recommended. I read the relevant passages from *A Companion to Homer* by Wace and Stubbings, written in the 1960s, where the authors list and describe the locations of all the major events of the Odyssey that take place in Ithaca. Then they summarise their findings:

'This complete and satisfactory setting for the story has been arrived at independently by a number of scholars – Leake, Bérard, G.Lang, Pavlatos – all with personal knowledge of the island; and anyone who visits Ithaki and re-reads the relevant parts of the Odyssey will need little imagination to fit the events and characters to the setting in the same way.'

My studies revealed that there was a striking consistency amongst Classical scholars on the location of the Homeric sites on Ithaca. Many suggested that Homer's descriptions of Ithaca are so accurate they could not have been based on second-hand information. When they looked carefully at the landscape of Ithaca, and assessed the evidence, they believed that Homer must have come himself to walk around the island before perfecting his epic poem of *The Odyssey*. Professor Luce, a Classics professor from Trinity College Dublin, came to this conclusion and wrote up the details of his observations on Ithaca in his book *Celebrating Homeric Landscapes* published in 1998.

Yet now not everybody sees it this way. Dr. Christina Souyoudzoglou-Haywood, director of the Irish School of Hellenic Studies at Athens and a lecturer at the School of Classics, at University College Dublin, currently heads up a team of archaeologists excavating at Livatho, near Argostoli in Kefalonia. She describes a 'bewildering complexity' and the 'apparent ambiguities in the textual references to the geography and topography of Homeric Ithaca'.

Scholars largely agree about the Homeric features of Ithaca. This contrasts in quite a startling way with the lack of agreement between those who put forward alternative theories on Kefalonia. Each Kefalonian theory is different and separate. Several areas of Kefalonia are competing to be Homeric Ithaca. Denis counted seven such claims, later Paizis-Danias counted ten, but now they are springing up like mushrooms. In 2018, Dr. Souyoudzoglou-Haywood explained, "fourteen hypotheses among those published at great length have identified Kefalonia with Homeric Ithaca. The hypotheses differ as to whether the island as a whole or just part of it was the Homeric island of Ithaca as opposed to just the home of Odysseus, consisting of city and palace."

Dr. Souyoudzoglou-Haywood's paper on the subject is carefully researched. The title is 'Archaeology and the Search for Homeric Ithaca. The Case of Mycenaean Kephalonia' . She explains that, although fourteen of the twenty-four books of the Odyssey contain references to the location or geography of Ithaca, "not only have they not led to an answer but over time they have made the relationship between text and geographical reality even more problematic and have led to the greatest of all conundrums."

As a result of this recent escalation of a controversy which was once quite small, the seed of doubt has been firmly planted in the minds of visitors to the Ionian Islands with an interest in the Classics. They come to Ithaca and ask whether that island was really the centre of Odysseus' kingdom. They search, as Alec did way back in the 1970s, for the Palace of Odysseus. But when they reach the site at Agios Athanassios they find it a disappointment. The excavation there is incomplete. The site is in a mess. And there is no literature to explain the finds.

Obviously I now needed to check the detail of the geography and landscape of Ithaca for myself to see whether Homer's descriptions fit the island still known as Ithaca (or Ithaki, or Θιάκη). I wondered whether my love for the island might have blinded me. Would I find, after all, that the Kefalonians have some real basis for their scepticism?

In Homer's story, twenty years passed from the time Odysseus left to fight in the Trojan War until he returned to Ithaca. His faithful wife Penelope waited patiently for him to come back and his son Telemachus, a baby when he left, grew up into a fine young man. After all this time, his people assumed that Odysseus must be dead and Penelope was besieged by suitors. They wanted to marry her and claim her husband's kingdom.

Homer tells us two stories of homecoming to Ithaca, both that of Odysseus and that of his son Telemachus. I researched and visited the sites on Ithaca where Homeric scholars believe Odysseus and Telemachus returned and finally met. At the beginning of *The Odyssey*, Telemachus travels to the mainland to ask his father's colleagues from the Trojan War if they have any news of him. On his return, father and son finally meet at the humble hut of Odysseus' faithful swineherd Eumaeus. I will start with the story of Odysseus himself.

As he was nearing the end of his gruelling journey Odysseus managed to scramble ashore exhausted, alone, and naked, on the land of the Phaeacians, which is thought to be the modern island of Corfu to the north of Ithaca. There the kindly King Alcinous befriended him. When Alcinous discovered Odysseus' true identity he showered him with gifts, including thirteen grand tripods, and arranged for his seamen to bring him home to Ithaca.

My younger grandson, the climber, was staying with me. He and I went to the place on Ithaca where, scholars say, Odysseus finally arrived back on Ithaca. Homer envisaged the Phaeacian sailors who brought him landing on a sheltered and barely-sloping sandy beach. They lifted the sleeping Odysseus, and his pile of treasure, out of their ship and slipped away. Homer describes their arrival on Ithaca:

> 'When the brightest of all stars came up, the star which often ushers in the light of early Dawn, the ship's voyage was done and she drew near to Ithaca. Now in that island is a cove named Phorcys, the Old Man of the Sea, with two projecting headlands sheer to seaward but sloping down on the side of the harbour. They protect it from the heavy swell raised by rough weather in the open and allow large ships to ride inside without tying up, once they are within mooring distance of the shore.'

(13: 93-102 Rieu)

So which is the cove on Ithaca that, in Homer's day, was named after Phorcys, the Old Man of the Sea? Where will we find a beach with two projecting headlands that protect it from the heavy swell raised by rough weather in the open to allow large ships to ride inside without tying up?

This beach has been identified by Professor Luce and others as the beach of Dexia, or Dexa, on the inner side of the Gulf of Molos adjacent to Vathi's deep harbour. [9] (See Map 4) Alec and I had often driven right by the end of Dexia Beach on our way into Vathi but we never stopped there. At first, I was surprised to read Homer's description of a shallow sandy beach as Ithaca's beaches are notoriously narrow, steep and stony, but when I parked beside the road, and we walked down the footpath at one end of the beach, there it was. The beach at Dexia is protected from the weather both by its position in the Gulf of Molos and by two head-lands. It is surprisingly sandy, wide, and very flat.

> 'It was here that the Phaeacians put in, knowing the place; and such was the headway of the ship, rowed by those able hands, that a full half of her keel's length mounted on the beach.' (13: 113-5 Rieu)

The sheltered beach of Dexia extends so far inland that houses are now built on the sand at the back of it. A small wall, about two foot high, has been built along the length of the beach adjacent to the sea, and behind it two rows of olive trees are growing. Without these modern impediments a half-length of a ship's keel could well have run up onto this wide, flat beach in ancient times. My grandson and I waded far out to sea in the shallow water and had a swim. Of course, it being Ithaca, there was no notice to say that this is the beach where Odysseus is said to have landed when he returned to the island after twenty years. The Kefalonians would not have missed an opportunity to make that connection for their tourists.

In Homer's story, the goddess Athena threw a mist over the place. When Odysseus awoke he didn't know where he had landed saying, "Oh no! Whose country have I come to this time?" He checked his gifts, the fine tripods and the cauldrons, his gold and his splendid woven fabrics, and found that none were missing. Now the goddess Athena appeared disguised as a young shepherd. Odysseus asked her anxiously where he had landed and this was her reply:

> *"Sir," said the goddess of the gleaming eyes, "you must be a simpleton or have travelled very far from your home to ask me what this country is. It has a name by no means inglorious... True, it is rugged and unfit for driving horses, and though not extensive it is very far from poor. Corn grows well and there is wine too. Rain and fresh dew are never lacking; and it has excellent pasture for goats and cattle, timber of all kinds, and watering places that never fail. And so, my friend, the name of Ithaca has travelled even as far as Troy."*

(13: 235-49 Rieu)

To convince Odysseus he was home at last, the goddess dispersed the mist. She showed him the Ithacan scene with Mount Neriton in the background. My grandson and I looked northwards over the Gulf of Molos at Mount Neriton rising steeply behind it, just as Homer had said. Then the goddess helped Odysseus stow the presents the Phaeacians had given him, the thirteen bronze tripods, the gold, and the fabrics, in a nearby cave, which she described thus:

> '...and nearby the pleasant, hazy cave that is sacred to the Nymphs whom men call Naiads. This is the broad vaulted cavern where you made many potent sacrifices to the Nymphs.'

(13: 348-9 Rieu)

Professor Luce identified the large ancient cave known as Marmarospilio (Marble Cave) on the hillside above Dexia beach as the cave that Homer had in mind, so we went to look at it. We stooped as we made our way through the narrow entrance, which could easily have been closed with a stone as it was in Homer's story, onto a narrow ledge. Two bats flew out. The steps down into the lower cave are supposed to be closed, but people go down there. Homer describes the goddess 'going down' into the cave and looking around for places to hide Odysseus' treasure. So my grandson and I went down the slippery steps into the base of the cave. A hole in the ceiling, which Homer described a 'second entrance for the gods', let in a dim light. The cave does have adjoining areas where treasure could be hidden, and my grandson searched them with the torch on his mobile phone. Archaeologists have found sherds in this cave showing that dedications were made to the Nymphs here in Hellenistic times, which would confirm Homer's description. It seemed to me rather high up the hillside, but no doubt both Odysseus and Homer were tougher walkers than I ever was.

I have heard many rumours. I have heard that the archaeologists from Washington State University under the archaeologist Symeonoglou in the 1980s found a passage, blocked by an earthquake in 373BC, which once led down from this cave to Dexia beach; that they also found bones of deer sacrificed to the nymphs in ancient times below the floor level of the cave; that another cave lower down the hillside was damaged by quarrying when the coastal road was built; that the Gaudiesque stalactites which Homer described as 'great looms of stone where the Nymphs weave marvellous fabrics of sea-purple' have recently been damaged. Professor Luce saw this cave in the 1970s and identified it with some certainty as the cave described by Homer. It seems to me to fit Homer's description pretty well.

After the goddess helped Odysseus hide his treasure in the cave, they sat down by the trunk of an olive tree. She gave him news of his wife and son, and together they began to plot the downfall of the presumptuous suitors. Finally, she told Odysseus to go to the house of his loyal swineherd Eumaeus near the Raven's Crag and the Spring of Arethusa. In Homer's story she explained:

'You will find him watching over his swine out at the pastures by Raven's Crag and at the Spring of Arethusa, where they find the right fodder to make them fat and healthy, feeding on their favourite acorns and drinking from deep pools.'"

(13: 406-10 Rieu)

Then she disguised Odysseus as a decrepit old beggar:

'She withered the smooth skin on his supple limbs, robbed his head of its dark locks, covered his whole body with an old man's wrinkles, and dimmed the brightness of his fine eyes. And she changed his clothing into a shabby cloak and tunic, filthy rags grimy with smoke. Over his back she threw a large and well-worn hide of a nimble stag; and finally she gave him a staff and a poor, shabby knapsack with a shoulder-strap.'

(13: 430-8 Rieu)

In Homer's story, Odysseus followed a rough track leading through the woods and up to the hills towards the place where his faithful swineherd lived, where he would at last meet up with his son Telemachus.

From the Marmarospilio Cave, a path leads southwards signed to Perahori, the old town above Vathi. Professor Luce walked from the cave down to the Marathias Plain, the Raven's Crag, and the Spring of Arethusa, on the very south of the island where, scholars believe, Eumaeus' hut once stood. There, in Homer's story, Odysseus found his loyal swineherd:

> 'He found him sitting in the porch of his hut in the farmyard, whose high walls, perched on an eminence and protected by a clearing, enclosed a fine and spacious courtyard.'

(14: 5-8 Rieu)

Let us leave Odysseus with his swineherd Eumaeus and move to the return journey of his son Telemachus. Of these two journeys, that of Telemachus is more carefully described. In the summer of 2007, the McCabes and Huxleys checked Telemachus' journey back from Pylos on the mainland Peloponnese. (See Map 3)

In Homer's story, the young Telemachus needed to know if his father was dead or alive, so he went to the mainland Peloponnese to consult others who had fought with Odysseus in Troy. He slipped away from Ithaca and sailed to Pylos where he visited the wise King Nestor. Later, he continued inland to visit King Menelaus of Sparta, who was now reunited with his beautiful wife Helen. There, the goddess Athena visited him in a dream, and told him to return at once to Ithaca. He should sail from Pylos on the southwestern coast of the Peloponnese.

Like Telemachus himself, the McCabes and Huxleys made their trip by boat. Alec and I had never done this. In spite of (or perhaps because of) his work as a maritime arbitrator Alec was never keen to go to sea. In all our years in Ithaca, he and I had never even been around the island in a private boat but I could see, as George Huxley described his journey, that his was the correct way to go about the task. He checked Homer's words against the landscape of the Ionian Islands just as Professor Luce had also checked this sea route previously.

Meanwhile, back on Ithaca, the suitors were horrified when they realised that Telemachus had managed to slip away secretly. The young man posed a direct threat to his mother's suitors. Homer described the reaction of the chief suitor Antinous when he heard the news:

> 'His heart was seething with black passion, and his eyes were like points of flame. "Damnation take it." he cried out. "What a coup Telemachus has had the audacity to bring off – this expedition that we swore would come to nothing. With all of us against him, the young puppy calmly sets out, after picking the best men in the place and getting them to launch a ship for him. He is going to give us still more trouble. I hope Zeus clips his wings before he reaches manhood. However, give me a fast ship and a crew of twenty, and I'll lie up for him in the straits between Ithaca and the bluffs of Samos, and catch him on his way. And a grim ending there'll be to this sea-trip of his in search of his father." '

(4: 660-72 Rieu)

The other suitors welcomed Antinous' plan, and they chose their best men to set an ambush for Telmachus' ship on his return journey. They assumed he would approach his island up the Ithaca Channel between Ithaca and Samos (the modern island of Kefalonia) to his home harbour of Polis (which is still known as Polis Bay) on Ithaca. But they were wrong. Telemachus gave them the slip and landed elsewhere.

In Odysseus' time seamen hugged the coast wherever possible. They headed for the next 'seamark', a strongly defined rock or island they could see from a distance. Night sailing, with no light other than that of the moon, was hazardous. They avoided sailing by night if they possibly could and came ashore to eat, drink, and sleep on-land. But Telemachus was advised by the goddess Athena to come home quickly. Her instructions were precise. To avoid the suitors' ambush she advised him to sail by night as well as by day, to keep away from the islands of his father's kingdom, and to keep close to the mainland shore of Elis. Then he should make for the 'pointed isles', from where he should head for the 'first foreland' of Ithaca. Telemachus did as he was told. He *sailed past the good land of Elis where the Epeians rule. After which Telemachus set a course for the Pointed Isles, wondering whether he would get through alive or be caught'.* (15: 298-300 Rieu)

The 'pointed' or 'sharp' islands are also called the Oxeiai or Thoai islands. They are conical in shape, with pointed summits. I can see them clearly from the east-facing terrace in front of my house in Kioni. Huxley showed me, in the Barrington Atlas of the Greek and Roman World, how they stand at the southern end of the Echinades at the mouth of the River Achelous. [10] Following the route of Telemachus, the McCabes and Huxleys headed for the island of Oxiá. From there they looked for the nearest point on Ithaca. They could see it easily.

"From the viewpoint of Oxiá," explained Huxley, "the 'first foreland' can only be the rocky headland of Cape St John at the south-eastern end of Ithaca. Homer's description indicates clearly that his destination was the real island of Ithaca. No other island can stand that test." [11]

The goddess Athena then told Telemachus to *'land in Ithaca at the first point you reach.'* (15:35 Rieu)

There is no landing stage on the rocky headland of Cape St John but immediately to the north is the small bay of Pera Pigadia. [12] Telemachus' crew rowed his ship into a nearby harbour and, after a meal on the beach, he sent them on to the city (polis) by sea whilst he himself walked up to the house near the Spring of Arethusa and Korakos Petra, where Eumaeus the swineherd lived. This is where, in Homer's story, he finally met his father, who had arrived the previous day.

14

The story of Eumaeus the swineherd

Alec and I had never been to the far south of Ithaca. In 2017, to make my first check, I went down by car. After leaving Vathi, the road becomes increasingly rural and precipitous until, some 10km later, there is a neat picnic hut and a sign saying to the 'Spring of Arethusa and Korakos Petra' (Raven's Crag). I stopped the car and looked along the path. It was nicely paved with close-fitting stones but it looked long. It snaked around the hillside and out along the next headland into the far distance. The early afternoon sun was hot, so I drove on. The road turned to a dirt track, which in due course led to a rough parking place. A number of smaller tracks led from there, one of which was also signed 'Korakos Petra'.

The un-cleared footpath was narrow and prickly but, when I reached it, the 'Korakos Petra' was massive. It wasn't just a 'stone', a 'rock', or a 'crag', but a wide east-facing cliff, falling some two hundred feet and spanning right across the top of a deep gorge which runs down to the sea, way below. I heard the distant crow of a cockerel and, as I looked towards the sound, I could see the silhouettes of strutting chickens outlined against the sky at the top of the cliff.

The Korakos Petra or Ravens' Crag

I scrambled back up the path and headed towards them. As I walked, the land became more agricultural. It was set with strange rounded rocks. I saw a rough little house next to a large courtyard surrounded by trees. A long-haired dog was draped like a hearth rug over the top of a rounded stone in a shady patch. Luckily it was friendly and quiet. A second dog, larger and black, stood in the wide opening beyond. It too was friendly, but it was coughing and its matted coat hung off it in clumps. Back in Kioni, I haven't seen dogs recently in that condition, although there were several when we first arrived in 1982. When Odysseus arrived, according to Homer, four fierce dogs rushed out barking. The swineherd threw stones at them to save his visitor. When I arrived, no shepherd came out of the humble dwelling, but I could see his pile of winter logs and his rough outside table with an aluminium washbowl laid out on it. His hut stood right next to and above the massive crag of the Korakos Petra.

In Homer's story, the swineherd Eumaeus welcomed the stranger, who was Odysseus disguised as a beggar, into his hut. Odysseus spent his first night back on his homeland swapping stories with him. Eumaeus' stories were true but those of the crafty Odysseus were false. While Eumaeus believed all Odysseus' lies he didn't believe the one true thing he said, that Odysseus would return to Ithaca to reclaim his kingdom. To which Odysseus replied that *'if...your master does not return as I say he will, you shall tell your men to throw me over a precipice...'* (14: 399-401 Rieu.)

The precipice of the Korakos Petra is right there next to the modern shepherd's hut.

Homer's Eumaeus built enclosures for his sows and piglets with rough fieldstones topped with hedges of wild pear. Around one side of the little house I found such a circular enclosure. Professor Luce photographed it in 1975, when it was still topped with spiny brushwood. It was just the type of animal-enclosure Nikóla would have built for his sheep or goats, before he decided he should be a master mason and use cement. The man who still lives in this house is surely a traditional Ithacan figure. Around the back, along with the chickens and roosters, I found a vineyard and fruit trees. I met a cluster of geese, so I turned back immediately. I have no doubt they would have performed their guarding job very well indeed.

How strange, I thought, that this place looks so absurdly similar to Homer's descriptions made in the eighth century BC. I could hardly believe it. It was a wee bit spooky. This wasn't a stage set. No-one had mocked this up. This definitely wasn't put here for tourists and, as far as I knew, none came. Was this place still here, and almost exactly the same, with a peasant farmer living in much the same way, since Old Testament times? Could this really be true?

A few days later I sat alone on our front terrace. Behind the headland of Kioni, with its three mills, I could clearly see the Pointed Isles, known also as the Sharp Islands, Thoiai, Oxeiai or, individually, as Oxia and Kutsilaris, at the southern end of the Echinades. I had often looked at these two pyramid-shaped islands. I had even included them in my paintings but I had never appreciated their Homeric significance. I wondered what I might find at the end of the path where the sign said to the 'Spring of Arethusa and Korakos Petra'. I thought it probably led to the base of the cliff where, in Homer's story, Eumaeus watered his pigs from the Spring of Arethusa.

The next day, as I set out at 6 am, the sky glowed pink behind the twin peaks of Kutsilaris and Oxiá. In my backpack I had a full bottle of water, sun-cream, and a fully charged mobile phone. I arrived at the posh roofed shelter with its picnic bench an hour later at 7 am. It looked a bit bourgeois, I thought, and out of place in this wild location. I later discovered it was one of several put up with money from the EU. I edged my little hired Fiat as close as I could to the rocky inner face of the single-track road, clambered out of the passenger side, and set out.

The smart paved path snaked its way along the contours of the hillside, which sloped steeply down to the sea. It seemed nobody had been along this way recently as spiders had built large, well-established webs across it at head height. Every two or three yards they spanned between the bushes growing on either side of the path. Each web had an owner, with a fat furry body and brown stripy legs, sitting centrally. After a few webs had wrapped themselves around my head like hairnets I began to walk along waving my arms in front of me to break them. This is when I first wished I had brought a stick. I had never quite seen the point of those smart hiking sticks that others use, but now I understood one use for them at least.

The stone paving soon petered out and, although the route was obvious, it became steeper and rockier. The sun, getting hotter by the minute, was blasting directly onto this east-facing hillside. Goats coughed and snuffled behind the bushes on either side and scattered when they saw me. As the path became more treacherous, its shaley surface slippery between rocky outcrops, I wished again I had one of those hiking sticks, this time for balance, and I began to wonder if I had been stupid to come here alone. Anyway, I reassured myself, if I fell and broke my leg my car was parked beside the road by the sign so it would be obvious to a potential searcher which way I had gone.

The path skirted around another inlet but as I came round the next headland I could clearly see the cliffs of Cape St John in the distance. Over and beyond it lay the conical silhouettes of Kutsilaris and Oxiá. Coming around the next headland I found myself in a huge gloomy gulley. There was no sun here. On the opposite side of the gorge a huge billy goat with twisting horns looked at me curiously before turning to scramble up a seemingly vertical rock-face. Way below, a yacht lay anchored in bright blue sea at a small sunlit beach at the southern end of Pera Pigadia Bay. At the head of the valley, the huge cliff face of Korakos Petra stretched wide across the skyline. Like the beach below, it was lit up by sunlight.

Ahead of me I could see some tumbled walls and cave-like openings and fallen masonry at the base of the cliff. I walked up to the 'Spring of Arethusa' and looked down into its deep pit. The small torch on my mobile phone didn't show water but I thought it best not to investigate further, without ropes and on my own. If I slipped down into that massive well shaft, I would be unlikely to be found alive. But it was easy to see that a winter torrent might come down from the cliff above and flow right down to Pera Pigadia Bay.

This place, so carefully assessed by William Gell in 1806, and by many others before Professor Luce came here in 1975, fits very precisely the descriptions given by Homer around 750 BC. The Kefalonian claim that there is nowhere on Ithaca resembling Homer's descriptions is odd. They must have forgotten this place or, more likely, they never came here.

In fact, I only came after George Huxley showed me the way.

Yet this place had been known and recorded since the earliest foreign Homerists came to Ithaca and, of course, known by the locals long before. The engraving made from William Gell's sketches, dated April 1806, shows water cascading from the centre of the Raven's Crag and, way below, in front of the walled Spring of Arethusa, four cows grazing with their shepherds.

Another beautiful water-coloured engraving of the scene, made by Joseph Cartwright in 1821, is now kept in the Gennadius Library at the American School of Classical Studies in Athens. It shows water cascading in the same way, with a scatter of shepherds, goats and a sheep near the fountain. The ancient pathway was in a better state in these engravings but Edward Lear's watercolour, made in 1848, shows a rougher path, more like the one before me, and no falling water.

The photograph of the same view, taken in 1975 and published in Professor Luce's book *Celebrating Homer's Landscapes*, shows 'the earthquake-damaged basin of the fountain' in the foreground. This photo was taken in September and, as he mentioned, the stream was dry but there was water to be had in the cave-like openings. I looked back towards the distant yacht in Pera Pigadia Bay. Pera Pigadia, meaning far away wells, is appropriate. The climb both up to the top and down to the bottom looked tough to me, but a young man like Telemachus would no doubt take it in his stride.

The place is surrounded by overhanging (or 'beetling') rocks as Homer describes. I didn't immediately see, through the undergrowth, a path around the edge of the Raven's Crag up to the shepherd's hut above it. I didn't look too hard as, outside this dark gulley, the sun was hammering down. It was getting hotter by the second and I was keen to get back.

Soon I sat down in the shade of a small tree to have a drink of water. When I looked back, a silvery moon, just waning from full, was floating in the sky above the Raven's Crag. There is something magical about these ancient places. As I got going again goats hid in the undergrowth, too shy to come out, ants tracked across my path, and small black grasshoppers jumped around my feet. I was glad when I finally reached the paved part of the track, and more so when I reached the picnic shelter I had considered out of place. Now I was glad to sit comfortably in the shade on one of its posh new benches as I finished my bottle of water.

My hair was still filled with sweat and cobwebs as I drove back into Vathi. I went into the baker's shop for a cappuccino and there I found Alexandros, my lawyer neighbour from Kioni. In explanation for my appearance I told him I had been to the Spring of Arethusa and he replied, "It's beautiful isn't it?" Glancing at me again, he added, "It's better to go in the evening when it's not so hot."

I am not someone who believes easily but the fit with Homer's description, made thousands of years ago, is too good to be a coincidence. I found I was beginning to agree with the many scholars who believe that Homer must have visited the island of Ithaca himself to make such accurate descriptions in his epic poem of the Odyssey. Some describe Homer as a blind poet but, if this was so, I think he must have gone blind after his visit to Ithaca.

I had found a shepherd's hut at the top of Korakos Petra and the ancient spring at the base, but where did the swineherd Eumaeus descend from his house to the fountain?

In June the following year, when my younger grandson, the climber, came out, I took him with me to show him what I had found. He was very interested in a prison-like bunker covered in rude graffiti but, when we had given that a good look, we followed a sign to Eumaeus' Cave. I wondered if we might find the area where, in Homer's story, Eumaeus spent the first night after Odysseus returned. The path descended steeply into the gorge on the north side of the Korakos Petra cliff and I admit that, after a bit, I sent my grandson on ahead with a camera. He found three caves, one near the path and two higher up the cliff above it, and took photographs.

"The main cave was about eight metres deep," he reported back some twenty minutes later. "The entrance was narrower than the inside width of the cave. I climbed up to two smaller caves higher up on the hillside. They were even better."

"Would it be have been a good place for a swineherd to spend the night?"

"Definitely. But how many pigs would he need to fit inside with him?"

"Good question. Homer said Eumaeus had three hundred and sixty white-tusked boars, but they didn't all need to fit into the cave. I don't think Homer mentioned a cave. He said that Eumaeus went out to spend the night where *'his white-tusked boars slept, under an overhanging rock sheltered from the northerly winds'."* (14:531-2 Rieu)

"Those white-tusked boars sound fierce."

"Odysseus had a huge scar on his leg where he was tusked by a boar when he was about your age. That is how the others were sure, when he returned, that it was really him."

"I'm not sure I'd like to sleep out with boars, but certainly there were plenty of overhanging rocks down there by the caves."

"Eumaeus' men drove the boars from there up to Odysseus' Palace, for the suitors to eat," I said.

We scrambled back up the path and walked along to the shepherd's hut I had visited the previous year. The setting is remote and agricultural, just as Homer explained. It is *'at the extreme limit of his land'* and *'a long way from the city'*. The city is thought to have been near Polis Bay in the north of Ithaca.

This time, when we reached his house, the shepherd was at home. I went up to him.

"Can we come through this way to get to Cape St John on the headland?"

"Yes. You can pass this way. Carry on along my path there. After a bit you will reach a larger track, which you can take to the headland. Where do you come from? How do you speak Greek?"

"I am English, but my husband was Greek. Sadly, he died. A few years ago now. I have been coming to Ithaca since the 1980s. I have a small house in Kioni. How far is it to the cape?"

"It will take you about forty-five minutes to get there."

It was a good walk with some old olives, wonderful views and, of course, many fat spiders. Some of their webs spanned ten or fifteen feet across our path. My grandson was much less brutish than me. He lifted the webs carefully to avoid breaking them and ducked under. I wondered how they got their webs to span such large distances and he had a view about that:

"First he fixes the web at his end with gluey spit. Then he makes a ball of silk and, with the help of the wind, he throws it to another fixing place. He walks across to the other side, and uses gluey spit to fix the line firmly at the other end. Then he comes back to the place where the web dips the most and drops another line of silk from there down to the ground to fix it. That is the basic structure. Some spiders take more lines out from the centre. Then he spins his web round and round onto this scaffold with special sticky web material to catch the insects. Richard Dawkins explained it."

After about fifty minutes, when we still hadn't reached the cape, I sent my grandson ahead again with the camera. He ran on and at the end of the road he found a small chapel with a couple of hand bells, a locked storage building, and a round threshing floor. He took a video and ran back. When we got back to the courtyard of our modern-day Eumaeus he was looking at his long-tailed sheep in an outhouse.

"You were quick," he said.

I didn't admit that only my grandson had reached the cape.

"How many sheep do you have?"

"Not many these days. Only forty."

The sheep were housed in an enclosure off the large round cleared area behind the shepherd's small house. In Homer's story the sows and piglets lived in twelve pens around a spacious courtyard. Could it really be that this layout hadn't changed since that time?

"Do you sell the milk?" I asked.

"I make cheese. I make it in the traditional way."

I asked the shepherd his name, which was Spiros, and he asked mine. His two dogs had Ottoman names. The large scruffy black female was Sultana and the smaller male hearthrug was Bey. Then I plucked up courage and asked him if we could go through to the front of his house to look at the view down to Pera Pigadia Bay. Three small kittens scattered as he took us through the yard in the front of his house. We passed the circular walled enclosure, which Professor Luce had photographed.

"Do you use that enclosure for your sheep?"

"I don't use it but my father used to use it for his goats. It is very ancient. It was built long before his time."

"Did your father and grandfather live here?"

"The great-grandfather of my great-grandfather owned the land all the way from here to Cape St John. It was all planted with vineyards in his day. The grapes were small. He made currants. We sold off a lot of land. When I go nobody will take over from me. Nobody wants to live this life any more. I will be the last."

We went through a gate and I took a photograph right down the valley to Pera Pigadia Bay.

"Have you been to the cave?" he asked, "and to the wells?"

"My grandson went to the cave. I went to the Spring of Arethusa last year but I couldn't see any water."

"You can't see the water from the top but there is water down there if you drop a bucket. It is fresh and tasty. A digestive, they say."

Spiros had been around the world with the merchant navy. The country he liked best was Japan. He explained how clean it was. He leaned down and touched a stone with his finger as he explained there was not a speck of dust anywhere in Japan. It is odd, I thought, that he should so admire cleanliness when he wasn't all that scrupulous about his own farmyard. He moved on to another subject.

"Years ago a professor from a university used to come up here."

"Was his name Professor Luce?"

"I don't remember his name. He said this was the place where the swineherd Eumaeus once lived. Those old stories that Homer told, they were true - you know - he just added a bit of…"

Spiros paused.

He rubbed his thumb in a circular motion against the tips of two forefingers.

"Pepper and salt," he said.

In Homer's story, when his son Telemachus reached Eumaeus' hut on the morning following his own arrival, Odysseus was still disguised as a beggar. After a brief conversation Telemachus asked the swineherd to go to the city to reassure his mother Penelope that he was safely home. Early in the morning Eumaeus left his hut by the Korakos Petra and set out for the

Palace of Odysseus to deliver his message. From his hut on the Marathias Plain in the south of Ithaca, up to Agios Athanassios/School of Homer in the north, is a walk of about fourteen miles. (See Map 4, page 11) To go there and back in a day is a fair distance but it would have been quite possible for a fit Ithacan farmer. To illustrate this I will tell you a story although, I admit, I am a bit ashamed of it.

Many years ago, back in the 1980s, Alec spoke to a Greek shepherd who said he knew of a Cyclopean wall (a wall built with huge stones which only a giant Cyclops could lift) high up in the hills between Kioni and Anoghi. "I will take you to see the wall," he said, "if you meet me at 5.30 am tomorrow morning at the top of the village near the path to Anoghi."

At 5.30 the following morning there was no sign of the shepherd at the meeting place, but we could hear the distant tinkling bells of his sheep. When we caught up with him Alec explained we had come to look at the Cyclopean wall he had found. The shepherd set off immediately at a cracking pace. Alec was in his fifties and a swift walker at that time, but he and I struggled to keep up with the shepherd. I can't tell you where we went, it was completely new territory to me but, after about an hour, we arrived. The wall had some very large stones, but neither Alec nor I were experts on ancient walls. I took a few photographs to show to a man on my Greek course in London who knew about these things. We thanked the shepherd and wondered how we would get back to Kioni. But by this time the sun was beating down and it was extremely hot. Way below we could see a small beach with tempting blue water. It didn't look enormously far, so Alec asked the shepherd how long it would take us to get there.

He turned towards us slowly. Then he looked us up and down with undisguised scorn. He gave a slight shrug before replying.

"For me it would take ten minutes. For you it might take twenty."

We set out towards the sunny little beach. We walked and walked but it never seemed to get closer. There was no clear path, only goat tracks. The scratches on our legs began to bleed. We found a curled grass snake in an old stone ruin. We finished the water we had brought but we carried doggedly on until, after about an hour and a half, we gave up the idea of a swim and turned for home. I have a poor sense of direction but Alec's was worse. We hadn't brought a compass. We never got our swim and, I am ashamed to say, it was about seven hours later, at around 4 pm, when we finally limped back into Kioni. By then we were thirsty, hungry, and utterly exhausted.

I am not proud of this episode but I am hoping it might serve as a warning to others to take care in the wild landscape of Ithaca. The island is quite small, but it is easy to get lost. Maps may be inaccurate, paths can be blocked or signs removed, and this can be deadly. As a result of this and similar experiences I have a great respect for the ability of an Ithacan shepherd to walk far and fast, and to find his way over the most difficult terrain.

On his visit to Ithaca in 2007, two Ithacans independently assured George Huxley that the journey from the site of Eumaeus' hut on the Marathias Plain in the south to the palace site in the north, and back again, could be completed on foot in eight to ten hours. I have no reason to doubt the truth of this.

While Eumaeus was walking up to the palace to give his message to Penelope, Odysseus and Telemachus were left alone at his hut by the Korakos Petra. Odysseus, with a little help from the goddess Athena, revealed himself to his son. At first Telemachus refused to believe the stranger was really his father, but finally:

'Telemachus flung his arms round his noble father's neck and burst
into tears. And now a passionate longing for tears arose in them both
and they cried aloud piercingly and more convulsively than birds
of prey, vultures or crooked-clawed eagles, bereaved when villagers
have robbed the nest of their unfledged young. So did these two let the
piteous tears run streaming from their eyes.'

(16: 212-20 Rieu)

Father and son spent the rest of the day discussing a plan to kill Penelope's suitors. They were up against a huge number of suitors, as Telemachus explained, one hundred and eight in all. Before the swineherd Eumaeus returned, late that evening, the goddess helped Odysseus back into his disguise as a beggar. Eumaeus then told his guests about his journey.

As Eumaeus was nearing the palace, he was joined by a messenger from Telemachus' ship, who was delivering a similar message. He didn't waste time at the palace. With a long walk ahead of him, he was eager to return. On the way home, when he had climbed up above the city onto the 'Hill of Hermes', he saw a ship coming in to 'our harbour'. It was the suitors returning from their attempt to intercept Telemachus' ship and murder him.

'On my way back, I had climbed up above the town as far as Hermes'
Hill when I saw a ship coming back into our harbour. She had a crowd
of men on board and a whole armoury of shields and two-edged
spears. I took it to be them, but I cannot say for certain.'

(16: 472-6 Rieu)

So can we locate the 'hill' or 'ridge' of Hermes on Ithaca? To the north of the modern town of Stavros a ridge of land extends to an area called Pilikata. The small Stavros Museum, erected by Heurtley and Benton in the 1930s, is located on this ridge.

"This ridge can satisfactorily be identified with the land Homer called the 'hill' or 'ridge' of Hermes," said Huxley.

Alec and I often walked along this ridge of land on the road running past the Stavros Museum. It ends shortly to the north of the museum in what, if these roads were larger, one might call a 'T junction'. On the far side of the 'T' is the ruin of a small church. It stands, as is so often the case, on the site of an ancient temple. In 2018 I stood there with my younger grandson, the climber. On three sides of this viewpoint the ground falls away down to the fertile plain that surrounds it. From there we had a clear view of three harbours: Polis and the Ithaca Channel to the west, Afales Bay to the north, and Frikes Bay to the east. We stood in Pilikata and looked across the shallow valley to the site of Agios Athanassios. The rock face separating the two main levels of the site stands out on the wooded hillside.

In *The Odyssey* Eumaeus the swineherd stood on the 'Hill of Hermes' and looked down towards 'our harbour'.

" 'Our harbour,' " Huxley explained, "where the suitors had arrived, can be satisfactorily identified with Polis Bay."

He went on to cross check this viewpoint.

"There is another mention of this ridge of land in the Odyssey, so we can cross reference its position. From the 'Hill of Hermes' the goddess Athena pointed down to her ship moored in the harbour of Rheithron."

I looked up the reference:

'My ship is not berthed near the city, but over there by the open
country, In Rheithron Cove, under the woods of Neion.'

(1:185-6 Rieu)

Archaeologists believe that 'the city' once stood on the lower western slopes of the modern town of Stavros. Rheithron lies to the east. Rheithron means a 'watercourse' or 'torrent gulley' in Greek. Scholars identify modern Frikes as ancient Rheithron. The watercourse from Agios Athanassios still, to this day, disgorges into the sea in Frikes harbour.

According to Homer the two harbours, 'our harbour' and Rheithron, are on opposite sides of the island but both can be seen from the 'Hill of Hermes'. These locations work perfectly with the words of Homer and with the landscape of Ithaca, as anyone who cares to walk northwards from the Stavros Museum can see.

We now need to locate the island of Asteris where, according to Homer, the suitors had been hiding in their effort to intercept and murder Telemachus.

Out in the Ithaca Channel beyond Polis Bay lies the tiny rocky island of Dascalio/Asteris. [13] It is the only island in the sea channel running between Ithaca and Kefalonia. It is small and low-lying. It looks like a little submarine. But, according to Homer, the suitors hid their ship in a 'double harbour' and kept watch by day and night from 'windy heights'. Dascalio/Asteris has neither a double harbour nor windy heights. So does this mean that ancient Asteris is to be found elsewhere? Or can this conundrum also be resolved by a more careful reading of the ancient words? Both Professors Huxley and Luce believe the latter. Both professors visited Dascalio by boat and, after considering the detail of Homer's texts, both independently concluded the 'double harbour' and 'windy heights' mentioned by Homer are to be found in, or on, the mountainous hillside of Kefalonia, directly behind Dascalio near the modern village of Evreti. Each independently concluded that Dascalio is the only respectable candidate for the island Homer called Asteris. [14]

Following the words of Homer can we now locate the Palace of Odysseus and Penelope? The area surrounding the 'Hill of Hermes' was thoroughly investigated by William Heurtley and Sylvia Benton from the British School at Athens in the 1930s. At that time, pottery finds from the Mycenaean Era had been made both at Pilikata and at Agios Athanassios, and at several other sites in the north of Ithaca as well. Amongst these other sites are Loïzos' Cave at Polis Bay, Treis Lagades (probably a fishing village from the Mycenaean Era) to the west of Polis Bay, and Stavros itself. The remains of defensive walls from the Mycenaean Era were found both at Pilikata and at Agios Athanassios, and both these sites had ancient water springs. When World War Two interrupted their work on Ithaca, Heurtley and Benton had not yet agreed which of these two places was the most likely site for the Palace of Odysseus. Heurtley (who was in charge) believed that Pilikata was the place where the palace once stood. Benton thought Agios Athanassios fitted the words of Homer better. It was work in progress.

My grandson and I were walking back along the 'Hill of Hermes' towards the Stavros Museum when he asked me an old question:

"Do you think that Odysseus really once existed?"

"Well yes, I think he probably did. We can't say *The Odyssey* is actual true history, but Homer's story of Odysseus was probably based on stories passed down to him, of a clever ancient king who fought in the Trojan War. The early Greeks, way before Christ, believed that Odysseus existed, and that he based his kingdom on this island of Ithaca where we stand."

At the museum we spoke about Sylvia Benton. We looked at the little pottery sherd from the second century BC dedicated to Odysseus. I explained how Benton believed that Odysseus himself was hero-worshipped in Loizos' Cave at Polis Bay, and that pre-Olympic 'Odyssean Games' took place there.

This year, on its museum shelf, the little sherd was rather overshadowed by a flashy pair of tasselled gold ear-rings and a large ring, all recently found up at the Agios Athanassios site, sitting next to it in the museum case. Although these are ancient (the archaeologists from Ioannina have tentatively dated them to the third century BC) they were left there hundreds of years after the time of Penelope. We looked at pots from before, during, and after the time of Odysseus. We looked at lamps, at little bronze animals, at weights used for spinning, and at tiny double axe heads. We looked at a terracotta plate from around the time of Homer with spectacular decoration of cockerels and lions.

"Are those really lions?" asked my grandson.

"They look like lions."

"They must be cats."

"No, I think they are lions."

Now my grandson did something very new. Probably this was the first year this would have been possible in North Ithaca. Right there, in the Stavros Museum, he looked up Wikipedia on his mobile phone. It told him that lions existed in Greece both in the time of Odysseus and in that of Homer, that lions are mentioned forty-five times in *The Iliad* and *The Odyssey*, and that they lived in northern Greece until around 100BC.

Then we looked at the tripods in the showcase at the far end of the room and I explained about their discovery buried below the floor of Loïzos' Cave. Another day we went to see the coins from Aetos, now in the Archaeological Museum in Vathi, which show Odysseus wearing his special little travellers' hat.

When I researched, and finally understood, Professor Huxley's explanation of the Homeric texts I found his explanation entirely convincing. Yet Dr. Souyoudzoglou-Haywood's paper expresses bewilderment at the 'baffling problems' and 'geographical incompatibilities' of the Homeric texts. Could it be that she hadn't seen, or understood, Professor Huxley's explanation? Does she really find 'geographical incompatibilities' between the Homeric texts and the Homeric sites on Ithaca? I am sure she has checked these sites more thoroughly than Robert Bittlestone, but her conclusions are at odds with my own observation.

Dr. Souyoudzoglou-Haywood briefly considers the archaeological finds at Agios Athanassios, but concludes:

"Although the evidence as presented by reputable archaeologists is persuasive, the identification has not been generally endorsed, mainly on account of the very small quantity of Mycenaean pottery associated with the building. Nonetheless, on Ithaki, in the face of high-profile theories put forward in the meantime equating Homeric Ithaca with Kephalonia, the identification has been fully embraced in defence of the heritage the Ithacans believe is rightfully theirs."

I suggest that a 'high profile theory' might simply have had more money, or effort, put into its promotion. High profile is evidence that people shouted loudly, but not that their theory was necessarily correct.

In her paper Dr. Souyoudzoglou-Haywood does not put forward any new theory or proof, but aims to summarize the theories put forward by others. To this end she highlighted The Odyssey Book 9 lines 25-26 whilst ignoring the earlier lines 21-25. However, as Huxley explained, the two sets of lines contradict each other. To say that Kefalonia, or anywhere else, could be Homeric Ithaca does not resolve this problem. Secondly she presents the possibility of a name change. There are examples of such changes. For instance it seems likely that the name Samos, or Same, was once the name of the whole island of Kefalonia, although it now denotes only the region around the modern port of Sami. It seems likely that the name of the white rock used in Homeric times as a 'seamark' on the south of the modern island of Lefkas (meaning white) was later extended to designate the entire island that Homer called Doulichion. However it seems unlikely that the names of Ithaca or Zakynthos were changed between the time of Homer and the time of Thucydides; between the 8th and the 5th centuries BC. There is no evidence to support such a change to the name of Ithaca in ancient times. Thirdly Dr. Souyoudzoglou-Haywood presents the idea that Homeric Ithaca could have been a peninsula, but she ignores Homer's insistence that Ithaca is a clear-seen island where the ancients arrived by ship, not on foot. I cannot agree with the Kefalonian arguments on these subjects, as I discussed in Chapter 12.

Dr. Souyoudzoglou-Haywood works as an archaeologist in Kefalonia, so I looked to her for a summary of the archaeological discoveries on that island. As Kefalonia was part of the Mycenaean kingdom of Odysseus we would expect archaeological excavation there to reveal pottery finds similar to those in Ithaca, and so it has. In the Livatho region near Argostoli, where Dr. Souyoudzoglou-Haywood herself is excavating, a number of tombs have been found, along with a small amount of pottery from the palatial period of Odysseus. Nearer to Argostoli the excavation of a second settlement is taking place and a rectangular building from the Mycenaean period has been discovered. In the locations suggested by Homerists as possible sites for a palace, or city, no Mycenaean domestic remains have yet been found. Dr. Souyoudzoglou-Haywood points out that the Livatho area, with good agricultural land and near the deep harbour of Argostoli, was occupied both during the time of Odysseus and in the following centuries. This makes sense. She does not suggest this site might have been the centre of Odysseus' kingdom.

She goes on to describe other, less extensive, Kefalonian sites from the Mycenaean Era. In Sami, in the west of Kefalonia, the remains of a Mycenaean house have been found. Near Poros, in the south-west of Kefalonia, a tholos tomb has been excavated. It is open to the public so I made a visit, but the remains found there were not from the time of Odysseus. Nearby, inland from Poros, an archaeological site was fenced and locked when I visited. There an oval building, possibly from the age of Odysseus, was found, along with a small amount of pottery from that period, but Dr. Souyoudzoglou-Haywood describes it as 'a very un-Mycenaean and un-palatial looking structure'. There is, so far, no evidence of any Mycenaean settlement in the area of Paliki (or Thinia), in the northwest of Kefalonia, which was chosen by Bittlestone to be the heart of Homeric Ithaca. Neither have Mycenaean sites been identified in the Erissos peninsula in the north-east of Kefalonia, which Cees Goekoop chose as Homeric Ithaca. So where, I am still wondering, do the archaeologists hope to find the Palace of Odysseus on Kefalonia?

Dr. Souyoudzoglou-Haywood concludes that "the evidence obtained through archaeology so far, and the new evidence that no doubt will be brought to light in the future, are unlikely to resolve the question for those Homerists who are convinced that archaeology holds the key."

From here she jumps to a curious conclusion.

"So," she says, "the debate is unlikely ever to die down."

The solution to this debate, I suggest, is that put forward by the eminent philologist George Huxley. In his view *The Odyssey* Book 9 lines 25-26 do not refer to Ithaca at all.

15

The Palace of Odysseus and Penelope

On the basis of my investigations to date I had to agree with the many classical scholars who firmly identify Homeric Ithaca with the modern island of Ithaca. I had found no 'baffling inconsistencies'. On the contrary, I discovered that Homer's descriptions fit very precisely with the landscape and topography of the island. The archaeologists from the University of Ioannina believed the Palace of Odysseus was truly located at Agios Athanassios/School of Homer on Ithaca, but I, as a habitual cynic, needed to check the detail for myself.

If, in Homer's story, Eumaeus the swineherd walked along the ridge extending to the north of Stavros, once called the Hill of Hermes, where did he then go to give his message to Penelope? My grandson and I went to the small road junction at Pilikata, to the small ruin where an ancient temple once stood, and looked across the valley to Agios Athanassios. Had the archaeologists really found the ruins of the Palace of Odysseus there?

Heurtley and Benton, from the British School at Athens, were pioneers. Since their excavations on Ithaca, in the early 1930s, palaces from Mycenaean times have been further excavated at Mycenae, Pylos, Tiryns, Thebes, Orchomenos and other places as well. The remains of these buildings, along with other finds from their age, such as the shipwreck at Uluburun off the coast of modern Turkey, indicate that the heroes from Homer's epic poetry probably did really once exist. The palaces of King Agamemnon of Mycenae and King Nestor of Pylos are known yet, until the archaeologists from Ioannina made their announcement in 2010, no archaeologist had complete confidence they had found the Palace of Odysseus on Ithaca.

In the nineteenth century, William Gell and Heinrich Schliemann were led by the local people to the top of the inaccessible conical hill now called the City of Alalkomenaï at Aetos but, by the end of that century, it was clear that the Palace of Odysseus would not be found there. In the 1930s Heurtley and Benton looked at several sites in North Ithaca, but they hadn't yet finally agreed whether Pilikata or Agios Athanassios was the most likely site of the palace when World War Two interrupted their work. Civil war, earthquakes, and emigration from the Ionian Islands followed. Some fifty years passed before the archaeological professors from Ioannina took up the baton in 1994. They looked at several sites, and made many trial pits, before deciding that Benton was more likely to be correct, and they would concentrate their work on Agios Athanassios/ School of Homer. There they worked for a month at a time, which was all they could afford, on seven separate years before making their announcement in August 2010. But then the work stopped, and I couldn't find the results of the excavations written up anywhere.

So what were the archaeologists from Ioannina looking for?

Agamemnon and Nestor, whose palaces have been found, were much richer and grander kings than Odysseus. According to the Catalogue of Ships Agamemnon took one hundred ships to Troy, and Nestor took ninety, but Odysseus took only twelve. Homer tells how Telemachus visited King Nestor's palace. We too can see it at Ano Englianos, outside the modern city of Pylos. It is said to be the best-preserved Mycenaean palace in Greece. The archaeologists from Ioannina would not be searching for such a grand place on Ithaca, perhaps just a large house. In Homer's story Odysseus was known for his wits, not his riches. However, one thing is certain. The palace would have needed a good supply of water.

Amongst the papers George Huxley had given me was a copy of a survey, commissioned by the professors from Ioannina from German Professor Jost Knauss of the Technical University of Munich, on the complicated underground water system at Agios Athanassios/School of Homer. Knauss is a leading authority on ancient hydraulic techniques and works. With an English translation of his paper in my hand I walked up to the Agios Athanassios site to check the system on the ground. As well as a scale drawing of the entire water system, the paper had a good measured drawing at a larger scale of a Mycenaean well house. This turned out to be the pit my grandchildren had rushed down into several years earlier. Now I went down myself through the corbelled-stone shaft into the domed cavity below. I looked into the circular pool of dark water. It was about six-foot diameter and, in the autumn, perhaps seven foot below the ground. I didn't taste the water but it smelled sweet. Knauss dated this corbelled stone underground well-house to the Mycenaean Era c.1300-1200 BC, the time of Odysseus. It lies below the position of the main hall, or 'megaron', of the palace, and within the Mycenaean defensive walls. No doubt this was a good precaution in case of a siege.

The hillside where the site of Agios Athanassios stands is filled with water. This is just one of several wells and fountains in the area, which flow all year round. In winter the water from these springs runs downhill in a large gulley. It finally disgorges into the sea several miles away in the harbour at Frikes, where Alec and I stayed with Helen and Gerry on our second visit to Ithaca in 1983. Frikes was called Rheithron in ancient times. Rheithron is the word for a watercourse in Greek and, every winter, torrents of water come down this gulley. Sometimes, in a wet winter, the harbour-side at Frikes is flooded by the water coming down from the Melanhydros wells (the dark water mentioned by Homer) at Agios Athanassios.

I was rather intrigued that Odysseus had sorted out his water supply so much better than Alec and I had managed some 3000 years later. In *The Odyssey* the huge cast of Homer's story wash and bathe at his palace with never a mention of water shortage. When the maidservants were preparing for a feast that the suitors were planning, twenty of them went to draw water *'from the dark waters of the well'*. (20: 156 Rieu) If the Palace of Odysseus once existed at the site now called Agios Athanassios/School of Homer on the island of Ithaca, we can be certain this site provided Odysseus, Penelope, and their retinue with plentiful supplies of fresh drinking water.

So, I wondered, why had Robert Bittlestone dismissed this site?

"Cities in Odysseus' time were about location, location, location - in a place secure from pirates, with water and farmland," he announced on his website.

I wouldn't have used those exact words but, basically, Bittlestone was right about this. Then he jumped straight on to conclude:

"Kasteli fits the bill. Dates of walls are uncertain but…sherds of Mycenaean pottery have been found."

Not so fast Mr. Bittlestone.

The Agios Athanassios and Pilikata sites on Ithaca both also fit this bill. Sherds of pottery from the Mycenaean Era have also been found at both these sites. In addition, archaeologists have discovered Mycenaean defensive walls surrounding both these sites on Ithaca and, as it turns out, an underground Mycenaean well structure too.

In August 2010, on the day that Alec and I had supper with Denis Sikiotis, the archaeologists from Ioannina, Litsa Kontorli-Papadopoulou and Thanasi Papadopoulos, announced that their finds at Agios Athanassios/ School of Homer fitted the descriptions of Odysseus' Palace given by Homer in *The Odyssey*. This should have been a high point for their work, but instead it was the last year in which excavation there took place.

It was difficult for me to find out what had been discovered on the site at Agios Athanassios, and precisely how this related to Homer's words. And I was not the only one. Even the two women who took groups of tourists up to the site on a regular basis seemed unsure of the facts. I was still looking for a description of their finds from the professors from Ioannina themselves. I couldn't find anything but, in the autumn of 2017, Ester van Zuylen, one of the two walk leaders, gave me a copy of an article written in 2011 for the archaeological journal *Corpus*. The article described the professors' work on Ithaca. The black and white photocopy was battered, incomplete, and written in quite difficult Greek, but it contained the information I wanted.

In October 2017, on the last day of my stay, I went to Vathi. I found the island librarian and, although he didn't speak English, I managed to ask him if he had a copy of this article. He replied that he did but, as it was a Monday, the library was closed. We swopped email addresses and I expected that would be the last I heard of it but, to my astonishment and delight, soon after my return to England, he sent me a scan of the full article. I translated it with the help of a Greek friend in London. At last I had some information from the archaeologists themselves.

The article in the archaeological journal *Corpus* stated that in 2011 the archaeologists' work was incomplete, but it confirmed the observations I had made myself years earlier when I first came to the site with two grandchildren. The site of Agios Athanassios is perfect for an ancient king. It overlooks the fertile plain of North Ithaca and it has a plentiful supply of fresh water. It has easy access to three alternative harbours for travel, trade and, if needs be, to escape from pirates. The archaeologists confirmed that the site was a powerful and affluent political centre and area for worship. It was inhabited from before the time of Odysseus, between the time of Odysseus and that of Homer, and for approximately a thousand years following. Then the church of Agios Athanassios was built on the same site in the 18th Century AD. As a result of this on-going habitation the stratification of the earth, used by archaeologists ever since Dörpfeld to date their finds, was very disturbed. Stones were used and re-used. New foundations and graves were dug down through areas where previous buildings once stood. This made their work much more difficult.

The archaeologists described how they managed to trace the remains of the Mycenaean defensive walls, which surrounded the Agios Athanassios site in the time of Odysseus and Penelope, and located three entrance gateways. They went on to briefly describe the Mycenaean buildings and objects discovered on the site, including foundations of a Mycenaean hall, or megaron, and the corbelled well structure identified by Professor Knauss.

Tombs and other finds from later Classical and Roman times were also described. Whilst these are interesting, they have led to confusion about the dating of the site to the time of Odysseus. The most obvious feature to cause confusion are the gigantic stones which form the base of the ruins of the church of Agios Athanassios, at the upper level where Penelope's bedroom is said to have stood. The archaeologists suggested these massive walls might date from the third century BC, almost a thousand years after the time of Odysseus and Penelope. I suspect it was these prominent walls from a later time that confused Wilhelm Dörpfeld and led to him develop his theory about Lefkas, the idea that has led to so many misunderstandings.

In early June 2018, I made another breakthrough. When I took my younger grandson up to Agios Athanassios I found a Greek archaeologist talking to a journalist from *Ithaca News*. I approached them in the area of the great hall. They were looking at a very good isometric drawing of the hall (or megaron) at the time of Odysseus and checking the positions of the paths, entrance, columns, and store rooms, against the evidence on the ground. Although it produces a three-dimensional image, an isometric drawing has accurate scaled dimensions both horizontally and vertically, so this was useful for their task.

The two women were in no doubt that this was the palace described by Homer.

"The more you look into the detail of Homer's story the more the detail of this site fits his words," one said.

The archaeologist explained that she had been part of Professor Litsa Kontorli-Papadopoulou's team during her excavation. As we stood there she leant down and picked a sherd of pottery up from the ground with a small mark incised on it.

"This is a piece of Mycenaean pottery," she said.

"Please hide it," I replied, "as it may be the vital part of a pot you want to piece together. If you leave it here some tourist might take it."

"We have boxes and boxes of pottery sherds from the site still waiting to be sorted. It is difficult specialist work and there isn't the money to pay someone suitably qualified to do it."

She showed me a well-preserved stone, a column base where a wooden column once stood to support the roof of the hall. It was one of several whose positions were precisely plotted and accurately scaled on the drawing. Then she pointed out some other features of the hall.

"This recess in the floor was once used for animal sacrifice," she said, "and this," she pointed to a circular recess, "is the position of the fire."

We walked together to the entrance to the hall complex. On the drawing there was a rough sketch of a man and a dog. In Homer's story, Odysseus met his old hunting dog at the entrance to his palace. He was walking with the swineherd Eumaeus when the dog nearly revealed his disguise.

'As they stood talking, a dog lying there lifted his head and pricked up his ears. Argus was his name. Patient Odysseus himself had owned and bred him, though he had sailed for holy Ilium before he could reap the benefit. In years gone by the young huntsmen had often taken him out after wild goats, deer, and hares. But now, in his owner's absence, he lay abandoned on the heaps of dung from the mules and cattle, which lay in profusion at the gate, awaiting removal by Odysseus' servants as manure for his great estate. There, full of vermin, lay Argus the hound. But directly he became aware of Odysseus' presence, he wagged his tail and dropped his ears, though he lacked the strength to come nearer to his master. Odysseus turned his eyes away and, making sure Eumaeus did not notice, brushed away a tear and said:

'Eumaeus, it is extraordinary to see a hound like this lying in the dung. He's a beauty, though I cannot really tell whether his looks were matched by his speed or whether he was just one of those dogs whom their masters feed at table and keep for show.'

Then you, Eumaeus the swineherd, said in reply: 'This dog did have a master, but it is all too plain he died abroad. If he was now what he was in the heyday of his looks and form, as Odysseus left him when he sailed for Troy, you'd be astonished at his speed and power. No game that he gave chase to could escape him in the deepest depth of the forest. He was a marvel too at picking up the scent. But now he's in a

bad way; his master has died far away from home and the women are
too thoughtless to look after him. With this Eumaeus left him, and,
entering the stately palace, passed straight into the hall where the
haughty Suitors were assembled. As for Argus, the black hand of
Death descended on him the moment he caught sight of Odysseus –
after twenty years.

(17: 312-27 Rieu)

A couple of days later, back at my house, my architect neighbour
Dimitris Skirgiannis walked up the track towards the vineyards. I don't
often see him, as this is his wife's county house. They live and work in Athens. He gave me a profuse welcome and said how much he misses Alec.

"So do I," I replied, "I can tell you." I sighed, tipped my head back,
shrugged my shoulders and spread my hands in the way that Greeks do.
"What can we do?"

As soon as he had gone, I remembered how, years ago, Dimitris had
come up onto our terrace to show Alec the photographs of the latest finds
at Agios Athanassios on the block-like mobile phone he had at the time.
He was helping the archaeologists record their finds. I had a moment of
inspiration. Dimitris might, I suddenly thought, know something about
that wonderful isometric drawing I had seen a few days earlier.

The following morning I walked along to his house. I took with me
a copy of Professor Luce's book on Homeric Landscapes. Dimitris offered
me a cup of coffee and gestured towards the chairs and table in a shady
spot under an old olive in his garden. He looked carefully at the photographs in Professor Luce's book.

"This looks like a very good account," he commented. "I have never
seen this book."

I told him about my meeting with the archaeologist up at Agios
Athanassios and about the excellent drawing they had.

"I did all the drawings for Professors Litsa Kontorli-Papadopoulou and Thanasi Papadopoulos from Ioannina," he replied.

All those years ago Alec had been on the case, but at last I had found his trail. I had hit the jackpot. Dimitris Skirgiannis was the key.

"There are boxes and boxes of finds from all periods of habitation on the site," he confirmed, "but nobody has sorted them yet."

"Do you know when the site will be fenced and the finds sorted?"

"The Ithaca Council has collected some money for this. Hopefully it will be enough."

"Will they be able to put new covers over the archaeologists' pits?"

"I don't think they have enough for that yet."

"Perhaps someone could do an aerial survey from a drone?"

"Someone has done a rough survey of the whole island. They found a shadow of an ancient stadium down at Polis Bay."

"That is wonderful. Sylvia Benton thought that ground was once used for competitive athletic games. Is anyone going on with the archaeological work on Ithaca?"

"Litsa Kontorli-Papadopoulou has died and Thanasi Papadopoulos is over eighty now. He has handed over to Professor Lolos at Ioannina. But the University of Ioannina has no money. Not a single euro."

He spread his empty hands.

We swopped email addresses and, a few days later, Dimitris Skirgiannis sent me a copy of his isometric drawing of the hall, or megaron, of Odysseus.

The following year, in 2019, when I thought my manuscript was finished, I sent Dimitris an email to ask if I could publish the drawing he had given me. He replied immediately. He had spoken to Professor Papadopoulos and he too gave permission for me to publish it. The following day the professor himself sent me a copy of a paper he wrote in 2016 for the archaeological journal Aegaeum. The paper, written in English, was dedicated to his wife Litsa. It compares Mycenaean citadels excavated over the whole of Western Greece. It then specifically compares Agios Athanassios/School of Homer with the palace at Ano Englianos near Pylos (assumed to be that of the great King Nestor), the palace of Mycenae (assumed to be that of King Agamemnon), and a palace structure at Tiryns. The article contained a large number of drawings made by my neighbour Dimitris Skirgiannis and photographs of some of the Mycenaean finds made up at Agios Athanassios/School of Homer. Professor Papadopoulos was in no doubt whatsoever that his wife's excavations had revealed a Mycenaean palace surrounded by defensive walls on Ithaca. He concluded, in rather charming English, "So, I agree with (the German archaeologist) Buchholz who says that 'the Ithacans of later times looked for the palace as described by Homer at this important and strategic place,' where I suggest that most probably existed the palace of Odysseus."

In June Dimitris Skirgiannis came to Ithaca again for a few days. We sat again in the shade of the magnificent olive tree in his garden and had another conversation.

"They found a bath," he said "in a room up by Penelope's bedroom. It is very similar to the bath found at King Nestor's palace. Have you been to see King Nestor's palace in Pylos?"

"I have. I went in 2017 when the site was reopened after the magnificent new steel roof was erected over the megaron. I looked down from one of the high-level walkways at the Mycenaean bathtub in the position where it was found. The drawings and explanations there are very clear, and well translated into several languages.

"The Mycenaean bath they discovered in Ithaca is far more complete than the one at King Nestor's palace. The archaeologists here found many more pieces."

Homer tells how, when Telemachus visits the palace of King Nestor, he is bathed by his beautiful daughter:

> *'The beautiful Polycaste, King Nestor's youngest daughter, now bathed*
> *Telemachus. When she had bathed him and rubbed him with*
> *olive-oil, she gave him a tunic and arranged a fine cloak around his*
> *shoulders, so that he stepped from the bath looking like an immortal*
> *god.'*

(3:464-468 Rieu)

Towards the end of our conversation Dimitris made a suggestion.

"Professor Papadopoulos lives quite near me in Athens. If you come to my house we can go together and see him."

I arranged to go the following week.

Meanwhile, with the archaeologists' two articles and Dimitris' isometric drawing of the main hall of the palace, I went up again to the site at Agios Athanassios. I wanted to check again Professor Papadopoulos' account of the Mycenaean finds there against Homer's descriptions of the Palace of Odysseus. The footpaths leading up to the site were overgrown. The site was still unfenced and weeds were growing all over it. The temporary covers to the open excavation pits were rotting, their flimsy corrugated roofs were bent, and some had blown off in the winter storms. The place looked both vulnerable and dangerous. But now I know my way around the site quite well. I began to check it against Professor Thanasi Papadopoulos' paper.

At Agios Athanasios the archaeologists recognised a pre-historic acropolis of around 23 hectares in area. The acropolis is surrounded by partly-preserved Mycenaean defensive walls with entrance gateways to the south-west, north, and north-east. [15] An extension to the walls was made in the late Mycenaean period to enclose the corbelled well dated by Professor Knauss. [16] Dimitris' plan of the site showed the Mycenaean walls extending far beyond the area covered by Penelope's bedroom at the upper level and the hall at the base of the cliff. I was surprised by the extent of it, by the area enclosed, and by the many buildings discovered but not yet fully excavated.

Within these walls the archaeologists identified the remains of a complex of buildings arranged in terraces on several levels. In Homer's story, Odysseus, who was still in disguise, walked towards the palace with Eumaeus. As they approached:

'Eumaeus,' said Odysseus, taking the swineherd by the arm, 'this must surely be Odysseus' palace: it would be easy to pick it out at a glance from any number of houses. There are buildings beyond buildings; the courtyard wall with its coping is a fine piece of work and those folding doors are true defences. No one could storm it.'

(17: 262-7 Rieu)

Homer's description fits.

The presumed site of Penelope's bedroom, where the ruins of the 18th century AD church of Agios Athanassios now stand, is at the upper level. It was located at the top of the cliff which rears up behind the position of the megaron, or great hall. Three staircases were found running between these two levels. The best preserved can easily be seen. It is steep, narrow, and cut into the bedrock. Over and over Homer refers to these two levels. Penelope's room, and that of her entourage, lay at the top of the staircase. The main drama was played out, and the suitors slaughtered, in the hall, or megaron, on the lower level.

'In her room upstairs Penelope...took in the words of his stirring ballad and came down from her quarters by the steep staircase.'

(1: 329-31 Rieu)

Professor Papadopoulos' paper reports that parts of the steep vertical face of the rock dividing the upper and lower terraces are embellished with large blocks of stone in pseudo-ashlar style similar to those used in the Cyclopean wall of King Agamemnon's palace at Mycenae, at the east side of the approach to the Lion Gate.

At the upper level, near the assumed site of Penelope's bedroom, the archaeologists discovered a bathroom and a metallurgical workshop from the Mycenaean Era. They also found a building that might be a second 'megaron', a separate upstairs hall for the women. The bathroom, to the south-east of the workshop, contained the remains of the Mycenaean bath Dimitris had described. [18] The metallurgical workshop contained a huge stone with, carved into the top of it, a long-shaped slot and three rounded pits of different sizes. Dimitris had photographed this stone years ago when it was first discovered, and showed his photograph to Alec. Professor G. Papademetriou of the National Metsoveian Technical University of Athens has recognised this as a Mycenaean casting stone for metals [17] but, as yet, he wasn't certain what objects were shaped from these castings.

Homer describes Penelope coming downstairs from the upper level to meet her husband Odysseus in the hall below. In the lower terrace the excavation revealed the foundations of a three-roomed rectangular building from the Mycenaean Era, in the form of a hall, or megaron. It is similar in construction and dimensions to those at Mycenae, Tiryns and Pylos. [18] Approaching from the south on a partly destroyed stone staircase, an entrance leads to the first room. In front of the opening to the next room a recess is cut into the surface of the rock bed. Professor Papadopoulos' paper confirmed this was probably used as an altar for sacrifices. The third room has a circular hearth sunk to a lower level in the floor. [19]

In Homer's story the hall, or megaron, is where Odysseus, still disguised as a beggar, strings his old bow and shoots an arrow through the rings of twelve axe heads, thus proving he is a worthy husband to Penelope. He then 'levelled a deadly shaft straight at Antinous', the leader of the suitors.

Antinous had just reached for his fine cup to take a draught of wine, and the golden, two-handled beaker was balanced in his hands, No thought of bloodshed entered his head. For who could guess, there in that festive company, that one man, however powerful he might be, would bring evil death and black doom on him against such odds? Odysseus took aim and shot him in the neck. The point passed clean through his tender throat. The cup dropped from his hand as he was hit and he lurched over to one side. His life-blood gushed from his nostrils in a turbid jet. His foot lashed out and kicked the table from him. His food was scattered on the ground, and bread and meat lay there in the dirt.

(22: 9-22 Rieu)

Homer went on to describe in detail how Odysseus and his small team of four killed every one of Penelope's suitors, until they lay in heaps 'like fish that the fishermen have dragged out of the grey surf in the meshes of their net on to a curving beach, to lie in masses on the sand longing for the salt water, till the bright sun ends their lives'.

Finally, Odysseus 'stood among the corpses of the dead, splattered with blood and gore, like a lion when he comes from feeding on some farmer's bullock, with the blood dripping from his breast and jaws on either side, a fearsome spectacle.'

Homer's story of the battle, and of Odysseus' meetings with Penelope, fit perfectly with the Mycenaean remains found at Agios Athanassios.

Close beside the base of the cliff, to the west of the megaron, the archaeologists found a cave-like underground storeroom. I looked through the Odyssey to where Telemachus left the main hall and 'went down to his father's store-room, a big and lofty chamber stacked with gold and bronze, *and with chests full of clothing, and stores of fragrant oil. There too, packed close along the wall, stood jars of mellow vintage wine...'* (2: 337-41 Rieu)

The archaeologists discovered a spacious pre-historic store, dug to a lower level, adjacent to the foundations of the great hall. A row of old terracotta wine jars were still aligned along the wall at the base of the cliff. [20] The jars were from a later period but the store room itself was from the Mycenaean era.

It is a perfect fit.

Professor Papadopoulos' paper describes other pre-historic discoveries made at Agios Athanassios. A large door opening was discovered in the northern wall of the megaron leading to a three-roomed building, orientated east-west. A tentative reconstruction of this building can be seen on Dimitris Skirgiannis' drawing. Judging from its architectural type, its position adjacent to the megaron, and the finds made there, Professor Papadopoulos suggests it could be a sanctuary from the time of Odysseus. [21] Also probably from pre-historic times is a further impressive but damaged monument [22] and other finds. [23].

In summary, the professor states that Agios Athanassios/School of Homer is an important and strategic Mycenaean citadel and residence. It has a commanding view over the undulating plateau, the most fertile area of the rocky island of Ithaca. It has easy access to the harbours of Polis, Afales, and Frikes. The architectural remains, and the finds, show evidence of the presence of workshops, knowledge of Mycenaean engineering, the existence of foreign contacts, a military presence, and religious activities. In addition, the inhabitants of the prehistoric citadel at Agios Athanassios/School of Homer could easily control the trading route from the adjacent area of Aetolia to the West. According to Professor Irad Malkin, who has made an extensive study of this subject, this route ran through the Ithaca Channel between Ithaca and Kefalonia in Mycenaean times. It is known that the Mycenaeans were competent and adventurous sailors and traders. Ithaca provided the possibility of obtaining food and water, and safe anchorage for the ships travelling along the Corinthian, Ionian, and Adriatic seas both westwards and to the north. [24] In conclusion, taking into account the finds as a whole, especially that of the preserved foundations of the megaron, and parts of the wall between the two levels which have exact parallels at Mycenae, Professor Papadopoulos states that the site of Agios Athanassios/School of Homer is probably the site of the Palace of Odysseus described by Homer.

In early July 2019 I went with Dimitris Skirgiannis to visit Professor Thanasi Papadopoulos. His house was in a leafy street in a northern suburb of Athens. The trees have been planted out into the road to allow parking but to prevent through traffic. They were heavy with sour oranges. His hallway was filled with small bikes belonging to his grandchildren, who live in the flat above him. The professor, who opened his front door to welcome us, was a tall, slim, distinguished-looking gentleman. The walls of his flat, like those of George Huxley's house, were lined with fully-packed bookshelves. Dimitris and I sat on comfortable chairs leaving the professor to move several very large teddy bears to make room for himself on the sofa opposite.

"They come from England," he said.

They were taking up a lot of space.

Professor Papadopoulos was in no doubt whatsoever that the excavations at Agios Athanassios/School of Homer in the north of Ithaca had revealed the Palace of Odysseus described by Homer. He intends to write up the results of the excavations in full, but he also has work at other sites to write up, and recently he has not been well. Meanwhile, he was delighted that I have checked the detail of the finds against the words of Homer and discovered, as he too believes, that they fit perfectly.

"What more can we do?" he asked. "Did anyone ask for absolute proof that King Nestor once lived at the Mycenaean palace structure the archaeologists discovered at Ano Englianos? Nobody can prove absolutely that King Nestor once lived there. Did anyone ask for absolute proof that King Agamemnon once lived in the Mycenaean palace in Mycenae? No."

I remembered the conversation Alec and I once had with Denis Sikiotis, who asked;

"How can the Ithacans prove absolutely that this was the Palace of Odysseus?"

We had joked about finding a stone recessed into the wall next to his front door with 'Odysseus and Penelope lived here' carved in the Linear B writing of their time. Of course no Mycenaean palace has such a thing. The professor continued:

"Have other palace structures from the Mycenaean Era been discovered? Yes, they have, for instance at Tiryns. Palace structures from the Mycenaean Era have not yet been discovered on Kefalonia but, if they were, would that prove that Odysseus centred his kingdom there? No. It wouldn't prove anything."

We went on to discuss funding and display of the finds made at Agios Athanassios.

"Could they be displayed in the existing Archaeological Museum in Vathi?" I asked.

"No, there are too many. That site was used from pre-historic right up to Roman times. We would need somewhere at least the size of the museum at Vathi. Ideally they should be displayed in Stavros."

I had no idea the finds had been so extensive.

"It would be good if the megaron at Agios Athanassios had a wonderful roof like that over the palace of Nestor," I suggested, "but smaller, of course."

"That would be completely splendid but we can't afford it. That roof was donated by the University of Cincinatti."

He picked a file from his bookshelves and showed me that he had neatly filed the notes from Professor Huxley's lecture at Senate House, along with Professor Luce's articles published in the Classical Association News.

Finally, we discussed both possible sources of funding for the archaeological work to continue, and for the display of the site, and the finds.

So what happened to Odysseus at the end of Homer's story? After the terrible fight with the suitors, where only the poet bard with his lyre and an innocent houseboy were spared, Odysseus' old nurse Eurycleia identified the twelve female slaves who had slept with the suitors during his absence. They were made to carry out the bodies of the dead suitors and clean up the blood and gore in the hall. When they had finished this work they were hanged. These were tough times for women. Only when this was complete Eurycleia was sent to give the news to Penelope, and the other women upstairs.

Penelope came downstairs from her bedroom. Odysseus was still disguised as a beggar until a slave woman washed him and rubbed him with oil, and the goddess Athena 'enhanced his comeliness from head to foot'.

> 'She made him look taller and sturdier, and she caused the bushy locks to hang from his head thick as the petals of a hyacinth in bloom....He came out from the bath looking like one of the everlasting gods, and went and sat down once more in the chair opposite his wife.'
>
> (23:156-65 Rieu)

But Penelope still needed to be certain that Odysseus was not an imposter. She made a final test – one worthy of Odysseus himself. Odysseus and Penelope's bridal bed was built into the base of an old olive tree firmly rooted into the ground. Odysseus had made it himself. Now Penelope asked for it to be moved. Odysseus protested. By insisting the bed could not be moved, a secret no imposter could have known, he confirmed his identity. Penelope's true husband had returned.

At his words her knees began to tremble and her heart melted as she realized that he had given her infallible proof. Bursting into tears she ran up to Odysseus, threw her arms around his neck and kissed his head...

Her words stirred a great longing for tears in Odysseus' heart, and he wept as he held his dear and loyal wife in his arms. It was like the moment when the blissful land is seen by struggling sailors, whose ship Poseidon has battered with wind and wave and smashed on the high seas.

(23: 205-8 and 231-5 Rieu)

Then,

the housekeeper Eurycleia, with a torch in her hands, lit them on their way to bed, taking her leave when she had brought them to their room, And blissfully they lay down on their own familiar bed.

(23: 293-6 Rieu)

Two famous ancient critics held that this was the end of *The Odyssey* and that the remainder of the story was written by later, lesser poets. There are many different versions of what happened next and the sources of these stories vary in their reliability. However Homer, whoever he might have been, is our oldest and most reliable source.

According to Homer, when Penelope pressed Odysseus about the future, he reluctantly told her about his visit to the soothsayer Tiresias, amongst the souls of the dead in the House of Hades.

'Tiresias told me to carry a well-balanced oar and wander from city to city, till I came to a people who know nothing of the sea, and never use salt with their food, so that crimson-painted ships and the long oars that serve those ships as wings are quite beyond their experience...As for my end, he said that Death would come to me away from the sea, and that I would die peacefully in old age, surrounded by a prosperous people. He assured me that all this would come true.'

(23: 266-72 and 281-4 Rieu)

These texts indicate that we should not expect to find Odysseus' tomb on either Ithaca or any of the neighbouring islands of his kingdom. On these islands no-one can ever roam far from the sea. In addition he would have been known and, no doubt, he would have had enemies too.

In *The Odyssey* as we know it, after the slaughter of the suitors, Odysseus envisaged only too well the probable consequences of his actions. He told his son Telemachus,

'In any community, when a man kills someone, even someone who has no friends at all to avenge him, he still goes into exile, abandoning his family and native state. But we have killed the best of Ithaca's young men, the mainstay of our state. Do consider this.'

(23:118-22 Rieu)

Odysseus set out from Troy with twelve ships and around two hundred and forty men from his kingdom. He returned on his own. In the twenty years he was away, he lost all his ships and all his men. Those families too had been waiting for their young sons to return from the war. In addition, Odysseus went on to kill every one of Penelope's suitors. According to Homer there were fifty-two suitors from Doulichion, twenty-four from Same, twenty from Zacynthus and twelve from Ithaca itself; one hundred and eight in all. These figures were no doubt exaggerated in the telling but, whatever the precise numbers, there is no doubt that

Odysseus' activities would have made him a great many enemies close to home.

People, both back in classical times and to this day, have wondered how Odysseus dealt with the problem that he himself had foreseen. Honour killing was practiced in Greece and Albania well into the twentieth century. There is no doubt that, back in Odysseus' day, the families of the suitors would come to avenge the deaths of their sons. In the remainder of *The Odyssey* the grieving families, led by Eupeithes the father of Antinous the chief suitor, do come after Odysseus. They catch up with him the following day at the farm of the old king, Odysseus' father Laertes. As they approach the farm Odysseus, with his father, his son, and a small band of supporters, arm themselves and prepare to fight the avengers:

> '*Odysseus raised a terrifying war-cry, gathering himself together and pounced on them like a swooping eagle.*'

Miraculously, the goddess Athina comes to his rescue once more.

> '*But at this moment Zeus flung a flaming thunderbolt...Athene called out to Odysseus: 'Odysseus favourite of Zeus, resourceful son of Laertes, hold your hand. Stop fighting your countrymen, in case you incur the wrath of Zeus the Thunderer.*'
>
> (24: 537-48 Rieu)

Odysseus obeyed her, and finally the goddess established peace between the two sides.

Mark Stevenson, with his partner Andy Pappas, runs a restaurant at Platreithias in the north of Ithaca. A nearby track leads up to the site of Agios Athanassios/School of Homer. A deep rainwater ditch, or gulley, runs beside the track. The restaurant is called Gefyra (the bridge) as the road there bridges over the gulley. The gulley carries the rainwater overflow from Agios Athanassios/School of Homer down to modern Frikes/ Homeric Rheithron. The word ρεῖθρο (reithro) means watercourse or torrent gulley. Paizis-Danias explained that you can see the word ρεῖθρο (reithro) hiding in the name Platreithias as well. It all fits together.

Mark and I sat together on the terrace in front of my house. He had heard on the grapevine about the book I was writing. So he came to see me.

"People often drop into the restaurant to ask about the Palace of Odysseus," he said.

When I had explained my research and what I had discovered, he said:

"This is very interesting. I have never heard about Professor Huxley's analysis and it makes a lot of sense."

Then he asked another question:

"Why has it been left to you to sort this out?"

"In the beginning it was Alec's search," I explained, "then I got hooked on it too. I'm a good sleuth, and I'm very dogged. Once I'm on the trail of something I like to run it to ground."

When I first came to Ithaca I was a bit sceptical about Homer's story but, during my journey (and in spite of the Laistrygonians) I find I have become a believer. I have come to believe that Homer, whoever he might have been, imagined Odysseus returning to the same modern island of Ithaca we can visit today. It seems to me quite probable that the poet himself visited Ithaca before finalising his song of *The Odyssey*. I believe that, when the archaeological team from Ioannina suggest that Homer envisaged his drama played out at Agios Athanssios/ School of Homer in the north of Ithaca, they are right. I believe they have finally nailed the location of the elusive palace of Odysseus and Penelope.

Now I asked myself another question:

If Alec were still here, how would he, as a trained barrister and experienced arbitrator, judge my conclusions? My views coincide with those of most respected philologists and archaeologists, but have I been able, based on the balance of probabilities, to prove them beyond all reasonable doubt?

In fact Alec had been hunting for the Palace of Odysseus on Ithaca since he first came to the island in 1975. He was on the trail in the conversations he had with Denis, with Liz, and with Dimitris Skirgiannis. Although we sometimes came by different routes he and I usually came to the same point at the end.

I think he would agree with me.

I hope he would agree I have completed his search.

Epilogue

The present Mayor and Vice-Mayor of Ithaca understand the importance of Agios Athanassios/School of Homer, site of the ancient Palace of Odysseus. They have built a road up to the site and they are erecting a fence to enclose it. They will clear the long grass and the weeds. When they have enough money they will renew the covers put up 'temporarily' nine years ago by the archaeologists. But Ithaca shouldn't be left to handle this on its own. The current situation at the Agios Athanassios site is a tragedy, not just for the little Greek island of Ithaca, but for our European cultural and literary heritage as a whole. Perhaps a Homeric site of this importance should be a UNESCO World Heritage Site. Instead it is neglected, vulnerable and dangerous.

So what should be done? This is a matter I discussed with Professor of Archaeology Thanasi Papadopoulos. We had the following ideas:

1. The Agios Athanassios site should be cleared, protected and secured.
2. Proper arrangements should be made for visitors, and information should be provided.
3. New covers should be made to protect the excavation pits on the site.
4. The archaeologists from the University of Ioannina, now under Professor Lolos, should continue the excavation, which is incomplete.
5. The University of Ioannina should also provide a team to sort, record, and restore the finds made by Litsa Kontorli-Papadopoulou and Thanasi Papadopoulos.

6. A museum should be provided on Ithaca to display the finds. Professor Papadopoulos suggested an existing building I know well in Stavros for this purpose. It is a lovely old building placed very centrally in Stavros. I had thought of the same building for this purpose and, when I returned to Ithaca, I discovered I was not alone in this. The Mayor and Vice-Mayor are already in discussion with the owner, who has agreed this building should be restored and used as a museum. The plan is to use it to display both the new finds from Agios Athanassios/School of Homer and the existing finds from Loizos' Cave and other sites in the north of Ithaca currently displayed in the Stavros Museum at Pilikata.

7. Precise non-invasive surveys should be made immediately to all known archaeological sites on Ithaca, to check the extent of ancient building. These areas should then be carefully designated to prevent damage, or further modern development, until proper archaeological investigations can be carried out.

These suggestions are neither in order of importance, nor in the order in which they should be done. They are all important. But how will this work be financed? I suspect that neither the Greek government, nor the new Greek Ephorate in Kefalonia, have much money to spare. The University of Ioannina, according to Dimitris Skirgiannis, has no money at all. Professor Papadopoulos suggests the European Union has a funding programme, ESPA, for this type of work, and that a grant might be obtained. The work might also attract foreign donations and student volunteers. For such an important site this should be possible.

Acknowledgements

Firstly I would like to thank the wonderful people of Ithaca for their warm welcome to their beautiful island. I have come to love it more and more.

For help in my research of the texts I would like to thank, most importantly, Professor George L. Huxley for his enormous generosity with his time and expertise. Thank you to Professor Robin Lane Fox for setting me on the right track. For help with archaeological research very many thanks to Professor Thanasi Papadopoulos and to the architect Dimitris Skirgiannis. Thank you to Ester van Zuylen, and Professor Geoffrey Sampson, for sharing information. Thank you to Dr Christina Souyoudzoglou-Haywood for explaining about the archaeological excavation on Kefalonia.

For help with writing and editing a particular thank you to Nick Davies for his patience, honesty, and extraordinary insight. Thank you Marsha Rowe and Gary Smailes for perceptive editorial work and advice, and to Mary Sandys and Duncan Fallowell for reading the whole manuscript, and for invaluable comments.

A huge thank you to Tabby Bourdier of Loco Design for her interest, expertise and endless care and patience with the typesetting and graphic design of the text and cover.

Thank you Frances Wilson for permission to publish your evocative poem, Phanis Koumpis for help with maps, my daughter Amy for your photo of Alec outside the Gate Cinema, my granddaughter Isabel for your photo of me for the cover and Mike Kozdon for your photo of the menhir. So many people have helped, both in Ithaca and in London, that I cannot hope to thank them all.

I wish I could thank Denis Sikiotis and Liz McGrath for their wonderful friendship, and for the good times we had discussing these subjects. Most of all I would like to thank my husband Alec for setting me off on this journey, and for sharing it with me for over thirty years. Sadly these three are no longer with us. I can only remember them with gratitude.

A note about transliteration

Because the Greeks use their own alphabet the same name can appear in alternative forms when written in English. For instance, in the 21st century, the commonest spelling for Ithaca's larger neighbouring island is Kefalonia, but you can also find it spelled as Kefalinia, Cephallinia, Cephallenia, Cephalonia and in several other ways.

For the names of Ancient Greece, there is a convention that, because the Romans were the first people to write Greek names in our Roman alphabet, that names are spelt as the Romans did. The word-endings are adapted to the structure of Latin. However Greek pronunciation has changed greatly over the millennia. Although Modern Greek is, on the whole, spelled phonetically there is nowadays a choice between spelling modern names by replacing Greek letters with corresponding Roman letters, or alternatively by reflecting their sounds. People do either, or mix different approaches. There is no ideal solution to this. I will try to spell modern Greek names as they are commonly spelled but I cannot promise consistency. In quoting from others I have used the spellings used in the original.

Ithaca, Ithaka, Ithaki, Ithake or Thiáki are not different names. They are different transliterations of the Greek names Ἰθάκη or Θιάκη. The many ways of spelling Kefalonia are different transliterations of the Greek name Κεφαλλωνιά.

A note about the characters

The places, events, and people described in this book are real, but I have changed a few names. There are many gaps in this account, both as a history and in what I have chosen to record. I accept full responsibility for any mistakes you may find.

Selected bibliography

BENTON S. Excavations in Ithaca lll. The Cave at Polis l.

BENTON S. BSA 47. Excavations at Stavros, Ithaca. 1937.

BENTON S. BSA 68 (1973) Excavations on Ithaca at Tries Lagades.

BITTLESTONE R. with DIGGLE J. and UNDERHILL J. Odysseus Unbound, The Search for Homer's Ithaca' Cambridge University Press 2005. Also www.odyseus-unbound.org.

DE GRUYTER W. Kadmos. Zeitschrift für vor- und frühgriechische Epigraphik. Walter de Gruyter 2005.

GELL W. The Geography and Antiquities of Ithaca – Primary Source Edition. 1807.

GOEKOOP C. 'Where on Earth is Ithaca'? Eburon Academic Publishers, Delft. 2010.

HEURTLEY W. BSA 35 (1935) pp.45-73. Excavations in Ithaca ll The Early Helladic Settlement at Pelikata,

HOPE SIMPSON and LAZENBY, The Catalogue of Ships in Homer's Iliad, Oxford 1970.

HUXLEY G. Ulixes Redux: Why the Island called Ithaki today is Homer's Ithaca. Unpublished lecture notes. Professor George Huxley for the Friends of the BSA on 7th November 2007.

KONTORLI-PAPADOPOULOU L. and PAPADOPOULOS T. Proceedings of the VIIIth conference (2-7th September 2000) on the Odyssey, issued by the Centre for Odyssey Studies, and collected in a volume titled 'Eranos'.

KONTORLI-PAPADOPOULOU L. PAPADOPOULOS T. OWENS G. A Possible Linear Sign from Ithaki (AB09 'SE')?

KONTORLI-PAPADOPOULOU and KNAUSS J. The Prehistoric underground well-house at Ithaka at the so-called School of Homer, L.

SELECTED BIBLIOGRAPHY

Kontorli-Papadopoulou, Eranos and Corpus 2001.

KONTORLI-PAPADOPOULOU L Corpus 28. Αρχαιολογια Ιστορια των Πολιτισμων Ζεύγμα. ΙΘΑΚΗ. 2011.

LUCE J.V. Homer and the Heroic Age.

LUCE J.V. Celebrating Homer's Landscapes. Troy and Ithaca Revisited, Yale University Press 1988.

LUCE J. The Classical Association News No.37 December 2007. 'The Identity of Ithaca: Decisive New Geological Information about the Thynia Isthmus in Kefalonia'.

MALKIN I. The Returns of Odysseus: Colonisation and Ethnicity, University of California Press, 1998.

MAROUKIAN X. et. al. Γεωμορφολογική - Παλαιογεωγραφική εξέλιξη της ΒΔ Κεφαλληνίας με έμφαση στην περιοχή μεταξύ του κόλπου Αργοστολίουκαι του Όρμου Αγίας Κυριακής, κατά το Ανώτερο Ολόκαινο. 2006.

ORMEROD H.A. Piracy in the Ancient World. 1924. Reprinted John Hopkins Paperbacks 1997.

PAIZIS-DANIAS D. 'Homer's Ithaca on Cephallenia? Facts and Fancies in the History of an Idea' Ithaca Friends of Homer Association.

PAIZIS-DANIAS D. 'Throwing Light on Homeric Ithaca'. Exhibition at Stavros Ithaca 2013 onwards.

PAIZIS-DANIAS D. The Archaeologiacal Treasures of Ithaca, pps 867-868.

PAPADOPOULOS T. Aegaeum 41. The Aegean seen from the West. Proceedings of the 16th International Aegean Conference, University of Ioannina, 18-21 May 2016. Mycenaean Citadels of Western Greece: architecture, purpose, their intricate role in the local communities and their relations with the West. Peeters Publishers, Leuven. Page 419 onwards.

RIEU D.C.H. Trans The Iliad and the Odyssey. Penguin Classics Revised

Translation 1991.

SAMPSON G. 'Odysseus' Home?'at www.grsampson.net

SCHLIEMANN H. 'Ithaka, der Peloponnes und Troja'. 1869.

SOUYOUDZOGLOU-HAYWOOD C. The Ionian Islands in the Early Bronze Age 3000-800 Liverpool University Press. 1999.

SOUYOUDZOGLOU-HAYWOOD C. ACTA Archaeologica Vol.89, Wiley 2018. Archaeology and the Search for Homeric Ithaca. The Case of Mycenaean Kephalonia.

STANFORD and LUCE, The Quest for Ulysses, 1974.

SYRMIS D. blog at dimos-syrmis.blogspot.co.uk/2015

TALBOT R.A. Ed, Barrington Atlas of the Greek and Roman World, Princeton 2000.

TSAKOS C.I. 'Ithaca and Homer (The Truth)' Athens 2005. Translated into English by Geoffrey Cox.

WACE and STUBBINGS, A Companion to Homer, Macmillan 1962.

WACE and STUBBINGS, Lands and People in Homer.

WATERHOUSE H. BSA 91 (1996) pp.301-317. From Ithaca to the Odyssey.

WILSON E. Trans. The Odyssey. Homer.

WOOD M. 'In Search of the Trojan War'. BBC Books 1985.

Notes

Comments marked GLH were made by Professor George L. Huxley. Archaeological information contained in notes 15-24 are taken from Professor Thanassi Papadopoulos' article in Aegaeum 41, by Peeters' Publishers, Leuven.

1. Aetos. If Odysseus and Penelope once lived in the fortified ruins at Aetos, at the southern end of the isthmus between the northern and southern parts of the island, the Homeric texts do not fit the landscape we find on Ithaca. There would scarcely be room there to accommodate all the structures mentioned by Homer as forming the great house of Odysseus. William Gell's companion Dodwell stated that the suitors could not have been lodged within the walls of the acropolis at Aetos, together with the household of Penelope, unless the building was several stories high.

2. Alalkomenaï. The ruined citadel at Aetos is also named 'City of Alalkomenaï'. Professor Huxley comments: GLH: Alalkomenaï is not named in the Odyssey but the origins of the name on Ithaca can be traced from other ancient sources. It is true that Strabo, according to our texts of the geographer, and following Apollodorus of Athens, stated that Alalkomenaï was a village (πολίχνιον)at the isthmus itself of Asteris. But Strabo's setting of Alalkomenaï on Asteris is unique and the text here is, almost certainly, corrupt. Other authors put Alalkomenaï in Ithaca. Two centuries before Strabo, Istros, a pupil of Callimachus, explained the name as follows: Antikleia the mother of Odysseus, having been given in marriage to Laertes, was

being taken to Ithaca. However she bore Odysseus near the
Alalkomeneion (a sanctuary of Athena Alalkomeneis) in
Boiotia. Hence the place in Ithaca was named, as though
after a mother city, after Alalkomenaï in Boeotia. References: Plutarch, Quaestiones Graecae (Greek Questions) 43.
"Whence did the city in Ithaca called Alalkomenaï get its
name?" Istros is given as authority: Antikleia, having been
given in marriage to Laertes, was being brought home. Near
the Alakomeneion in Boeotia she brought forth Odysseus.
Thence came the name to Ithaca. (Istros the Callimachean,
F.Gr.Hist. 334 F 58b Jacoby). As for Aetos, Leake reasonably
insisted, the remains there can be identified with Alkomenai or Alalkomenaï, which according to Apollodoros lay on
the isthmus of Ithaca. Leake 'Travels in Northern Greece 1'
London 1835, 263-268; Apollodorus, F. Gr. Hist. 244 F 202
Jacoby; Strabo 456-457 Casaubon (10.2.16). The point of the
story is that Alalkomenaï was in Ithaca. Why then did Strabo
say it was in Asteris? Either Strabo has made a mistake in his
reading of Apollodoros, or there is a lacuna before the sentence beginning 'in it'. There is no good reason to doubt that
Alalkomenaï was in Ithaca, and there is no room for a village
on Asteris-Dascalio.

3. Laertes, and his son Odysseus, belonged to a race, or tribe,
called Kephallenians. His kingdom included both Ithaca and
the island now called Kefalonia, Zacynthos, and several other
places as well. Many years after the time of Laertes, Odysseus,
and Homer, the name of the Kephallenian race attached itself
solely to the island we now call Kefalonia. Homer referred to
that island as Samos, or Same.

4. Nericus (or Nerikos) is an area to the north of modern Lefkas.

It became part of Odysseus' kingdom on its mainland territory as noted in the Odyssey 24: 375-380. Nericus must not to be confused with Neritos (sometimes translated as Niritos or Neritum) the main mountain on Ithaca.

5. Akarnania. GLH: Laertes wishes he had the strength he had formerly, when ruling the Kephallenians, when he captured the city of Nerikos together with the shore of the mainland - ἀκτὴν <τ'> ἠπείροιο (Od. 24: 375-380.) Thus Nerikos became part of the Ithacan kingdom on its mainland territory in Akarnania. Aktē as we learn from the author of the portulan of Pseudo-Skylax, is the low-lying land south of the cape of Aktion.

6. GLH: Aktē is on the mainland of Akarnania and it forms part of the mainland territory, the peraia, ascribed to Odysseus in the Catalogue of the Ships (Iliad 2:635) Aktē is indeed furthest to the north in the Kephallenian realm of Odysseus. Geologically it was once an island but it was joined to the mainland of Akarnania by an encroaching spit. Here, close to sea level, the runway of the Aktion-Preveza airport extends from east to west. Odysseus contrasts with the far Aktē the other islands, including Ithaca, Doulichion, Same, and Zakynthos.

7. GLH: The Echinades together with Doulichion form the realm of Meges (Iliad 2: 625-630). This area is large enough and it sits well as the northerly part of a unitary kingdom extending southwards to include the Echinades.

8. GLH: Doulichion was not part of the kingdom of Odysseus. Meges ruled there until he went to Troy. (Iliad 2: 625-629.) He did not come home from Troy, and in his absence Akastos ruled there. But Same (Kephallenia) and Zakynthos were parts of the kingdom of Odysseus. Ithaca and the islands around

it are to the south; Akte and Nerikos are towards the gloom. The contradiction in the words of Odysseus is thus removed. Where then is Doulichion? Homer thought of it as a large place, because more suitors came from Doulichion to woo Penelope than from any other island. It is sometimes said that because Homer calls Leukas 'Leukas' Doulichion cannot be there. But Homer speaks only of Leukas Petre, the white rock at the south-western extremity of what is now called Leukas. Leukas replaced the name of Doulichion when, during the Dark Age before the coming of the Corinthian colonists, the name of the White Rock, a prominent sailing mark, was extended to the whole island. Doulichion is the strongest candidate for the principal part of the realm of Meges and Akastos. Doulichion, then, is the old name of Leukas. In Pliny Hist. Nat. Ithaca and Dulichium are clearly distinguished. References to Odysseus as Doulichian are anachronistic rather than mistaken when events before the slaughter of the suitors are described. When the flower of Doulichian manhood had been killed in the great house of Odysseus, the territory inevitably fell to him. When the kingdom of Odysseus included Doulichion, he too could correctly be called Doulichian. We have no need to look for Homeric Doulichion anywhere except in the island later called Leukas. As for the insular character of Leukas, Leukas is now no more and no less of an island than it was in antiquity.

9. Some people suggest that Odysseus' ship probably landed at the harbour now known as Vathi, and this harbour would suit the words of Homer equally well. These days, due to modern harbour construction, Vathi no longer has a long, shallow, sandy beach. As Professor Luce discusses, nowadays

the shallow, sandy slope of the neighbouring beach of Dexia fits Homer's description more precisely. However this is not to say that, in Homer's day, Vathi beach may not have resembled that of Dexia. Both Vathi and Dexia harbours have 'two projecting headlands sheer to seaward but sloping down on the side of the harbour' as described by Homer. Both Vathi and Dexia face out onto Mount Neritos, on the far side of the Gulf of Molos. The Gulf of Molos fits the description given by Homer as the 'cove named after Phorcys, the Old Man of the Sea' (Od.13:95-96). The Gulf of Molos protects both Vathi and Dexia harbours 'from the heavy swell raised by rough weather in the open and allows large ships to ride without tying up, once they are within mooring distance of the shore (Od.13: 96-102). Both Vathi and Dexia harbours are within easy reach of the cave known as cave of the Nymphs or Marmarospilio. There evidence of worship of the nymphs has been discovered by archaeologists at the Marmarospilio, which is also known as the Cave of the Nymphs.

10. GLH: We know the position of Elis, upwards from the modern port of Killini on the Peloponnesian mainland. The exact positions of the Pheae and of the land of the Epeans are disputed but we know that the Sharp Islands are the southern Echinades near the mouth of the river Achelous. The Thoiai or Oxeiai are part of this group. The Thoai are also called Oxeiai and are part of the Echinades Islands (Strabo 10.2.19 [458 Casaubon]) The Thoas river is another name for the Achelous (Strabo 10.2.1).

11. GLH: It is noteworthy that in the Homeric Hymn to Apollo the first island to be sighted by the mariners is the 'steep mountain of Ithaca' as they move northwards. The island can

only be Ithaca. The Paliki Peninsula of Kefalonia is hidden by Mount Ainos for anyone looking from the entrance of the Corinthian Gulf. The first foreland of Ithaca is the Cape of St John in the southeast of the island.

12. Homer doesn't describe Telemachus' precise landing place. Access to the Korakos Petra can be made either from Pera Pigadia Bay or from St Andrew's Bay in the south of Ithaca.

13. Asteris. The only island now in the Ithaca Channel is the small island now called Dascalio. It lies between Polis bay in Ithaca and the opposite coast of Kefalonia. It is a small star-like rock, as the ancient name Asteris reflects. The problem with Dascalio is that there is no 'harbour where ships may lie, with an entrance on either side' (Od:4: 844-847.) Schliemann visited Dascalio in 1869, and McCabe, Huxley and their group visited in 2007. There are no twin harbours on Dascalio, however there are two deep inlets very close to Dascalio on the eastern shore of Kefalonia. Between them is a steeply sloping hillside with the village now known as Evreti. These inlets, which would make excellent hiding places for pirates, were also thoroughly investigated by Professor Luce. GLH: There are two harbours offering a safe mooring where the Achaeans (the suitors) lay in ambush μεγάλη· λιμένες δ᾽ ἔνι ναύλοχοι αὐτῇ ἀμφίδυμοι· τῇ τόν γε μένον λοχόωντες Ἀχαιοί. However it is unclear from the text whether the harbours are 'within' Asteris or 'on either side' of it. The Homeric description, as we see from Strabo, was much debated by Hellenistic scholars. Strabo's account is brief, but the outlines of the dispute over the harbours can be discerned. Demetrios of Skepsis, who was much interested in seismic and other changes in physical geography, argued that in Homer's time Asteris had been larg-

er than in his own day, about 200BC. He so argued because there was no room on contemporary Asteris for harbours. Apollodoros of Athens, criticising Demetrios of Skepsis, said that Asteris had not changed in the course of time. It follows that he didn't place the harbours in Asteris, but on either side of the sea channel or sound (porthmos) between Ithaca and Kephallenia.

14. GLH: By day the suitors kept watch on the windy heights of Kephallenia near Asteris. (Od 16:365-368) By night, with the white rock of Asteris as a clear sailing mark, they rowed in ambush on the 'watery paths'.

15. Professors Litsa Kontorli-Papadopoulou and Thanasis Papadopoulos were able to recognize a prehistoric acropolis at Agios Athanassios/ School of Homer of around 23 hectares in extent. It has partly preserved walls, the construction of which typifies the Cyclopean technique, and a complex of buildings arranged in two terraces (άνδηρα), dating from the Bronze Age to the Late Hellenistic and Roman periods.

16. During the final Mycenaean building phase, Professor Papadopoulos notes, the defensive walls of the citadel were enlarged to the east of the megaron to include the Mycenaean underground well investigated by Professor Knauss. Knauss compared this well to those from other palatial prehistoric sites at Mycenae, Tiryns, Ayia Eirini-Keas and Hatusa. He concluded that it was a 'sophisticated example of urban technical infrastructure of the Mycenaean world' and dated it to the 13th century BC. The Ithaca spring provided water to the residents of the Mycenaean acropolis in times of drought. In times of war its position protected it from disclosure to the enemy and made it safe from attack.

17. The metallurgical workshop was recognised as such by Professor G. Papademetriou of the National Metsoveion Technical University of Athens. Relevant products were bronze pins and nails, fish- hooks, an awl, a needle, a flat (or 1/2 of double axe?) and most importantly one broken low-stemmed monochrome LH IIIB2 early kylix, two lamps - one of bronze (Catling's Form 27b, LM/LH IIIA), the other of lead with a skillet handle, broken and badly corroded.

18. The bathroom, SE of the metallurgical workshop, has an entrance to the east and a low inner dividing wall. Immediately after the entrance part of a slab-paved floor is preserved, while several sherds of Late Mycenaean pottery and parts of a broken clay bath-tub (asaminthos) were found.

19. In the lower terrace or άνδηρον the foundations of a three-roomed rectangular building in the form of a megaron dating from late Middle Helladic to LH IIIC period were revealed. It is similar in type, construction, and dimensions to those of Mycenae, Tiryns and Pylos. One can approach the megaron from the south through a partly destroyed stone staircase and an entrance leads to the first room (aithousa). Before the opening leading to the next room (prodomos) a rough, irregular "oxhide ingot" (talanton) has been recognised. It is cut out in the surface of the rock bed. This could possibly have been used as an altar. In the northern room (domos) the floor with the hearth (estia) (diam. 3 m.) was sunken. It was built with a ring of big porous stones. Professor Papadopoulos especially mentioned the preserved foundations of the megaron, and parts of the wall dividing the two άνδηρα, as having exact parallels at Mycenae. He agrees with Buchholz who said that "the Ithacans of later times looked for the palace

as described by Homer at this important and strategic place," and suggests that the palace of Odysseus probably existed on the site of Agios Athanassios/School of Homer. His suggestion is strengthened, he states, by the opinions of Tsountas, Nilsson, Lorimer, Pausanias, Iakovidis, Camp, Immerwahr, and O. Komninou-Kakridi, who argue that later constructions covered the prehistoric residence after the collapse of the Mycenaean palatial centres, and that sanctuaries or temples dedicated to local deities were constructed in the place of the palaces.

20. To the west of the megaron the archaeologists discovered auxiliary rooms, where a broken Mycenaean IIIC kylix and sherds were found, also prehistoric handmade sherds, big broken pithoi from later times, a circular destroyed bothros, remains of prehistoric walls and an underground cave-like storeroom were found.

21. The archaeologists found a large door opening in the northern wall of the megaron, leading to a three-roomed building, orientated E-W. Judging from its particular type of architecture, its adjacency with the megaron, and the few, but very important finds (two triton shells, one Minoan lead votive idol of a worshipper, a stone altar-shaped seal, two stone feet and a model column in ivory) Professor Papadopoulos suggests it could be a Late Bronze Age sanctuary.

22. One further impressive prehistoric monument, probably prehistoric, is the so-called kykloteres or tholos. It lies further to the East of the underground spring and outside the area that has been fenced in 2019. It has been badly destroyed and looted. It produced, however, many interesting finds. Amongst the most important was a clay tablet bearing incised figures

of a ship and a man tied on its mast accompanied by mythical creatures and symbol(s) of Linear B(?) It also contained (AB09 "SE") pottery sherds and a great number of animal bones. It is worthy of special note that among these bones were two bucrania (oxen crania) that may be related with bull sacrifices, and bones of Bos primigenius.

23. Other prehistoric finds from Agios Athanassios/School of Homer include Middle and Late Bronze Age pottery, mainly sherds of 1 jar, 4 kylixes, 1 stirrup-jar, 2 deep bowls, 1 stemmed bowl, and 2 kraters. Also a bronze spear head, leaden rivets of the 'double rivet' type, broken stone vases, a clay seal, and a small spoon and fragments of an ivory pyxis and a pin. Professor Papadopoulos notes that the relative scarcity of prehistoric/Mycenaean finds at Agios Athanassios is most likely due to the continuous habitation of the site. As Hope Simpson and Dickinson observed "later (Hellenistic and Roman) remains on the hill above the spring may have removed much of the LH (Mycenaean) level."

24. Some bronze items found on Ithaca are regarded as imports from abroad, for example two swords now in the Neuchatel and British Museums.

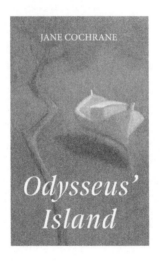

JANE COCHRANE

*Odysseus'
Island*

If you enjoyed reading 'Odysseus' Island' please consider leaving a
review on Amazon UK, Amazon US, or on my website:

www.janeocochrane.co.uk

Even a line or two would be incredibly helpful.

Thought provoking and captivating

This elegantly written, honest book is a combination of memoir, travelogue and archaeological investigation. Jane Cochrane writes with genuine affection for the people and culture of Ithaca. Her family's love affair with the island is evident on every page, but she does not shy away from the sometimes challenging times she and her husband faced in making a home there. Her gradual immersion in the quest for Odysseus' home, part tribute to her late husband, part unshakeable intellectual curiosity, is told with clarity and force. Cochrane makes no claims to be an expert, but patiently explains the findings of professionals, and politely challenges theories with which she disagrees. By the end, I was completely persuaded that Homer meant Odysseus' home to be the island we know as Ithaca today - and that he set foot on the island himself. I can't wait to go there! Highly recommended.

David Horspool *History Editor at the Times Literary Supplement*

Clear, objective, thorough and well-documented

Odysseus' island is a book full of love for Ithaca and I enjoyed it very much indeed. I would suggest to every Greek or foreign visitor to Ithaca to get a copy of this book. It combines elements of everyday life of the inhabitants of modern Ithaca with archaeological data for the identification of modern Ithaca with the Homeric, and the palace of Odysseus. She has presented in a clear, objective, thorough and well-documented way her opinion, which coincides with that of eminent scholars such as Heurtley, Benton, Wace, Stubbings, Knauss, Alexiou et.al. I think that it will be a constant and valuable guide for all those who love this small, but beautiful and historical, island.

Thanasis J. Papadopoulos *Professor of Archaeology, University of Ioannina*

How to live the myth

This book is a great read. It describes the author's relationship with Ithaca, the fabled island of Odysseus/ Ulysses. It's part personal narrative, part archaeological, part exploration of the island. Jane Cochrane arrives in Ithaca in the early 80s, not speaking a word of Greek. The island does not yet know tourism and her only link to everyday life is her Greek husband. They fall in love with the place as well as with the locals. The couple buy a ruin and the author, an architect, designs and sets about building a house. This is an adventure in itself, as her plans are continually inflected or deflected by Ithakan reality. But the optimism of the author and her good will finally triumph. The years pass, she learns Greek and her husband dies. The second part of the book is a hunt for Odysseus, as he is known locally, the Homeric king of ancient Ithaca. These days the large and more powerful island next door, Kefalonia, is seeking to appropriate this ancient son of Ithaca for monetary gain. The story and the history can be used to attract and entertain tourists. Several theories compete for scarce archaeological funds and block the promising work already begun in Ithaca. Cochrane sets out to defend the classic view, basing herself on the text of the Odyssey. Again her courage and optimism triumph. She visits Greek and English academics, studies in libraries, masters the detail of the argument and presents cogently and without jargon the fruit of her research. The final part of the book is an exploration of various sites mentioned in the Odyssey. This again is informed by guidance and knowledge from archaeologists and she uses the textual evidence in the Odyssey to produce surprising echoes in the present. In a ghostly but unpretentious way, she makes the Odyssey live. This book is an excellent example of how an outsider can not only enjoy with respect but also bring a valuable offering to the people and culture of that place.

George Paizis

A perfect informal guide to Ithaca

Full of lively character portraits and vignettes of life on a small Greek island by an observant architect and artist who has had a long association with the island. She recounts with warmth and beautiful illustrations the places and people the intrepid traveller longs to find and only occasionally does. It's a perfect informal tour guide to Ithaca, its churches, historical sites and, of course, the reader will be convinced by the evidence that this was indeed the home of Odysseus.

Jennifer Skilbeck

Enough to send you to Ithaca immediately

Half of this highly readable book dwells on the purchase and restoration of a ruin on a hillside by Jane Cochrane and her Greek-speaking husband Alec. But two important things lift it out of that fairly crowded category - the artist author's own beautiful illustrations, and her involvement in researching Ithaca's claim to have been the island kingdom Odysseus left and returned to twenty years later. Her conclusions are persuasive.

Her writing is unfussy and direct, and all the more effective for it, leaving the reader latitude to absorb and react to the characters, landscapes, events and ideas that make up this deeply personal and utterly delightful story.

tonstantouida

Don't hesitate...

... and snap up this wonderful book! Jane Cochrane's memoir and quest for Odysseus is an absolute gem.

Daphne Hyman

Printed in Great Britain
by Amazon